Commonomics II:

The Sheep, Sheepdog and Evil Shepherd

Dr. Ridgely Abdul Mu'min Muhammad

With a Forward by Dr. Ava Muhammad

Kemetic Research Institute of Science and Technology

DEDICATED

To our fallen warriors and anonymous victims who have suffered during this 6,000 years of the absence of light.

Contents

Forward

By Dr. Ava Muhammad

The Honorable Minister Louis Farrakhan is truly a light-giving Sun, producing an endless variety of life-sustaining mind food from his students and followers. Because of the Minister's determination to lift the Name and Work of the Honorable Elijah Muhammad--- when a racist America was doing and continues to do everything it can to defame his Teacher --- such a work as this one is being published when we truly need it.

Dr. Ridgely Muhammad's exhaustive research is presented in a way that is as entertaining as it is enlightening. It has the quality of a textbook and the appeal of a work of fiction. It is impossible to overestimate how critical a real knowledge and understanding of global finance is to the goal of economic independence. We handle money every single day of our lives, yet nothing is taught about finance in the public school system of America. This book helps to close that lethal educational gap and culminates in helping us see why we must support Muhammad's Economic Blueprint.

We are living in the fullness of Time and the revelation given through *"The Time and What Must Be Done"* by the Honorable Minister Louis Farrakhan. "The Sheep, Sheepdog and Evil Shepherd" is a practical aid to the consistent references in the Bible to God's people as "sheep". It can be used, not only by devotees of Christianity and Islam, but nationalists, intellectuals and anyone who loves to get to the root cause of a condition. It repeats and then answers the nagging question: Why have Black people made absolutely no economic progress whatsoever, though chattel slavery ended more than 150 years ago? Could it be that we truly are inferior? If you don't know the history laid forth here, you may think such is the case.

The Minister has been the point person for the Truth and has withstood relentless false charges of anti-Semitism for decades. He has taken heat that no ordinary human being could have survived.

Brother Ridgely has used his God-given skill set to produce a superb work of compilation in the sciences of business, economics and finance to support the original exposition of the Teachings of the Honorable Elijah Muhammad. How important is this? Our children's future depends upon it.

ACKNOWLEDGMENTS

I must first acknowledge Master Fard Muhammad for coming Himself and bringing us The Supreme Wisdom that has allowed me to see beyond the devil's lies. I must acknowledge The Most Honorable Elijah Muhammad who was bold enough to deliver His Message, then grew into first, The Messiah, then later, The Christ. And of course I must acknowledge the best student of The Messenger, the Honorable Minister Louis Farrakhan who used the Teachings, the history taught by The Messenger, and his faith to bring us back to the light.

Then I must thank my wife, Sister Anne Mu'min, for taking the time to help edit the manuscript and critique my ideas. I thank Minister Farrakhan for allowing me to work at Muhammad Farms which introduced me to hard work, but also provided me with a sanctuary away from the foolishness of this dying world so that I could think and write. I thank Sister Dr. Ava Muhammad for seeing the value in this work and writing an insightful Forward to this book.

Commonomics II: The Sheep, Sheepdog and Evil Shepherd

(The Secret Biblical Code used to manipulate financial markets)

Introduction:

The white people who call themselves "Jews" are lying about who they are and are playing a wicked game on humanity. These white or Ashkenazi Jews have stolen the identity and sufferings of God's Chosen People to force the rest of humanity to accept their economic dominance.

The Most Honorable Elijah Muhammad said that Jesus was ahead of time to destroy the Jewish civilization. In his book, *Our Saviour Has Arrived*, The Messenger wrote these weighty words **about** the **historical Jesus**:

"Jesus came to the Jews and not to us and then he got disappointed that he was ahead of the time of the Jews to preach the doctrine of the destruction or judgment and the setting up of a New Kingdom of Heaven after the destruction of the Jew's civilization. Jesus was born two thousand years ahead of the judgment of the Jews." (Muhammad 1992: 166)

In his *Theology of Time* lecture series **in 1972** the **Honorable Elijah Muhammad** said:

"Jesus was not able to bring Pharaoh to a naught, none of the leaders at that time, because it was not Time for the Kingdom of Heaven of righteous and justice to be set up. The Jews had

1

two more thousand years to live. And Paul, when he was questioned about the Jesus teachings, he said: 'I saw him as a man born out of due season.' It was not Time that the Jews be brought to Judgment in Jesus' day and time, but I'm on Time."

In fact at the time of Jesus the Jews of that day were confined to the Levant. They had yet to dominate the Roman Empire, the Orient and Africa below Egypt. These Jews knew nothing of the Americas or Australia. However, 2,000 years later their economic tentacles through their international control of banks and money allows them to dictate the policies of countries throughout the world and through their control of the media and communications, they are able to lead the masses in all these various countries as a herder would herd cattle. In fact the Jews call the non-Jews "goyim" which literally means "cattle."

Jesus, according to the Bible, knew who they were and called them out. However, he could not overcome them. They overcame him:

John 8:31-33 (KJV)

31 To the Jews who had believed him, Jesus said, "If you hold to my teaching, you are really my disciples. 32 Then you will know the truth, and the truth will set you free."

33 They answered him, "We are Abraham's descendants and have never been slaves of anyone. How can you say that we shall be set free?"

If we were to take the Jews to court accusing them of identity theft, we would surely ask them to explain "…never been slaves of anyone." So what about your slavery to Pharaoh in Egypt for 400 years? What about your exile and slavery for 70 years in Babylon? So are you saying that these events never happened or are you saying

2

that you are not the descendants of those people that were enslaved?

Jesus goes on to point out the identity of these Jews, particularly the Pharisees with whom he had a continuing battle:

John 8:44

44 You belong to your father, the devil, and you want to carry out your father's desires. He was a murderer from the beginning, not holding to the truth, for there is no truth in him. When he lies, he speaks his native language, for he is a liar and the father of lies.

So the father of these people who claimed to be of Abraham's seed was a liar, we say identity thief. These Pharisees, priests and elders represented the House of Israel, but according to The Most Honorable Elijah Muhammad Jesus did not go to Jerusalem to teach the leadership but to find and redeem the "lost sheep of the house of Israel." These leaders conspired against Jesus. Matthew 26:3-5 reads:

"3 Then the chief priests and the elders of the people assembled in the palace of the high priest, whose name was Caiaphas, 4 and they schemed to arrest Jesus secretly and kill him. 5 'But not during the festival,' they said, 'or there may be a riot among the people'"(Matthew 26:3-5).

If we analyze this passage, there are three distinct classes of people: (1) the chief and high Priests, (2) the Elders of the people, and (3) the people. It is clear that the priests and elders are not just conspiring against Jesus, they are also conspiring against "the people." The Honorable Elijah Muhammad pierces through the confusion and exposes the cause of this division when he writes in *Message to The Blackman In America*:

3

- "As Jesus comes close to revealing the whereabouts of the lost members of a great nation in these words, **'that he was sent to the lost sheep of the house of Israel, or in the house of Israel.'**
- He did not say that he was sent to the lost Israel, but to the lost sheep in the house of Israel. The lost sheep are not Israel. The lost sheep were in the house or government of Israel and were swallowed up by Israel so thoroughly that they were always overlooked." (Muhammad 1965: 251)

Here we see that "the lost sheep" and Israel are not the same. Who were these "lost sheep" and how did they end up in Israel? Where did Israel or, rather, the governing body of Israel come from? If you look at a map of Israel or Palestine, you will see that it lies between two continents, Africa and Asia, on the overland trade routes between the two. If we go back to ancient times, we find that at one time Ancient Egypt (Kemit) held dominion over Palestine, and Jerusalem was used as an outpost to protect the borders of Egypt and secure the trade routes to Asia. Eventually the Egyptians lost control of Palestine when Nebuchadnezzar, king of the Babylonians, swooped through Palestine and took prisoners back to Babylonia in 597 BC. This phase of Jewish history is referred to as the "captivity". In this book we will question this so-called "captivity."

However, continuing the party line of the Jews, this forced exile ended in 538 BC, when according to the Bible, the children of the captives or slaves were allowed to go back to Palestine and to rebuild the Temple. Later, Ezra led another group of "returnees" with a new Torah, because the original book had been destroyed (Ezra 7-10 and Neh. 8). However, they were admonished by their "liberator," the Persian King Cyrus the Great, not to allow the natives of Palestine, many of them Jews, to participate in the rebuilding of the Temple or intermarry with those "returning" from Babylon. This ruling class, called Pharisees, who came from Babylon, now ruled over "the people" of Palestine for the Persian rulers who now occupied Israel.

When the Romans conquered Palestine and took over Israel, the priests and elders ruled over "the people" for the Romans. This division between the priests, also called the Scribes and Pharisees, is highlighted in this conflict that Jesus had with them where they told him: "We be Abraham's seed, and were never in bondage to any man..." (John 8:33). Therefore, the Scribes and Pharisees exposed that they did not consider themselves returned captives, but a separate class ruling over the people in Israel. In fact, the word "Pharisee" in Hebrew means "set apart."

The Pharisees were the Rabbis that later developed the Babylonian Talmud. And according to the *Jewish Encyclopedia*: "Henceforth Jewish life was regulated by the teachings of the Pharisees; the whole history of Judaism was reconstructed from the Pharisaic point of view, and a new aspect was given to the Sanhedrin of the past. A new chain of tradition supplanted the older, priestly tradition (Abot i. 1) (http://www.jewishencyclopedia.com/articles/12087-pharisees). Like Jacob who supplanted his brother Esau in the Book of Genesis, the Pharisees of Jesus' time had replaced the older priesthood.

A reason for Black people being reluctant to compete against or criticize Jews is that we have been taught that the Jews are God's Chosen People. We have been taught they, the Jews have suffered just like Blacks and are our natural allies. We will bring evidence to show that the Jews are liars and identity thieves.

The Most Honorable Elijah Muhammad and his best student, the Honorable Minister Louis Farrakhan, have given us the keys to unraveling the false history of the Jews and other white people that has acted as a veil over the minds of Black people and the world. The first colleges set up in this New World, America, were set up to teach and spread the Bible. It was through the Bible and its interpretation of how man began and how he got to where he is today that they were able to conquer the minds and souls of the indigenous people of America and now the world. The Messenger said that we as a people were "buried" in this "poison" book. He writes on the

5

back of Muhammad Speaks and now on the inside cover of The Final Call under "What The Muslims Believe": "4. WE BELIEVE in the truth of the Bible, but we believe that it has been tampered with and must be reinterpreted so that mankind will not be snared by the falsehoods that have been added to it."

The Teachings of The Most Honorable Elijah Muhammad breaks through the clouds of confusion produced by the Bible and gives us a proper lens to see through and evaluate that book. With this lens and keys we can then go to the libraries and find the morsels of truth that bear witness to The Messenger's Teachings and allows us to piece together the real history of the world using the road markers provided in our lessons. We can essentially fill in the gaps between firm historical markers given to us by The Messenger's Teachings.

We must thank the Jews themselves for motivating us to get on this journey of exposing their identity theft. Even though The Messenger made the statement about Jesus being ahead of his time to judge the Jewish civilization, he did not go into much detail about the Jews. However, when the Honorable Minister Louis Farrakhan stood up to rebuild the Nation of Islam, he fell into a dispute with the Jews. We say "fell into" because he was defending Rev. Jesse Jackson as he was running for the office of President of the United States in 1984. Jesse Jackson had made the "mistake" of calling New York City "Hymietown". The Jews in New York went berserk and started chants such as "Ruin Jesse Ruin." When Minister Farrakhan came to stand with Jesse and offer the protection of the Fruit of Islam (FOI), the Jews began chanting "Who do we want? Farrakhan! How do we want him? Dead!" That was over 30 years ago, but it motivated those who love Minister Farrakhan and Black people to investigate why did these Jews who had supported the Civil Rights Movement want Minister Farrakhan dead?

Why is it important to understand the secret science behind Jewish financial dominance? The Honorable Minister Louis Farrakhan announced the launch of Muhammad's Economic

6

Blueprint in February of 2013. He asked Black people to donate $.05 per day into a national treasury to be used for economic development for Black people. Every other people on our planet understand the five principles outlined by The Most Honorable Elijah Muhammad in his economic blueprint. A person called in to Min. Ava Muhammad's blogtalk radio program called "Elevated Places" and asked: "Is Muhammad's Economic Blueprint divine?" I answered by pointing out that the five principles outlined in Muhammad's Economic Blueprint are designed to get Black people to do what is normal for every other people on our planet. Why would such simple instruction have to be given to a whole people unless someone like a devil has come and distorted the natural and normal behavior of a people? Since a devil has interfered with the natural development of a people, then only God can step in to reverse the works of such a devil. So yes, it is divine.

Someone asked me why did I take up the field of economics? I had to think about that one for a while. Jews dominate the field of economics and dominate the financial industry in capitalist countries. Most Black people shy away from economics because of its heavy dependence on mathematics. Coming out of high school I was good in mathematics and I wanted to help Black people make some money because we are inordinately poor.

Economic development requires investment and investment requires confidence and security. Black people do not feel that their own people are smart enough to handle "big business", yet they believe that Jewish people are good at business. They are smart. So when The Minister asked for our financial support, we may hold back because we do not believe that we can handle the money, whereas Jews can do a better job. So Black people's strategy has been to find some good Jews or other white people to believe in and seek economic well-being from them.

However, what if we learn that the secret to the Jews' economic success is not so much that they are smarter, but they have developed an economic gambling game that they control and have lured the world into. Within this economic or financial "game" they cheat by planning secret moves together as insiders to this "game." What happens if, in a tall office building everybody flushes the toilets on each floor at exactly the same time? Pipes would burst. What would happen if a number of major players in this financial "game" all knew when to make a move at the same time without telling the "outsiders" what time it was and what needed to be done. These "insiders" could cause the system to crash right after they had taken their winnings out of the system. The "outsiders" would not only loose the money that they had in the "game", but now will have to sell some assets not originally in the game to pay off their debts. These same "insiders" could then turn around and use their ill-gotten gains to purchase real assets and businesses at bargain discount rates and walk off with the money, real estate and stocks of the "suckers." We will expose this "game" in this book. We will trace the history of this game of "financial raiding" and reveal the mathematical cipher used to regulate the moves of the "insiders" of the game as they fleece their "goyim", i.e. cattle, sheep and sheepdogs.

Also this book is a follow up to "Commonomics: Developing a Post Yakub Economy" that we published in 2009, right after the financial system melt down at the end of 2008. In that book we describe the economic system set up by the children of Yakub and produce a competing model for economic development. In this book we will show how some of the principles of the model advocated in "Commonomics…" actually prevent the "game" to take hold that has siphoned off the people's wealth . These so-called Jews are masters at using the weaknesses of the people to corral them within an economic pen in which they can periodically fleece them of their assets and suck their financial blood. We will expose their "playbook" and schemes, then show the way to an alternative system where everyone can enjoy freedom, justice and equality.

What is "Commonomics"?

A new paradigm is needed to replace the economic "wisdom" of the present day rulers. *"Commonomics"* is *common* sense eco*nomics* needed for personal and group survival and righteous "success". It is based on a fundamental understanding of the nature of man and his preferred relationship with God, the universe and each other. It is presented in a simple mathematical form. Underlying the analytical model is a set of assumptions and principles that have been inspired by the Economic Blueprint developed by The Most Honorable Elijah Muhammad.

Underneath western economic theory is a set of basic assumptions: 1. **The goal of life is to acquire riches** (consumption, **mammon**), 2. Well-being is measured in money, 3. Man has unlimited wants, 4. There are limited resources, 5. Therefore competition is how people must interact and 6. Life is a "zero sum game", i.e. winners and losers, winner takes all.

We have categorized the real reasons for the economic success of the Western World: 1. **Stealing and enslaving indigenous peoples, 3. Stealing, then renting or reselling land back to indigenous peoples, 4. Stealing gold, silver and productive assets from indigenous peoples, 5. Lending money at usury, 6. Starting wars among tribes then *selling* them "weapons of mass destruction"** and 7. **Unfair exchange rates.**

Commonomics assumes a Universe based on laws:

- Every cause has an effect.
- Every effect has a cause (known or unknown).
- For every action there is a reaction.
- The universe is *knowable,* yet not known.
- Mathematics unlocks the universe's mysteries and treasures.
- There is no such thing as a coincidence.
- The universe was created by God.

- The universe submits to the Laws of God.
- Man must submit to God's laws to **benefit** from God's universe.
- God is *just*.

Basic Commonomics Principles for living include:

- 1. Live to Serve not just consume.
- 2. Define "progress" and "success" for self.
- 3. Plan or be Planned.
- 4. Enjoy producing a superior product or service.

We go much more into details in *Commonomics: Developing a Post Yakub Economy*.

Chapter 1

Why "Sheep, sheepdog and evil shepherd?"

Before we get into the behavior of sheep and the training of a sheepdog, let us ask why would we use this shepherd, sheepdog and sheep analogy to describe human behavior? Most people are familiar with the trio of the sheep, the wolf and the sheepdog as portrayed in cartoon characters. It was a pretty straight forward relationship. The wolf wanted to kill and eat the sheep and the sheepdog was there to protect the sheep from the wolf. Not much information is given on the shepherd or the farmer that owned the sheep.

In a human context one can see the sheep as the masses of basically good people. The wolf could be a thief, murderer or a whole tribe bent on taking the land from another people. In such an analogy the sheepdog would be the watchmen or the authorities chosen by the people to protect them and work in the people's best interest.

The Honorable Minister Louis Farrakhan has pointed out to us that the "snake" described in Genesis seducing the woman out of the Garden of Eden has grown in the book of Revelations into a giant "dragon" bent on devouring the woman and her child. In the same way, could the wolves have learned how to herd the sheep as though they were the legitimate shepherds over the sheep and then trained the sheepdog to continue their work of keeping the sheep boxed in for this "snake" hiding in human form?

Why did The Most Honorable Elijah Muhammad and Jesus refer to their people as "sheep"? The Messenger describes himself as a "lamb" and his people as sheep in the October 20, 1956 Pittsburg Courier article, "THE ONE HUNDRED AND FORTY-FOUR THOUSAND..." In it he writes:

"The messenger is called a lamb due to certain characteristics of his (the messenger) being similar to that of a sheep, and the tender love of Allah for him like that of a good shepherd towards his sheep.

Though the love of Allah (God) for the so-called Negroes is not equaled by anyone. Describing us as sheep is about the best way of putting it, as sheep are dumb, ignorant and humble, not aggressive.
They will not fight even if attacked by the wolf. So, are the so-called Negroes and Allah has to do the fighting for them."

Here the "good shepherd" is characterized by Allah (God) Himself and the so-called Negroes as "dumb, ignorant, not aggressive" sheep. Jesus gives a similar description of the people who he comes to save and also hints at this "evil shepherd" under the name of "thief and robber."

John 10:1-16: King James Version

> **10** *Verily, verily, I say unto you, He that entereth not by the door into the sheepfold, but climbeth up some other way, the same is a thief and a robber.*
>
> *2 But he that entereth in by the door is the shepherd of the sheep.*
>
> *3 To him the porter openeth; and the sheep hear his voice: and he calleth his own sheep by name, and leadeth them out.*
>
> *4 And when he putteth forth his own sheep, he goeth before them, and the sheep follow him: for they know his voice.*
>
> *5 And a stranger will they not follow, but will flee from him: for they know not the voice of strangers.*
>
> *6 This parable spake Jesus unto them: but they understood not what things they were which he spake unto them.*
>
> *7 Then said Jesus unto them again, Verily, verily, I say unto you, I am the door of the sheep.*

⁸ All that ever came before me are thieves and robbers: but the sheep did not hear them.

⁹ I am the door: by me if any man enter in, he shall be saved, and shall go in and out, and find pasture.

¹⁰ The thief cometh not, but for to steal, and to kill, and to destroy: I am come that they might have life, and that they might have it more abundantly.

¹¹ I am the good shepherd: the good shepherd giveth his life for the sheep.

¹² But he that is an hireling, and not the shepherd, whose own the sheep are not, seeth the wolf coming, and leaveth the sheep, and fleeth: and the wolf catcheth them, and scattereth the sheep.

¹³ The hireling fleeth, because he is an hireling, and careth not for the sheep.

¹⁴ I am the good shepherd, and know my sheep, and am known of mine.

¹⁵ As the Father knoweth me, even so know I the Father: and I lay down my life for the sheep.

¹⁶ And other sheep I have, which are not of this fold: them also I must bring, and they shall hear my voice; and there shall be one fold, and one shepherd.

According to this scripture the sheep will know the voice of the "good shepherd" and not follow a "stranger." However, what if the "stranger", the "thief and robber" and the "hireling" have been taken over by a "snake" in human form that is so crafty he can mold the enemies of the sheep into a form that looks and sounds like the "good shepherd" but is indeed the "evil shepherd" who has fooled both the sheep and the sheepdog.

The Most Honorable Elijah Muhammad teaches how the white man was taught how to control the Original Man (sheep) using tricknology. He also taught us to "study the white man, he is successful." So in studying the most successful ethnic group among white people, European Jews, we find that they have peculiar ways of looking at all non-Jews. According to their rabbis as formulated

13

in their Babylonian Talmud, all non-Jews are called "goyim" which literally means "cattle". Therefore it is most appropriate to then study the relationship between a shepherd and his sheep to get a glimpse of the mind of the Jew (shepherd) as he relates to non-Jews (sheep). However, a successful shepherd must also have a good sheepdog to help look after and herd his sheep "goyim" to him, the master.

Now let us explore how the Jews view their "goyim". Later we hope to also clear up how these "Jews" recently came into existence around 526 B.C and how white Russians, Khazars converted to Judaism about 740 A.D.

According to the "Father of Spin", Edward Louis Bernays:

"If we understand the mechanism and motives of the group mind, is it not possible to control and regiment the masses according to our will without their knowing about it? The recent practice of propaganda has proved that it is possible, at least up to a certain point and within certain limits."
(Bernays 2004: 71)

In *Propaganda* (1928), Bernays argued that the manipulation of public opinion was a necessary part of democracy:

"The conscious and intelligent manipulation of the organized habits and opinions of the masses is an important element in democratic society. Those who manipulate this unseen mechanism of society constitute an invisible government which is the true ruling power of our country. ...We are governed, our minds are molded, our tastes formed, our ideas suggested, largely by men we have never heard of. This is a logical result of the way in which our democratic society is organized. Vast numbers of human beings must cooperate in this manner if they are to live together as a smoothly functioning society. ...In almost every act of our daily lives, whether in the sphere of politics or business, in our social conduct or our ethical thinking, we are dominated by the relatively small number of persons...who understand the mental processes and social patterns of the masses. It is they who pull the wires which control the public mind." (Ibid.: 37)

Before we get into the behavior of sheep and the training of a sheepdog, let us ask why would we use this shepherd, sheepdog and sheep analogy to describe human behavior? The Most Honorable Elijah Muhammad teaches us that at the root of the relationship between white people and Black people is the concept of "white supremacy" and the white race ruling over Black people for 6,000 years. According to the Messenger a Black scientist named Yakub who lived 6,600 years ago said as a little boy of six, "*Uncle, when I get to be an old man, I am going to make a people who shall rule you.*" The Messenger continued teaching on the motive behind the actions of Mr. Yakub by stating:

> "*He learned from studying the germ of the black man, under the microscope, that there were two people in him, and that one was black, the other brown.*
>
> *He said if he could successfully separate the one from the other he could graft the brown germ into its last stage, which would be white. With his wisdom, he could make the white, which he discovered was the weaker of the black germ (which would be unalike) rule the black nation for a time (until a greater one than Yakub was born).*
>
> *This new idea put him to work finding the necessary converts to begin grafting his new race of people. He began by teaching Islam, with promises of luxury to those who would believe and follow him.*
>
> *As Mr. Yakub continued to preach for converts, he told his people that he would make the others work for them. (This promise came to pass). Naturally, there are always some people around who would like to have others do their work. Those are the ones who fell for Mr. Yakub's teaching, 100 per cent.*

15

The Messenger goes on to describe how a race of white people were made from the original Black people by using a form of grafting over a 600 year period. What is important here is that built into the fiber of white people is the desire to rule over Black people. And this desire is rooted in them the same as the desire to herd sheep is in the DNA of a sheepdog. The Messenger goes on to teach what Mr. Yakub taught his new race of white people that would allow them to rule over their former brothers and sisters. The Messenger teaches us that Mr. Yakub lived only 150 years, left instructions for his made race of people which included:

"That -- when you go back to the holy black nation, rent a room in their homes. Teach your wives to go out the next morning around the neighbors of the people, and tell that you heard her talking about them last night.

When you have gotten them fighting and killing each other, then ask them to let you help settle their disputes, and restore peace among them. If they agree, then you will be able to rule them both. This method the white race practices on the black nation, the world over. They upset their peace by putting one against the other, and then rule them after dividing them."(Muhammad 1965: 116,117)

In these statements we find that Yakub taught the truth, Islam, to get his potential followers to listen to him. Then he added promises of luxury. What is wrong with luxury? But then he added that he would "make the others work for them." In other words, the way his followers would receive luxury is that they would enslave those who did not follow them. He appealed to a latent desire of both laziness and an inordinate sense of self-worth to believe that they were better than the ones they were willing to enslave.

To accomplish this goal he taught them more than simple brutish warfare. He taught them to lie, steal and how to master the original people of the planet by giving them a false understanding of God. The Messenger teaches us that this new white race of people came back into the company of black people 6,000 years ago and

16

used this method of lying to cause trouble among them. After 6 months, the righteous black nation discovered that these white people were the cause of their problems. They then rounded all the whites up that they could find and put them behind the Caucasus Mountains and placed guards on the sides of the mountains to keep them from re-entering the Holy Land. These white people stayed up in those mountains for 2,000 years and lost the knowledge of civilization and lived a beast's life. After this 2,000 year period a half-original (mulatto) named Musa (Moses) was sent amongst them to teach them how to live a respectful life, how to build homes and some of the forgotten "tricknowlogy" that Yakub taught them, which was "devilishment, telling lies, stealing and how to master the original man." (F. Muhammad, 1992: 11)

If we follow the Children of Jacob (Yakub) from Genesis all the way to their confrontation with Jesus, we find a people that are living up to a special covenant with a god that allows his "Chosen People" to lie, steal, murder and rape other nations to become the rulers over humanity. Could it be that we have found Yakub and his reliance on tricknology under the Bible character of Jacob?

In the Bible, commandments are given to Jacob's children to use debt as a weapon to take over land of other nations. Let's read Deut. 23:20; *"Unto a stranger thou mayest lend upon usury; but unto thy brother thou shalt not lend upon usury: that the Lord thy God may bless thee in all that thou settest thine hand to in the land whither thou goest to possess it."* And Deut. 15:6 *"For the Lord thy God blesseth thee, as he promised thee: and thou shalt lend unto many nations, but thou shalt not borrow; and thou shalt reign over many nations, but they shall not reign over thee."*

Here we have the "god" of the Bible allowing for his "Chosen", so-called Jews, to see themselves above and separate from other humans. These Jews are allowed to use special lending tactics such as usury to steal the wealth of other nations. Later we will deal with the banking system and stock market system through which the Jews herd their sheep and sheepdogs then periodically fleece them both.

Some scholars even attribute the aggressive nature of the West to their dependence on meat animals and herding instead of plants and cultivation. According to an article posted on www.nonhumanslavery.com entitled "How Did We Get Here? The Rise of The Dominator/Herding Culture," Will Tuttle describes how agrarian or partnership societies, where men and women are essentially equal, had worked together cooperatively for many tens of thousands of years before the expansion of patriarchal dominator cultures that were based on herding animals. This new culture is only five to seven thousand years old and was forced onto indigenous societies in central Asia, Eastern Europe and the Mediterranean basin by the invasion of Kurgan (Aryan, white) warlike herders coming out of the Caucasus Mountains.

For these herding cultures, confined animals were not just food; they were also wealth, security and power. The first money and forms of capital were sheep, goats and cattle. In fact the word "capital" derives from *capita*, Latin for "head," as head of cattle and sheep. The first capitalists were the herders who fought each other for land and capital. The ancient Roman coin, the *denarius*, was named because it was worth ten asses.

Raiding others to take their cattle and sheep was the primary way to obtain more capital; the ancient Aryan Sanskrit word for war, *gavyaa,* means literally "the desire for more cattle." A shepherd in those days, when farming required a lot of hand labor, could dominate a lot more land than could a dirt farmer. Therefore the mentality of conquering other peoples and societies went hand in hand with the expansion of the herding culture including sheep herding.

SHEPHERD:

In the early days of settlement in Palestine the chief occupation of the Israelites was that of shepherding. Traces of the importance of this occupation are found throughout the Old Testament. The shepherd's function was to lead the flocks of sheep to the pasture and the stream (Ps. 23. 2), and protect them from wild beasts (I Sam. 11. 24) and robbers (Job 1. 14 *et seq.*), in which latter task he was sometimes assisted by a sheep-dog (Job 30. 1). At night the shepherds kept watch, sometimes in the open air (Nah. 3. 18), and at other times in the shepherd's tent (Isa. 38. 12) or in a special

18

stone tower (Gen. 35. 21). At times he would collect the sheep in caves (I Sam. 24. 3), or in sheepfolds built of stones (Judges 5. 16; Zeph. 2. 6); and a lamb that had fallen sick or become lame he would carry in his bosom (Isa. 40. 11).

The shepherd generally wore a single garment (Jer. 43. 12), clad in which he walked forth at the head of his flock (John 10. 4), carrying his shepherd's bag or wallet; his weapons were a staff and a sling (Gen. 32. 10; I Sam. xvii. 40). When agriculture became the prominent industry of the country, the shepherd, instead of being independent, was generally hired by a farmer, who paid him wages in kind (Gen. 30. 28), or sometimes in money (Zech. 11. 13). The number of sheep returned to the master's fold was checked by being made to pass under the shepherd's staff (Jer. 33. 13; Ezek. 20. 37). As **farming increased** in importance, the shepherd became **less respected**, just as in Egypt, where he was regarded "as an **abomination**" (Gen. 46. 34). In Talmudic times it was even declared that a shepherd was incapable of bearing witness, owing to his habit of encroaching upon other persons' pastures (Sanh. 25a).

(http://frumheretic.blogspot.com/2009/03/sheep-worship-in-ancient-egypt.html)

> *"And Joseph said to his brothers, and to his father's household: I will go up, and tell Pharaoh, and will say to him: 'My brothers and my father's household who were in the land of Canaan have come to me; and the men are shepherds, for they have been keepers of cattle; and they have brought their flocks, and their herds, and all that they have.'"* (46:31-32)

Joseph then coaches them with instructions to tell Pharaoh a similar story when they are summoned before him:

> *"And it shall come to pass, when Pharaoh shall call you, and shall say: 'What is your occupation?' then you will say 'Your servants have been keepers of cattle from our youth even until now, both we, and our forefathers'; so that you may dwell in the land of Goshen; for every shepherd is an abomination to the Egyptians."* (Genesis 46:33-34)

One reason for the Egyptians not liking shepherds is due to the possibility of sheep overgrazing thereby destroying the land. Sheep can graze very close to the ground and like other livestock will overgraze, if they are allowed to. Overgrazing can lead to loss of vegetation, soil erosion and depleted soil. Fragile soil can be turned into a desert.

Why do sheepherders herd sheep? All the above information does not answer this very important question. Sheepherders herd sheep to fleece them and eat them.

As a young boy every Saturday morning I would look at cartoons. One of my favorites was about a sheepdog protecting sheep from a wily old wolf. Every morning the sheepdog would come to work and sit watching the sheep. The sheepdog had a lot of hair over his eyes so it was always amazing and funny when the wolf would try and sneak up to steal a sheep and the sheepdog would always have a trap set for the wolf.

However, I never saw the shepherd who owned the flock. Therefore the hidden agenda of the shepherd is never exposed for scrutiny. The people assume that the wolf is evil and the sheepdog is good, but no one questions the motives of the shepherd that they never see. In this book we will explore motives and systems designed to satisfy these motives.

Sheep behavior: (taken from:
http://www.sheep101.info/201/behavior.html)

Behavior is defined as an animal's response to its environment.

(When reading the following information on the behavior of sheep and sheepdogs, we want the reader to make the connections with human behavior. Humans can be domesticated. Indeed the so-called American Negro has been domesticated, dominated and castrated. Our enemy studies our behavior and our responses to his stimuli to determine his next phase of manipulation.)

Flocking behavior

Sheep are best known for their strong flocking (herding) and following instinct. They will run from what frightens them and band together in large groups for protection. This is the only protection they have from predators. There is safety in numbers. It is harder for a predator to pick a sheep out of a group than to go after a few strays. Flocking instinct varies by breed, with the **fine wool** breeds being the most gregarious.

Follow the leader

When one sheep moves, the rest will follow, even if it is not a good idea. The flocking and following instinct of sheep is so strong that it caused the death of 400 sheep in 2006 in eastern Turkey. The sheep plunged to their death after one of the sheep tried to cross a 15-meter deep ravine, and the rest of the flock followed. Even from birth, lambs are taught to follow the older members of the flock. Ewes encourage their lambs to follow. The dominant members of the flock usually lead, followed by the submissive ones. If there is a ram in the flock, he usually leads.

Social

Sheep are a very social animal. In a grazing situation, they need to see other sheep. In fact, to prevent excess stress when moving or handling them, you should ensure that sheep always have visual contact with other sheep. According to animal behaviorists, a group of **five** sheep is usually necessary for sheep to display their **normal** flocking behavior. A sheep will become highly agitated if it is separated from the rest of the flock. (Note: *Black codes and later street gang codes were set up to prevent 5 or more Blacks congregating together without white supervision.)*

In addition to serving as a protection mechanism against predators, this flocking and following instinct enables humans to care for large numbers of sheep. It makes sheep **easier to move** or drive and enables a **guardian dog** to provide protection for a large flock. Domestication and thousands of generations of human contact has further strengthened this trait in sheep.

Domestication has also **favored** the **non-aggressive**, **docile** nature of sheep, making it easier for people, especially women and children, to care for sheep. Sheep were one of the earliest animals to be domesticated, and they have been thoroughly domesticated. It is **doubtful** they could survive in the wild, if a predator risk existed.

Sight

Sheep depend heavily upon their vision. With only slight head movement, sheep are able to scan their surroundings. Their field of vision ranges from 191 to 306 degrees, depending upon the **amount of wool** on their face.

On the other hand, sheep have poor depth perception (three dimensional vision), especially if they are moving with their heads up. This is why they will often stop to examine something more closely. Sheep have **difficulty picking out small details**, such as an open space created by a partially opened gate. They tend to avoid shadows and sharp contrasts between light and dark. They are reluctant to go where they can't see.

For many years, it was believed that sheep and other livestock could not perceive **color.** But, it has since been proven that livestock possess the cones necessary for color vision. Research has shown that livestock can differentiate between colors, though their color perception is not equal to humans.

Hearing

Sheep have excellent hearing. They can amplify and pinpoint sound with their ears. In fact, sound arrives at each ear at a different time. Sheep are frightened by sudden loud noises, such as yelling or barking. In response to loud noises and other unnatural sounds, sheep become nervous and more difficult to handle. This is due to the release of stress-related hormones. To minimize stress, the handler should speak in a **quiet, calm voice**. Sheep should not be worked in the presence of **barking dogs.**

Normal sheep behavior

Changes in normal behavior can be an early sign of illness in sheep. The most obvious example of this relates to the sheep's most natural behavioral instinct, their **flocking instinct.** A sheep or lamb that is **isolated** from the rest of the flock is likely showing early signs of illness (unless it is lost). Even the last sheep through the gate should be suspected of not feeling well, especially if it is usually one of the first.

Appetite

Appetite is another strong indicator of health. Healthy sheep display normal eating and cud-chewing behavior. They will chew their cuds for several hours each day. Healthy sheep are eager to eat. They are almost always hungry. They will overeat, if we let them. Sheep bleat in anticipation of being fed and will **rapidly approach** the feeding area.

Lack of appetite is probably the most common symptom exhibited by a sick sheep. At the same time, food is an excellent motivator. Next to a good **herding dog**, a **bucket of grain** is usually the best way to gather and move sheep. Grain feeding tends to make sheep friendlier and less intimidated by people.

Sheep spend about fifteen percent of their time sleeping, but may lie down and rest at other times. Upon rising, they often defecate and stretch. A sheep that is reluctant to get up is probably in pain. A sheep takes a long time to lie down is probably in pain. A sheep that cannot relax is under stress. Teeth grinding is another common sign of pain in sheep.

Watch out for rams

While sheep are generally a docile, non-aggressive animal, this is not usually the case with **rams**, especially during the breeding season. Rams can be very aggressive and have been known to cause serious injuries, even death, to people. A **ram should never be trusted**, even if it is friendly or was raised as a pet. **It is important to always know where the ram is and to never turn your back on him.** Children should be restricted access to rams during the breeding season.

Head butting is both a natural and learned behavior in sheep. Classic head butting among rams is highest during the rutting season which precedes the onset of heat in ewes. It is a way for rams to get into physical shape for the breeding season and to establish (or re-establish) the dominance hierarchy. To discourage butting, you should avoid petting or scratching a ram on the head. Otherwise, the ram may see this as a challenge or aggressive behavior. In general, the **ram** sees you as part of the flock and wants to **dominate you.**

The only time ewes may exhibit aggressive behavior is after lambing -- to protect their young.

Bell-wether (scared to death Negro leader)

Herders are known to make use of a **tame and trained** animal from the herd to go to the front of the herd and move according to the **instructions of the herder**, while the rest of the herd follows it. This use of a "flock leader" or **'bell-wether'** is widespread in shepherding. These particular sheep 'work as **mediators** between the shepherd and the flock' (Tani 1989: 196). Through training, flock leaders become '**obedient agents** reacting to the shepherd's vocal order' (ibid.)

This **'bell-wether'** sheep is a ram that has been **castrated** and a **bell put around his neck** so that the shepherd will know where he is at all times. (*Unfortunately, just like this 'bell-wether' sheep, many of the so-called leaders placed in front of Black people have been emasculated and trained to respond to the master's command*). As long as the sheep follow the shepherd's "flock leader", everything seems peaceful in the **corral**. However, if he finds that there is a ram in his herd that has **not been castrated** and is attempting to lead the flock in **another direction,** he is quick to **sic the dogs** on that bad sheep.

Training a sheepdog: (taken from http://www.sheepdogsonline.com/getstarted.html)

Pup training *(think of white folk):*

The most important lesson that a pup can learn while they are being raised is what is a **"correction"**. A correction shouldn't

24

frighten or confuse the pup; it should help to get the pup to think what the **right response** to do is. That means that if an individual is asked to do a task, and chooses another task instead, a correction will make him stop doing the wrong task and **search out** to find what the correct or right task is.

With a proper correction, the individual learns that he has made the wrong choice and must choose the right decision to **please his leader**. Many people get confused and misguided in how to train as they think that a positive response will always get the dog to make the right choice. This is true as long as that positive response is always available and is more enticing than the other responses. For example, training positively by food is a good way to start pups in simple obedience commands. You might ask them to sit or stay, and the pup is readily available to do this as long as you have some food in your hand. It is when you **don't have the food** that the problem usually arises. The dog also needs to be taught at the same time, that not only does the correct command please himself, but also it **pleases his leader**.

First exposure to sheep:

There are many different ways dogs will react to sheep in their first exposures but these are some common ones. The "why" is much more important than the "how" in determining how to proceed with your dog. Most dogs just need gentle guidance in understanding the "rules to work by" and to have their confidence built up. Dogs without the confidence problem generally just need some guidance. **Overconfident dogs** might need to be **taken down a peg** or two but also need to be shown how this all works and what is and is not allowed and expected.

A round pen, an inexperienced handler and an inexperienced dog can make for a wild scene! If you can remember some basic rules it'll be easier though. Most important is to **keep the dog on the other side of the sheep**. Do what you have to do to block him from coming around, but do it! Every time he "beats" you he is rewarded for it so just decide it's not allowed. If he was running for the street and a car was coming, you wouldn't worry about what method you used to stop him, you just would. So approach this the same way -it's just not allowed. You can make it easier for him and you by moving and **turning appropriately**, the same way you could make it easier to stop him before he got to the street if you'd taught him to come instantly on command. Don't expect him to do it right if you don't help him. And make sure to **read your dog**, pay attention to what he's doing, why he's doing it, what's going through his head. Help him when he needs it, fuss at him when he's wrong, and tell him he was a brave boy when he was. The whole idea is to **mold** what you've got.

Remember – Training a herding dog isn't so much about teaching him anything. It's all there **in the dog already**. You've just got to figure out how to ask for it in a way he can understand and listen to him when he's trying to tell you something. It's all about teaching you and opening that two-way communication between you and your dog.

Chapter 2

The Power of the Poison Book

The Most Honorable Elijah Muhammad referred to the Christian Bible as "The Poison Book." Although this book was written and rewritten hundreds of years ago, it still effects how people deal with each other underneath the labels attached to them by the dominant society. As we write there is ongoing bloodshed in the land of Palestine in which another people were injected based on the Bible.

In his book, *The Fall of America*, he wrote:

> **"America and England deposited their little brother, Israel, on foreign soil, Palestine, which is Arab land. They deprived the Arabs of their own land and sent them into exile. This injustice against the Arabs is now costing America the power and authority that she once exercised in the East. She is on her way out of the Near East. This means bloodshed and plenty of it."** (Muhammad 1973:171)

Some years ago I was watching The Phil Donahue Show. On this episode he had two guests, one a Jewish Rabbi and the other a Catholic Priest. They were discussing the issue of the Jews claiming divine rights to occupy Palestine and set up Israel as a Jewish state. The Jewish Rabbi asked the Catholic Priest if he believed that the Bible was the word of God. Of course the Catholic Priest answered, "Yes." The Rabbi continued his interrogation of the Priest: "Do you believe that all of the Bible is the truth?" The Priest answered: "Yes." Then the Rabbi said to the Priest: "Well, God promised that land to us." End of story.

Another incident happened recently to me in Americus,

27

Georgia. I was visiting a Black Baptist church with a friend of mine, not knowing that this particular Sunday a Jewish White woman was the guest speaker. Her subject was: "Egypt is Sin." What is a white woman doing in a Black church talking about a country in Africa, Egypt, being "Sin"? That would be like me going to a white church talking about "England is Sin." Jews seemingly have the right to come to a church filled with the great great-grandchildren of real slaves to denigrate a whole people based on their supposed enslavement to them 3500 years ago. That is real spiritual and psychological power using a book written with their own hands.

Even more recently, Prime Minister Netanyahu of Israel instructed President Obama to read the book of Ester in the Bible so as to encourage the U.S. to make a preemptive strike against Iran to destroy her nuclear facilities. Imagine that, what a political weapon that you can use the "word of God" to force present day leaders to go to war for you.

Herbert Berg in his 2005 *Journal of the American Academy of Religion* article titled "Mythmaking in the African American Muslim Context: The Moorish Science Temple, the Nation of Islam, and the American Society of Muslims" (http://www.academia.edu/2254441/Mythmaking_in_the_African_American_Muslim_Context_The_Moorish_Science_Temple_the_Nation_of_Islam_and_the_American_Society_of_Muslims) states:

> "Simply put, mythmaking is a social activity in which the group authorizes its identity and the role it sees for itself in the larger scheme of things (Mack 1995: 11). It is one of the key ways in which a group forms and perpetuates itself...
>
> More elaborately stated, mythmaking can describe any rhetorical act whose goal is to create, renew, sustain, or radically re-envision a group identity—whether within a

street gang, a nation, a religious community, or in this case a people identified by the color of their skin...In other words, they are revising the past, in light of present circumstances from a particular point of view to support a critical judgment about the present state of affairs."(Ibid.)

It is hard to get Black people who have been raised believing that the Bible is the unadulterated word of God to accept that it is a giant "myth" produced by Jews to give white people a new identity and make black, brown and yellow worship and fear white people as they should fear God. If God could not stop Jews (white people) from producing a lie in His name then He must not be real. To them, not to believe in the Bible is the same as not believing in God.

The Honorable Elijah Muhammad boldly writes on the back of the Muhammad Speaks Newspaper and on the inside back cover of the Final Call Newspaper beneath "What The Muslims Believe" point number 3: "WE BELIEVE in the truth of the Bible, but we believe that it has been tampered with and must be reinterpreted so that mankind will not be snared by the falsehoods that have been added to it."

To bear witness to the truth of what The Messenger teaches about the Bible we call upon one of the prophets of the Bible, Jeremiah. According to Jeremiah 8:8 **New International Version (NIV):**

> *⁸ How can you say, "We are wise,*
> *for we have the law of the LORD,"*
> *when actually the lying pen of the scribes*
> *has handled it falsely?*

Now let us show you how wicked these people really are in case you have not figured it out yet. If we look at the same verse Jeremiah

8:8 in the Kings James Version, it reads:

> *8 How do ye say, We are wise, and the law of
> the LORD is with us? Lo, certainly in vain made he it;
> the pen of the scribes is in vain.*

Or the New Revised Standard Version:

> *8 How can you say, "We are wise,
> and the law of the LORD is with us,"
> when, in fact, the false pen of the scribes
> has made it into a lie?*

Or the Wycliffe Bible which was the first English translation
published in 1382:

> *8 How say ye, We be wise men, and the law of the
> Lord is with us? Verily the false stylus, either writing,
> of scribes wrought leasing.* (How can ye say, We be
> wise men, and the Law of the Lord is with us? Truly
> the false stylus, or the deceitful writing, of the writers
> hath wrought lies.)

The word "leasing" in Old and Middle English according to the
Merriam-Webster Dictionary means "the act of lying."

Now you know that this King James Version translation of
this particular verse is confusing as hell and does not tell you with
clarity, like the New International Version, that the "…lying pen of
the scribes has handled it falsely…" The Messenger called the Bible
the "Poison Book" for it is indeed a poison venom for the mind.

30

The Bible as history:

Now let us recount the history of the world as given by the Bible, preached from the rostrum each Sunday and given to the members in Sunday school classes. The world was created 6,000 years ago in 6 days. On the seventh day God rested. Adam and Eve, the first humans were created on the sixth day and placed in the Garden of Eden somewhere in the Middle East. A snake slid up to Eve and tricked her into eating the forbidden fruit. She gave some of this fruit to Adam. God got upset and threw them out of the garden. Adam and Eve had two sons, Cain and Able. Cain was jealous of Able and killed him. Cain was driven away into the wilderness, but somehow beget children. To replace Cain, Adam and Eve gave birth to Seth. Seth begot Enoch and Enoch begot etc,, etc,. etc., until Noah was born. The world had fallen into sin because of the fall of Adam and God decided to destroy all living things except a pair of each species which he saved from the flood on the arc.

After the flood, Noah begot Shem, Ham and Japheth, who became the Semites, Blacks and Whites of the world. A descendent of Shem was born, Abraham, who became the friend of God and to whom was given the Divine Covenant sealed with blood, circumcision of the male child. Abraham begot Isaac and Ishmael. Isaac begot Esau and Jacob. Jacob stole Esau's birthright, wrestled with God or an angel, prevailed and was renamed Israel.

Jacob had 12 sons. One of them, Joseph, was sold into slavery to the Egyptians. Joseph was a dream interpreter and warned Pharaoh about a **seven year** famine. Pharaoh rewarded Joseph by placing him over the grain warehouses. Joseph later persuaded Pharaoh to allow his other brothers to move to Egypt to the land of Goshen. The Children of Israel grew in the land, but were persecuted by a Pharaoh who knew not Joseph.

Pharaoh ordered the killing of all male babies of the Children of Israel. However, one was saved by his mother by placing him in a basket and floating him down the Nile until he was picked up by Pharaoh's daughter who raised him as her son, Moses. Moses grew up in Pharaoh's house and learned all the ways of the Egyptians. However, one day he witnessed the brutal beating of a Hebrew and came to his defense slaying an Egyptian. For this murder of an Egyptian, Moses had to flee to the land of Midian. In Midian he met Jethro who taught him about Yahweh. One day Moses saw this burning bush on Mt. Sinai and went to take a better look. A voice came from the burning bush and told Moses to take off his sandals because he was standing on holy ground.

God, Yahweh, told Moses that he was not an Egyptian but a Hebrew child of Israel. God told Moses to cast his staff to the ground. It became a snake. God told Moses not to be afraid and to reach down and pick up the snake which turned back into a staff or rod. God told Moses to take his rod and go to Pharaoh and tell him to "let my people go." Moses claimed to not speak very well and asked if he could take along his brother, Aaron. God agreed and Moses and Aaron both went into Egypt and told Pharaoh what God, Yahweh, had instructed them to say.

Well Pharaoh did not accept the power of the God of Moses and refused to let the Children of Israel go. Then Moses used his rod and brought about ten plagues on Egypt until Pharaoh decided to let the Children of Israel go. However, after Pharaoh sent the Children of Israel on their way, he changed his mind and went after Moses and the Children of Israel as they journeyed to the Red Sea. Pharaoh must have forgot about that rod that Moses still had. Moses stretched his rod across the Red Sea and God's hand came down from the clouds and parted the sea, leaving dry ground through which the Children of Israel fled headed to the Sinai peninsula. Pharaoh and his chariots were held back by a pillar of fire until the Children of Israel had safely passed through the Red Sea. When the pillar of fire was lifted, Pharaoh and his army pursued Moses and the Children of Israel, but God closed the sea walls over Pharaoh and his army, killing all of them including Pharaoh.

On the other side of the Red Sea Moses went up into Mt. Sinai to meet with God. God used a finger of fire to write out the Ten Commandments on a slab of stone. While Moses was gone to meet with God, the people grew restless and some even wanted to go back to Egypt. They made Aaron make for them a Golden Calf as a god besides Yahweh or Jehovah. Yahweh was jealous and therefore made the Children of Israel to walk around in circles in the desert for 40 years before they could enter the Promised Land which was Palestine, which was already inhabited by a people who had done nothing to the Children of Israel. Moses died and Joshua took over. Joshua led the Battle of Jericho and other battles as the Children of Israel pushed into Palestine killing tribe after tribe until they dominated the Promised Land.

As time went on, Israel was attacked by the Philistines. The Philistines had a great giant warrior named Goliath. All the Children of Israel were afraid of Goliath except little David. David put a rock into his sling and hit Goliath in the middle of his forehead, knocking him out. David then took Goliath's own sword and cut his head off. David then built Israel into a great kingdom. His son, Solomon, had Hiram the king of Tyre, to help him build the Great Temple of God.

The Children of Israel grew disobedient to God, Yahweh, taking on other gods. God, Yahweh, then rose up the Babylonians led by Nebuchadnezzar to come into Palestine and destroy the Temple of Jerusalem in 586 BC. He took the leading families of Israel back to Babylon as slaves. The Children of Israel, now called Judah, were commissioned by the Persian King Cyrus who had defeated the Babylonians, to go back to Jerusalem and rebuild the temple and begin practicing Judaism back in Palestine.

The Children of Israel, now called "Judah" and later "Jews", although they had been disobedient to God, God promised them a Messiah from the line of David to restore Israel to her former greatness. In the time of King Herod a star was seen in the East by

33

three wise men (Magi). These wise men from the East knew that this star foretold of a Messiah being born. They followed this star to Bethlehem where Jesus was born in a manger from a "virgin" named Mary. Even though Joseph was not supposed to be the biological father of Jesus, both the book of Matthew and the book of Luke trace the ancestry of Joseph back to David. This is a little awkward, for this "born of a virgin" thing, but they needed to tie Jesus back to David to fulfill prophecy, but could not use Mary because kingship descended through the man and not the woman.

Jesus grew up to become a great wise man who was seen at an early age teaching the priests in the Temple of Jerusalem. As he grew older and developed a great following, he was seen as a threat by the Pharisees, priests and elders of Israel. They claimed that Jesus had blasphemed against God and went to Pontius Pilot, Rome's representative in Palestine, to demand that Jesus be crucified. Pontius Pilot did not want to do it, so he washed his hands and turned Jesus over to be crucified. Jesus was crucified on Good Friday, but arose three days later on Sunday morning. The Christians believe that when Jesus was crucified his sacrifice meant that he had died for the sins of the world. Now all one had to do was say that Jesus Christ was your personal Savior, and you could be guaranteed to go to heaven after you died and live in the presence of God and all your good relatives for eternity; wearing gold slippers, drinking milk and eating honey all day.

Oh, did I say that Jesus taught that we should "love everybody" no matter how mean they have been to you. Well even though a computer search of the Bible will not find the phrase "love everybody", the preachers know what Jesus meant.(smile) Oh, Jesus was the Son of God, yet also part of the three parts of God, the Father, the Son and the Holy Ghost, three in one. Don't worry about understanding it, just believe, because man can never know God nor his ways. Just do what the authorities tell you to do and go to church each Sunday.

Well as a young black boy in Winston-Salem, N.C., I did just

34

that until the assassination of Dr. Martin Luther King, Jr. I went to my church right after the murder of Dr. King and witnessed my lifelong preacher with his mouth literally condemning the young black people to eternal hell fire, who had thrown some bricks in white folk's stores after he was assassinated. I told my mother that I was going to talk to that preacher, because in all my days of going to this church each Sunday and me even teaching Sunday school, I never heard him say a mumbling word about the wrongs and injustices perpetrated by whites against black people. My mother told me not to confront my preacher, so I decided then and there never to go back to church. It took a little Black man from Georgia, Elijah Muhammad, to change my mind by giving me a new and more realistic interpretation of the Bible and human history.

However, those people still trapped in the grave of the Bible can be manipulated by Jews and Christian preachers, the shepherds of the human flock, to accept Whites and Jews as superiors to the darker people of our planet because their god made it that way. And this is the power of the Poison Book. It is the evil shepherd's crook or the snake's venom.

Some people may argue that our young black people are not going to church and are therefore not affected by the Poison Book. However, I would argue that the Poison Book has developed a civilization and a culture, where its world view is at the base of all movies, T.V. programs, plays and music. Every Christmas and Easter a string of old and new movies are broadcasted to remind the American people that this is a society based on Judeo-Christian ideas and ideals.

Now add to these influences the fact that a lot of black people, old and now young, are dying. Family and friends are obligated to attend these funerals and now the preacher has a new chance to proselytize and save another soul from hell. The message that the preachers give at the funerals are passionate and confusing. They usually start out by saying the dead person, say Aunt Sally, is in a "better place", she is in the "bosom of Abraham" etc. Then a few

35

hoops later the preacher will say, "But on that great getting up morning when the dead rise to glory, Aunt Sally will be in that number." Why would Aunt Sally want to come from this "better place" in the "bosom of Abraham" just to go back to the same place?

The Poison Book preys on people's bewilderment over life and death along with appealing to a sense of greed, because each person wants to have his life forever. Of course no one has ever come back from the dead to tell the living what they can expect, but the preacher sells the people on this lottery ticket, "well what if there is a heaven and hell that you will sit in for eternity, can you afford to be wrong and not buy what I am selling?"

Chapter 3

A New Historical Paradigm

The Most Honorable Elijah Muhammad has been teaching a completely different history of man and mankind since he received these teachings from his teacher Master Fard Muhammad in the 1930s. This revised history, which is given to the members of Nation of Islam as "Lessons" to study, produces different reasons for things being as they are. It gives the reader a different road map of cause and effect. If one has been misinformed as to how people got from point A to point B, then the misinformed person will continue to make plans but never get to his planned destination because of this false historical road map. The Most Honorable Elijah Muhammad straightens out this road map allowing us to have a better understanding of the past, how we got where we are and therefore, what are the best routes to take as we move forward.

Unlike the Bible which tries to limit the creation of the heavens and the earth to 6 earth days, The Messenger in his lecture series captured in *The Theology of Time* gives a more realistic and scientific approach to understanding the beginnings of our universe, earth and man. He states:

> .. Light came unto the total darkness of our Created
> Man. There was no such thing as God saying, "Let us make a
> Black Man." No man knows when the first Black Man was made.
> The Atom out of which Man was created came from space. It
> was out in space where He originated. An Atom of Life was in
> the darkness of the space and He came out of that Atom that
> was in the space. Now you may wonder; how did that Atom get
> in space? The history of space teaches us that at one time it was
> nothing but darkness. If there had been light for us to use our
> glasses on, to find out if there was an Atom of Life in the
> darkness, before the Atom exploded, to show what it was, we

would tell you so. But we can't go that far. We don't know how the Atom formed in space. What came out of space was a Human Being. That is as far back as we can go with it...(Muhammad 1992: 105)

The God created Himself out of matter (which still exists here) that He took out of the darkness of space...(Ibid.: 108)

Time is motion. We can't make Time without a motion. Whenever we make a motion it is registering Time. This is the way the Universe is made. There was no such thing as Time before the Creation of God. The Universe, as we call it now, was not a Universe. It was just darkened, unlimited space. (Ibid.: 110)

We will take excerpts from The Messenger's monumental book ***Message to the Blackman in America*** so that the reader can get a glimpse of a new mind. We start off from the chapter entitled "Original Man Know Thyself":

Who is better knowing of who we are than God, Himself? He has declared that we are descendants of the Asian black nation and of the tribe of Shabazz.

You might ask, who is the tribe of Shabazz? Originally, they were the tribe that came with the earth (or this part) 66 trillion years ago when a great explosion on our planet divided it into two parts. One we call earth and the other moon.

This was done by one of our scientists, God; who wanted the people to speak one language, one dialect for all, but was unable to bring this about. He decided to kill us by destroying our planet, but still He failed. We were lucky to be on this part, earth, which did not lose its water in the mighty blasting away of the part called moon.

We, the tribe of Shabazz, says Allah (God), were the first to discover the best part of our planet to live on. The rich Nile Valley of Egypt and the present seat of the Holy City, Mecca, Arabia.

The origin of our kinky hair, says Allah, came from one of our dissatisfied scientists, 50,000 years ago, who wanted to make all of us tough and hard in order to endure the life of the jungles of East Asia (Africa) and to overcome the beasts there. But he failed to get the others to agree with him.

He took his family and moved into the jungle to prove to us that we could live there and conquer the wild beasts, and we have. So, being the first and the smartest scientist on the deportation of our moon and the one who suffered most of all, Allah (God) has decided to place us on the top with a thorough knowledge of self and his guidance. (Muhammad 1965:31, 32)

And starting on page 108 of the chapter called "The Making of Devil" he writes:

We make such history once every 25,000 years. When such history is written, it is done by twenty-four of our scientists. One acts as Judge or God for the others and twenty-three actually do the work of getting up the future of the nation, and all is put into one book and at intervals where such and such part or portion will come to pass, that people will be given that part of the book through one among that people from one of the Twelve (twelve major scientists) as it is then called a Scripture which actually means script of writing from something original or book...

Six thousand years ago, or to be more exact 6,600 years ago, as Allah taught me, our nation gave birth to another God whose name was Yakub. He started studying the life germ of man to try making a new creation (new man) whom our twenty-four scientists had foretold 8,400 years before the birth of Mr. Yakub, and the scientists were aware of his birth and work before he was born, as they are today of the intentions an ideas of the present world.

According to the word of Allah to me, "Mr. Yakub was seen by the twenty-three Scientists of the black nation, over 15,000 years ago. They predicted that in the year 8,400 (that was in our calendar year before this world of the white race), this man (Yakub) would be born twenty miles from the present Holy City, Mecca, Arabia. And, that at the time of his birth, the satisfaction and dissatisfaction of the people would be:--70 per cent satisfied, 30 per cent dissatisfied"

And, that when this man is born, he will change civilization (the world), and produce a new race of people, who would rule the original black nation for 6,000 years (from the nine thousandth year to the fifteen thousandth year).

After that time, the original nation would give birth to one, whose wisdom, Knowledge and power would be infinite. One, whom the world would recognize as being the greatest and mightiest God, since the creation of the universe. And, that He would destroy Yakub's world and restore the original nation, or ancient nation, into power to rule forever...

Yakub was the founder of unlike attracts and like repels, though Mr. Yakub was a member of the black nation. He began school at the age of four. He had an unusual size head. When he had grown up, the others referred to him as the "big head scientist."

At the age of 18 he had finished all the colleges and universities of his nation, and was seen preaching on the streets of Mecca, making converts. He made such impressions on the people, that many began following him.

He learned, from studying the germ of the black man, under

40

the microscope, that there were two people in him, and that one was black, the other brown.

He said if he could successfully separate the one from the other he could graft the brown germ into its last stage, which would be white. With his wisdom, he could make the white, which he discovered was the weaker of the black germ (which would be unalike) rule the black nation for a time (until a greater one than Yakub was born).

The new idea put him to work finding the necessary converts to begin grafting his new race of people. He began by teaching Islam, with promises of luxury to those who would believe and follow him.

As Mr. Yakub continued to preach for converts, he told his people that he would make the others work for them. (This promise came to pass). Naturally, there are always some people around who would like to have others do their work. Those are the ones who fell for Mr. Yakub's teaching, 100 per cent...

...So, the Government began to make preparation for the exiling of Mr. Yakub and His followers. The King ordered everyone rounded up who was a believer in Mr. Yakub. They took them to the seaport and loaded them on ships.

After rounding them all up into ships, they numbered 59,999, Yakub made 60,000. Their ships sailed out to an Isle in the Aegean Sea called "Pelan" (Bible "Patmos"). After they were loaded into the ships, Mr. Yakub examined each of them to see if they were 100 per cent with him; and to see if they were all healthy and productive people. If not, he would throw them off. Some were found to be unfit and overboard they went...

After the first 200 years, Mr. Yakub had done away with the black babies, and all were brown. After another 200 years, he had all yellow or red, which was 400 years after being on

"Pelan." Another 200 years, which brings us to the six hundredth year, Mr. Yakub had an all-pale white race of people on this Isle...

After Yakub's devils were among the Holy people of Islam (the black nation) for six months, they had our people at war with each other. The holy people were unable to understand, just why they could not get along in peace with each other, until they took the matter to the King.

The King told the holy people of the black nation that the trouble they were having was caused by the white devils in their midst, and that there would be no peace among them until they drove these white made devils from among them.

The holy people prepared to drive the devils out from among them. The King said: "Gather every one of the devils up and strip them of our costume. Put an apron on them to hide their nakedness. Take all literature from them and take them by way of the desert. Send a caravan, armed with rifles, to keep the devils going westward. Don't allow one of them to turn back; and, if they are lucky enough to get across the Arabian Desert, let them go into the hills of West Asia, the place they now call Europe.

Yakub's made devils were driven out of Paradise, into the hills of West Asia (Europe), and stripped of everything but the language. They walked across that hot, sandy desert, into the land where long years of both trouble and joy awaited them; but—they finally made it. (Not all; many died in the desert.)

Once there, they were roped in, to keep them out of Paradise. To make sure, the Muslims, who lived along the borders of East and West Asia, were ordered to patrol the border to keep Yakub's devils in West Asia (now called Europe), so that the original nation of black men could live in peace; and that the

42

devils could be alone to themselves, to do as they pleased, as long as they didn't try crossing the East border.

The soldiers patrolled the border armed with swords, to prevent the devils from crossing. This went on for 2,000 years. After that time, Musa (Moses) was born; the man whom Allah would send to these exiled devils to bring them again into the light of civilization...

Being deprived of divine guidance for their disobedience, the making of mischief and causing bloodshed in the holy nation of the original black people by lies, they became so savage that they lost all their sense of shame...

They became shameless. In the winter they wore animal skins for clothes and grew hair all over their bodies and faces like all the other wild animals.

In those days, they made their homes in the caves and hillsides. There is a whole chapter devoted to them in the Holy Qur-an. They had it very hard, trying to save themselves from being destroyed by wild beasts which were plentiful at that time.

Being without a guide, they started walking on their hands and feet like all animals; and, learned to climb trees as well as any of the animals. At night, they would climb up into trees, carrying large stones and clubs, to fight the wild beasts that would come prowling around at night, to keep them from eating their families.

Their next and best weapons were the dogs. They tamed some of these dogs to live in the caves with their families, to help protect them from the wild beasts. After a time, the dog held a high place among the family because of his fearlessness to attack the enemies of his master. Today, the dog is still loved by the white race and is given more justice than the so-called Negroes, and, is called the white man's best friend. This comes

43

from the cave days.

After 2,000 year of living as a savage, Allah raised up Musa (Moses) to bring the white race again into civilization; to take their place as rulers, as Yakub had intended for them. Musa (Moses) became their God and leader. He brought them out of the caves; taught them to believe in Allah; taught them to wear clothes; how to cook their food; how to season it with salt; what beef they should kill and eat; and how to use fire for their service. Moses taught them against putting the female cow under burden.

He established for them Friday as the day to eat fish, and not to eat meat (beef) on that day. And, fish is the main menu on Fridays in many of the whites' homes today..."(Ibid.:108-120)

In the above history The Messenger makes it very clear that the Jews did not fulfill the prophecy of being enslaved for 400 years in Egypt. Moses delivered them from their 2,000 year exile from behind the Caucasus Mountains, not from a supposed enslavement in the land of Egypt. The Messenger further states on page 268 that it is America's enslavement and treatment of the Negro that fulfills scripture:

"America has fulfilled this to the very letter and spirit with her slaves (the so-called Negroes) under the type of Israel. The Egyptians did nothing of the kind to Israel when they were in bondage to them. In fact, and as God taught me, the Bible is not referring to those people as His People, it is referring to the so-called Negro and his enemy (the white race)..."(Ibid.: 268)

As stated earlier Jesus came 2,000 years after Moses but was 2,000 years ahead of his time. However, the life of Jesus was a prototype of the modern Jesus of today. The Messenger states on page 251:

44

"As Jesus comes close to revealing the whereabouts of the lost members of a great nation in these words, 'that he was sent to the lost sheep of the house of Israel, or in the house of Israel.' He did not say that he was sent to the lost Israel, but to the lost sheep in the house of Israel. The lost sheep are not Israel. The lost sheep were in the house or government of Israel and were swallowed up by Israel so thoroughly that they were always overlooked." (Ibid.: 251)

Here we see that "the lost sheep" and Israel are not the same. Who were these "lost sheep" and how did they end up in Israel? Where did Israel or, rather, the governing body of Israel come from? If you look at a map of Israel or Palestine, you will see that it lies between two continents, Africa and Asia, on the overland trade routes between the two. At one time Ancient Egypt (Kemit) held dominion over Palestine, and Jerusalem was used as an outpost to protect the borders of Egypt and secure the trade routes to Asia. Eventually the Egyptians lost control of Palestine when Nebuchadnezzar, king of the Babylonians, swooped through Palestine and took prisoners back to Babylonia in 597 BC. This phase of orthodox Jewish history is referred to as the "captivity". This supposed forced exile ended in 538 BC, when according to the Bible, the children of the captives or slaves were allowed to go back to Palestine and rebuild the Temple. Later another group led by Ezra came to Jerusalem to "reintroduce" the Torah, which had been destroyed according to the Bible (Ezra 7-10 and Neh. 8).

These "returnees" were admonished by their "liberator", the Persian King Cyrus the Great, not to allow the natives of Palestine, many of them Jews, to participate in the rebuilding of the Temple or intermarry with those "returning" from Babylon. The ruling class, called Pharisees, who came from Babylon, now ruled over "the people" of Palestine for the Persian rulers who now occupied Israel.

So Jesus was locked into a fight with these Pharisees over the lost sheep. He was not victorious over these Pharisees, nor was he on time to destroy the Jews' civilization. A key to understanding this battle centers on the identity of the "sheep", who were the people taken to Babylon by Nebuchadnezzar and who came back. It took the coming of Master Fard Muhammad and the raising up of The Most Honorable Elijah Muhammad to give us the keys to solve this puzzle over the identity of God's "chosen people."

Which History is Correct?

In these two chapters we dealt with historical paradigms presented in the "Poison Book" and in "Message to the Black Man." I would like to deal with these two points of view under the headings of: 1. The creation of the planet earth, 2. Creation of man and races, 3. Enslavement and Exodus from Egypt, 4. Babylonian Captivity and 5. Searching for the Messiah.

1. Creation of the planet earth:

The Bible claims that the heavens and the earth and all living creatures on the earth were created in 6 earth days. On the seventh day God was a little tired and so he rested. However, The Honorable Elijah Muhammad describes the first God as creating himself from "darkness" and the earth and moon as we know it were here for at least 66 trillion years.

We say in the Nation of Islam that "Islam" is mathematics and "mathematics" is Islam. We believe that there is no conflict between true science and true religion. They should back up each other. Indeed the latest astrophysics backs up The Messenger's creation paradigm completely as described in two articles below: 1 "Dark energy, dark matter" and 2. "Was the Moon created by a nuclear explosion?"

Dark energy, dark matter:

(http://science.nasa.gov/astrophysics/focus-areas/what-is-dark-energy/)

In the early 1990's, one thing was fairly certain about the expansion of the Universe. It might have enough energy density to stop its expansion and re-collapse, it might have so little energy density that it would never stop expanding, but gravity was certain to slow the expansion as time went on. Granted, the slowing had not been observed, but, theoretically, the Universe had to slow. The Universe is full of matter and the attractive force of gravity pulls all matter together. Then came 1998 and the Hubble Space Telescope (HST) observations of very distant supernovae which showed that, a long time ago, the Universe was actually expanding more slowly than it is today. So the expansion of the Universe has not been slowing due to gravity, as everyone thought, it has been accelerating. No one expected this, no one knew how to explain it...

Theorists still don't know what the correct explanation is, but they have given the solution a name. It is called dark energy...

WHAT IS DARK ENERGY?

More is unknown than is known. We know how much dark energy there is because we know how it affects the Universe's expansion...It turns out that roughly 68% of the Universe is dark energy. Dark matter makes up about 27%. The rest - everything on Earth, everything ever observed with all of our instruments, all normal matter - adds up to less than 5% of the Universe...

Einstein's theory of gravity may not be correct. That would not only affect the expansion of the Universe, but it would also affect the way that normal matter in galaxies and clusters of galaxies behaved. This fact would provide a way to decide if the solution to the dark energy problem is a new gravity theory or not: we could observe how galaxies come together in clusters...

47

What Is Dark Matter?

By fitting a theoretical model of the composition of the Universe to the combined set of cosmological observations, scientists have come up with the composition that we described above, ~68% dark energy, ~27% dark matter, ~5% normal matter. What is dark matter?

We are much more certain what dark matter is not than we are what it is. First, it is dark, meaning that it is not in the form of stars and planets that we see. Observations show that there is far too little visible matter in the Universe to make up the 27% required by the observations. Second, it is not in the form of dark clouds of normal matter, matter made up of particles called baryons. We know this because we would be able to detect baryonic clouds by their absorption of radiation passing through them. Third, dark matter is not antimatter, because we do not see the unique gamma rays that are produced when antimatter annihilates with matter...

Was the Moon created by a nuclear explosion on Earth?

http://www.dailymail.co.uk/sciencetech/article-1246872/Was-moon-created-nuclear-explosion-Earth.html#ixzz0eIrKMSYe

By Lucy Waterlow

Last updated at 7:04 PM on 31st January 2010

How the Moon was created and came to orbit the Earth has long puzzled scientists.

The most commonly held theory is that when the solar system was first formed, an object collided with Earth, knocking off a chunk of rock that fell into orbit around it.

But now two scientists have come up with a new explanation. They believe the Moon did not break away from the Earth because of an impact or an explosion in space, but because of a nuclear explosion on Earth itself.

Their idea is based on the fission theory which was first outlined in the 19th century.

The fission theory suggested that the Earth and Moon were both created out of the same blob of spinning molten rock - with a part becoming separated which later became the moon.

However, aside from an impact, scientists couldn't explain how the blob which became the moon spun off.

Rob de Meijer at University of the Western Cape and Wim van Westrenen at VU University in Amsterdam believe the Moon was blasted out of the Earth by a nuclear explosion on our planet. In their research paper, "An alternative hypothesis for the origin of the Moon", they explain that if the moon had been separated from the Earth by an impacting external force, the moon would be composed of whatever knocked into it and the Earth.

"Models of solar system evolution show that it is highly unlikely for the chemical composition of the Earth and impactor to be identical," they state.

Yet recent lunar samples show that the moon is almost identical in chemical composition to the Earth - suggesting there was no impactor involved.

"A more likely possibility for the large degree of compositional similarity... is that the moon derives directly from terrestrial material," the research paper states.

2. Creation of man and races

White skin:

One of the strangest yet fundamental parts of the Teachings

of the Honorable Elijah Muhammad is the history of Yakub and the making of the white race. Where did the white race come from? In our lessons the question is asked, "Who is the colored man?" The Answer is, "The colored man is the Caucasian (white man) or Yakub's grafted devil, skunk of the planet earth." These are hard and, some say, "racist" words. But are they true?

In the Holy Qur'an reference is made to human-like creatures called "jinn". These jinn are sometimes represented as spirits of evil, mountain tribes or devils. A whole chapter of the Holy Qur'an is dedicated to them (Surah 72). No real description is given of them except that they were created of a "flame of fire"(Surah 55:15). In the history of Yakub the Honorable Elijah Muhammad teaches us that 6,600 years ago Mr. Yakub discovered that there were two natures or people within the original Black man, one black, the other brown. This brown germ could be isolated and formed into a human with a fiery, unalike nature.

In Ancient Kemet they had a story or legend about two brothers, Ausar and Set. The human being was said to have these two fighters in their bodies, one Ausar or the Black and the other Set, or the Red. The human had to maintain the balance between these two warriors within the body.

In the Bible the authors try to give an explanation for the three major categories of man or races. The human race was destroyed by a flood. Only Noah and his three sons and their wives were saved. After the flood the earth was divided and populated from his three sons, Shem, Ham and Japheth. Shem representing what is called the "Semites", Ham, "Cushite" or black, and Japheth, "Gentiles" or white. Japheth is said to populate what is called in the Bible, the "isles of the Gentiles" (Genesis 10:2-5). The "-iles" part refers to the mountainous islands in the Aegean Sea, but what does the "gen-" part refer to? Could this be the "jinn"?

The Honorable Minister Louis Farrakhan has taught us that the Holy Qur'an was revealed by Allah (God) to and through

Prophet Muhammad (may Allah be pleased) 1400 years ago. Minister Farrakhan has also taught us that the Holy Qur'an is a Message from God that can only be understood more clearly as we develop our understanding of the science of God's universe.

This brings us to what is this "jinn"? Could the "jinn" actually be talking about the "gene", a part of man that has been unseen until recently? The word "gene" comes from the Greek "genea" which means "generation" or "race". So could a "gene"(race) representing a fiery (red) nature of man have been locked within the chromosomes of Black people? Remember that the Honorable Elijah Muhammad taught that before 6,600 years ago there was no white race of people, just Black. Starting 6,600 years ago on the Island of Patmos (Pelan) in the Aegean Sea, it took Mr. Yakub and his laborers 600 years of grafting to finally produce a completely white race.

Now let us fast-forward to today and the latest genetic research:

"Still Evolving, Human Genes Tell New Story", by NICHOLAS WADE, March 7, 2006:

> "There is ample evidence that selection has been a major driving point in our evolution during the last 10,000 years, and there is no reason to suppose that it has stopped," said Jonathan Pritchard, a population geneticist at the University of Chicago who headed the study...
>
> Their data is based on DNA changes in three populations gathered by the HapMap project, which built on the decoding of the human genome in 2003. The data, though collected to help identify variant genes that contribute to disease, also give evidence of evolutionary change...
>
> Dr. Pritchard estimates that the average point at which

the selected genes started to become more common under the pressure of natural selection is 10,800 years ago in the African population and 6,600 years ago in the Asian and European populations.

Skeletons similar in form to modern Chinese are hard to find before that period, Dr. Klein said, and there are few European skeletons older than 10,000 years that look like modern Europeans.

Dr. Pritchard's list of selected genes also includes five that affect skin color. The selected versions of the genes occur solely in Europeans and are presumably responsible for pale skin. Anthropologists have generally assumed that the first modern humans to arrive in Europe some 45,000 years ago had the dark skin of their African origins, but soon acquired the paler skin needed to admit sunlight for vitamin D synthesis.

The finding of five skin genes selected 6,600 years ago could imply that Europeans acquired their pale skin much more recently.

Dr. Pritchard also detected selection at work in brain genes, including a group known as microcephaly genes because, when disrupted, they cause people to be born with unusually small brains."
(http://www.nytimes.com/2006/03/07/science/07evolve.html?pagewanted=all&_r=0)

Blue eyes:

According to a February 1, 2008 article published on www.foxnews.com entitled

"Scientist: All Blue-Eyed People Are Related", Danish researchers have concluded that all blue-eyed people share a common ancestor, presumably someone who lived 6,000 to 10,000 years ago.

Eiberg and his team analyzed 155 individuals in a large Danish family, plus several blue-eyed people born in Turkey and Jordan.

"Originally, we all had brown eyes," Professor Hans Eiberg of Copenhagen said in a press release. "But a genetic mutation affecting the OCA2 gene in our chromosomes resulted in the creation of a 'switch,' which literally 'turned off' the ability to produce brown eyes."

Eiberg figures the mutation took place on the northern side of the Black Sea, but that's an educated guess, assuming the first blue-eyed humans were among the proto-Indo-Europeans who subsequently spread agriculture into Western Europe and later rode horses into Iran and India...

Blue eyes are a recessive trait, and the gene must be inherited from both parents. It wasn't until the original mutant's grandchildren or great-grandchildren hooked up that the first blue-eyed person appeared."
(http://www.foxnews.com/story/2008/02/01/scientist-all-blue-eyed-people-are-related/)

White race migration into Europe: "Kurgan Invasion"

Professor Hans Eiberg mentioned the proto-Indo-Europeans who in 4,000 B.C. spread a form of agriculture into Western Europe and who later after 2,000 B.C. rode horses into Iran and Iraq subduing the native or indigenous populations. This brings us to the archaeological work of American and Russian scholars as they try to find the beginnings of the white race. Some of their research findings were published in "The 'Kurgan Culture', Indo-European Origins and the Domestication of the Horse: A Reconsideration" by

David W. Anthony (Current Anthropology Volume 27, Issue 4 (Aug.-Oct., 1986) 291-314).

According to David Anthony "The concept of a 'Kurgan Culture' derives ultimately from *The Aryans,* Childe's (1926) seminal study of Indo-European origins. Childe assumed that large-scale migrations would have been associated with the prehistoric diffusion of Indo-European languages, and he therefore searched the archaeological record for a material culture horizon that was distributed widely enough to qualify as the archaeological manifestation of that diffusion." (Ibid.: 291) The phrase "Kurgan culture" was coined by Marija Gimbutas who constructed the picture of this culture which most Western European and many Eastern European archaeologists rely.

In general outline the Kurgan culture is a patriarchal, seminomadic, Indo-European-speaking group of stock breeders who originated in the vicinity of the lower Volga river just north of the Caucasus and migrated westward across much of Europe, eastward across Central Asia, and southward into Anatolia (Turkey) and Greece starting in about 4,000 to 3,500 B.C. Before the Kurgan invasion the inhabitants are described by archaeologists as "Mediterranean types" which is a euphemism for "dark skinned oval headed" while the conquering Kurgan's were "white-skinned square headed." After Kurgan had conquered an area the primary changes are said to have been "…the emergence of ranked, highly competitive societies dominated by localized elites who controlled local production and enriched themselves through trade and war." In other words they developed a stratified caste system as we find in India today, light-skinned on top and dark-skinned on the bottom.

The indigenous people were farmers who grew a variety of grains whereas the invaders were mostly sheep herders who had domesticated the sheep, the wolf into a **sheepdog** and the horse. According to Gimbutas (Ibid.: 305) the basic features of the Kurgan culture –"patriarchy, patrilineality, ranking, animal domestication (including that of the horse), pastoralism, mobility, and armament (bow and arrow, spear, thrusting and cutting flint dagger, and later bronze) and a **poor** ceramic and **architectural** tradition—correspond with what has been reconstructed as Proto-Indo-European by means of linguistic studies. These features stand *in opposition to* the Old European matricentric, sedentary and ceramic traditions." This change was accompanied by the "hybridization of the Old European pantheon of lunar and chthonic goddesses with the Indo-European male pantheon of sky gods typical of **shepherds**."

Now if we tie this back into The Messenger teaching us about how the white people were driven across the dessert into the Caucasus Mountains in 4,000 B.C., we find them emerging on the north side of the Caucasus Mountains attacking a more civilized darker society. 2,000 years later these same white folk were raised up by Moses to roll out of the south side of the Caucasus Mountains as the "shepherd kings" or Hyksos who attacked Egypt and the Aryans or Scythians who attacked Iran and India.

One of the telling aspects of these Aryans or Scythians was their caste system with the whitest on top and the darker below. Herodotus also mentioned a royal tribe or clan, an elite group which dominated the other Scythians:

> Then on the other side of the Gerros we have those parts which are called the "Royal" lands and those Scythians who are the bravest and most numerous and who esteem the other Scythians their **slaves**. (Herodotus. *History* . Book IV, verses 19-20)

The Wall and Gate at Derbend

Map of Caucasus Mts: Derbend (right side)

Earlier in this chapter we related the history of Yakub's grafted people who after returning to the Holy Land started mischief and were kicked out and placed behind a wall in the Caucasus Mountains. The Honorable Elijah Muhammad taught us that there is a whole chapter or Surah in the Holy Qur'an titled "The Cave" and is dedicated to the cave dwellers in Europe. Both Greek legend and the Holy Qur'an mention some type of wall being built at the foot of the Caucasus Mountains. From
http://www.theoi.com/Ther/DrakonKholkikos.html

"The Drakon Kholkikos (or Colchian Dragon):

> Diodorus Siculus, Library of History 4. 47. 3:
>
> "He [Aeetes] also threw a **wall** about the precinct [where the Golden Fleece was kept] and stationed there **many guardians**,

these being men of the Tauric Chersonese, and it is because of these guards that the Greeks invented monstrous myths. For instance, the report was spread abroad that there were fire-breathing Tauroi (Bulls) round about the precinct and that a sleepless Drakon (Dragon) guarded the fleece, the identity of the names having led to the transfer from the men who were Taurians to the cattle because of their strength and the cruelty shown in the murder of strangers having been made into the myth of the bulls breathing fire; and similarly the name of the guardian who watched over the sacred precinct, which was Drakon, has been transferred by the poets to the monstrous and fear-inspiring beast, the dragon."

Holy Qur'an Surah 18: The Cave verses 83-101:

18:83 And they ask thee about Dhu-l-qarnain. Say: I will recite to you an account of him.

18:84 Truly We established him in the land and granted him means of access to everything;

18:85 So he followed a course.

18:86 Until, when he reached the setting-place of the sun, he found it going down into a black sea, and found by it a people. We said: O Dhu-l-qarnain, either punish them or do them a benefit.

18:87 He said: As for him who is unjust, we shall chastise him, then he will be returned to his Lord, and He will chastise him with an exemplary chastisement.

18:88 And as for him who believes and does good, for him is a good reward, and We shall speak to him an easy word of Our command.

18:89 *Then he followed a course.*

18:90 *Until, when he reached (the land of) the rising sun, he found it rising on a people to whom We had given no shelter from it —*

18:91 *So it was. And We had full knowledge of what he had.*

18:92 *Then he followed a course.*

18:93 *Until, when he reached (a place) between the two mountains, he found on that side of them a people who could hardly understand a word.*

18:94 *They said: O Dhu-l-qarnain, Gog and Magog do mischief in the land. May we then pay thee tribute on condition that thou raise a barrier between us and them?*

18:95 *He said: That wherein my Lord has established me is better, so if only you help me with strength (of men), I will make a fortified barrier between you and them:*

18:96 *Bring me blocks of iron. At length, when he had filled up the space between the two mountain sides, he said, Blow. Till, when he had made it (as) fire, he said: Bring me molten brass to pour over it.*

18:97 *So they were not able to scale it, nor could they make a hole in it.*

18:98 *He said: This is a mercy from my Lord, but when the promise of my Lord comes to pass He will crumble it, and the promise of my Lord is ever true.*

18:99 *And on that day We shall let some of them surge*

against others and the trumpet will be blown, then We shall gather them all together,

18:100 And We shall bring forth hell, exposed to view, on that day before the disbelievers,

18:101 Whose eyes were under a cover from My Reminder, and they could not bear to hear.

Scholars and translators of the Holy Qur-an including Maulana Muhammad Ali and A. Yusuf Ali have ventured to determine where this wall or iron gate was located and who was Dhu-l-Qarnain or Zul-qarnain. A. Yusuf Ali in appendix VII gives the meaning of the name Zul-qarnain: "Lord of the two Qarns..." "'Qarn' may mean: (1) a horn in the literal sense, as in the case of a ram or bull; (2) a horn in a metaphorical sense, as in English, the horns of the crescent, or by a further metaphor (not used in English), the horns of a kingdom or territory, two portions on opposite ends..."

Starting from the two kingdom metaphor Yusuf Ali and Muhammad Ali disagree on the personage of Dhu-l-Qarnain. Yusuf Ali argues for Alexander the Great and Muhammad Ali argues for King Darius of Persia. Both kings conquered and ruled over vast territories and both kings had a run-in with the Scythians who were based north of the Caucasus Mountains. Maulana Muhammmad Ali takes the reference to the sun setting in a "black sea" in the Surah of The Cave to refer to the Black Sea which is on the west side of the Caucasus Mountains and considers the Caspian Sea to represent the place of the "rising sun" which is on the east side of the Caucasus. Both authors point out the existence of a great Wall, 29 feet high, which stretched for 50 miles between the Caucasus and the Caspian Sea at Derbend (see map). Muhammad Ali prefers the Scythian tribes as representing Gog and Magog, while Yusuf Ali prefers the Mongol tribes. Both commentaries are a fascinating read which is worth taking your time and reading each.

Although both scholars are correct at the meaning of "Dhu-l-Qarnain" and recognize the wall and iron gate built at Derbend, they have overlooked another dual kingdom kingship and a king given credit for dealing with these same Scythians from the Caucasus. In Ancient Egypt since the unification of the "North and South" into one kingdom 6,000 years ago and stretching for almost 4,000 years of the Egyptian Civilization, the King (not Pharaoh) was called "Lord of the Two Lands", "Lord of Upper and Lower Egypt" and "Wearer of the Double Crown." Of course this fact is overlooked by Arab scholars and European scholars when it comes to this verse from the Holy Qur'an, because it would place the conflict between the Black Africans and White Europeans at an earlier stage which would destroy the white man's mythological history and fit into The Messengers historical paradigm. Later in this chapter I will present to you what the Greek historian Herodotus saw at the foot of the Caucasus Mountains which linked an Ancient Egyptian king by the name Sesostris to the need for keeping white folks locked up in Europe from 4,000 B.C. to 2,000 B.C.

3. Enslavement and Exodus from Egypt: Did the Exodus ever happen?

This question is so important and anything that I might write would be called Anti-Semitic, I felt it best just to reprint an article written in an Israeli news journal written by Jewish Israeli scholar and professor, Ze'ev Herzog:
http://www.truthbeknown.com/biblemyth.htm

Ha'aretz.com Friday, October 29, 1999

Deconstructing the walls of Jericho: Who are the Jews

By Ze'ev Herzog

Following 70 years of intensive excavations in the Land of Israel, archaeologists have found out: The patriarchs' acts are legendary, the Israelites did not sojourn in Egypt or make an exodus, they did not conquer the land. Neither is there any mention of the empire of David and Solomon, nor of the source of belief in the God of Israel. These facts have been known for years, but Israel is a stubborn people and nobody wants to hear about it.

This is what archaeologists have learned from their excavations in the Land of Israel: the Israelites were **never** in Egypt, did not wander in the desert, did not conquer the land in a military campaign and did not pass it on to the 12 tribes of Israel. Perhaps even harder to swallow is the fact that the united monarchy of David and Solomon, which is described by the Bible as a regional power, was at most a small tribal kingdom. And it will come as an unpleasant shock to many that the God of Israel, Jehovah, had a female consort and that the early Israelite religion adopted monotheism only in the waning period of the monarchy and not at Mount Sinai. Most of those who are engaged in scientific work in the interlocking spheres of the Bible, archaeology and the history of the Jewish people - and who once went into the field looking for proof to corroborate the Bible story - now agree that the historic events relating to the stages of the Jewish people's emergence are radically different from what that story tells.

What follows is a short account of the brief history of archaeology, with the emphasis on the crises and the big bang, so to speak, of the past decade. The critical question of this archaeological revolution has not yet trickled down into public consciousness, but it cannot be ignored.

Inventing the Bible stories

The archaeology of Palestine developed as a science at a relatively late date, in the late 19th and early 20th century, in tandem with the archaeology of the imperial cultures of Egypt, Mesopotamia, Greece and Rome. Those resource-intensive powers were the first target of the researchers, who were looking for impressive evidence from the past, usually in the service of the big museums in London, Paris and Berlin. That stage effectively passed over Palestine, with its fragmented geographical diversity. The conditions in ancient Palestine were inhospitable for the development of an extensive kingdom, and certainly no showcase projects such as the Egyptian shrines or the Mesopotamian palaces could have been established there. In fact, the archaeology of Palestine was not engendered at the initiative of museums but sprang from religious motives.

The main push behind archaeological research in Palestine was the country's relationship with the Holy Scriptures. The first excavators in Jericho and Shechem (Nablus) were biblical researchers who were looking for the remains of the cities cited in the Bible. Archaeology assumed momentum with the activity of William Foxwell Albright, who mastered the archeology, history and linguistics of the Land of Israel and the ancient Near East. Albright, an American whose father was a priest of Chilean descent, began excavating in Palestine in the 1920s. His declared approach was that archaeology was the principal scientific means to refute the critical claims against the historical veracity of the Bible stories, particularly those of the Wellhausen school in Germany.

The school of biblical criticism that developed in Germany beginning in the second half of the 19th century, of which Julian Wellhausen was a leading figure, challenged the historicity of the Bible stories and claimed that biblical historiography was formulated, and in large measure actually **"invented,"** during the **Babylonian exile**. Bible scholars, the Germans in particular, claimed that the history of the Hebrews, as a consecutive series of events beginning with Abraham, Isaac and Jacob, and proceeding through the move to Egypt, the enslavement and the exodus, and ending with the conquest of the land and the settlement of the tribes of Israel, was no more than a later **reconstruction** of events with a theological purpose.

Albright believed that the Bible is a historical document, which, although it had gone through several editing stages, nevertheless basically reflected the ancient reality. He was convinced that if the ancient remains of Palestine were uncovered, they would furnish unequivocal proof of the historical truth of the events relating to the Jewish people in its land.

The biblical archaeology that developed from Albright and his pupils brought about a series of extensive digs at the important biblical tells: Megiddo, Lachish, Gezer, Shechem (Nablus), Jericho, Jerusalem, Ai, Giveon, Beit She'an, Beit Shemesh, Hazor, Ta'anach and others. The way was straight and clear: every finding that was uncovered would contribute to the building of a harmonious picture of the past. The archaeologists, who enthusiastically adopted the biblical approach, set out on a quest to unearth the "biblical period": the period of the patriarchs, the Canaanite cities that were destroyed by the Israelites as they conquered the land, the boundaries of the 12 tribes, the sites of the settlement period, characterized by "settlement pottery," the "gates of Solomon" at Hazor, Megiddo and Gezer,

"Solomon's stables" (or Ahab's), "King Solomon's mines" at Timna - and there are some who are still hard at work and have found Mount Sinai (at Mount Karkoum in the Negev) or Joshua's altar at Mount Ebal.

The crisis

Slowly, cracks began to appear in the picture. Paradoxically, a situation was created in which the **glut of findings** began to undermine the historical credibility of the biblical descriptions instead of reinforcing them. A crisis stage is reached when the theories within the framework of the general thesis are unable to solve an increasingly large number of anomalies. The explanations become ponderous and inelegant, and the pieces do not lock together smoothly. Here are a few examples of how the harmonious picture collapsed.

Patriarchal Age: The researchers found it difficult to reach agreement on which archaeological period matched the Patriarchal Age. When did Abraham, Isaac and Jacob live? When was the Cave of Machpelah (Tomb of the Patriarchs in Hebron) bought in order to serve as the burial place for the patriarchs and the matriarchs? According to the biblical chronology, Solomon built the Temple 480 years after the exodus from Egypt (1 Kings 6:1). To that we have to add 430 years of the stay in Egypt (Exodus 12:40) and the vast lifetimes of the patriarchs, producing a date in the 21th century BCE for Abraham's move to Canaan.

However, no evidence has been unearthed that can sustain this chronology. Albright argued in the early 1960s in favor of assigning the wanderings of Abraham to the Middle Bronze Age (22nd-20th centuries BCE). However, Benjamin Mazar, the father of the Israeli branch of biblical archaeology, proposed identifying the historic background of the Patriarchal Age a thousand years later, in the 11th century BCE - which would place it in the "settlement period." Others rejected the historicity of the stories and viewed them as ancestral legends that were told in the period of the Kingdom of Judea. In any event, the consensus began to break down.

The exodus from Egypt, the wanderings in the desert and Mount Sinai: The many Egyptian documents that we have **make no mention** of the Israelites' presence in Egypt and are also **silen**t about the events of the **exodus**. Many documents do mention the custom of nomadic **shepherds** to enter Egypt during periods of drought and hunger and to camp at the edges of the Nile Delta. However, this was not a solitary phenomenon: such events occurred frequently across thousands of years and were hardly exceptional.

Generations of researchers tried to locate Mount Sinai and the stations of the tribes in the desert. Despite these intensive efforts, **not even one site** has been found that can match the biblical account.

The potency of tradition has now led some researchers to "discover" Mount Sinai in the northern Hijaz or, as already mentioned, at Mount Karkoum in the Negev. These central events in the history of the Israelites are not corroborated in documents external to the Bible or in archaeological findings. Most historians today agree that at best, the stay in Egypt and the exodus occurred in a few families and that their private story was expanded and "nationalized" to fit the **needs of theological ideology**.

The conquest: One of the shaping events of the people of Israel in biblical historiography is the story of how the land was conquered from the Canaanites. Yet extremely serious difficulties have cropped up precisely in the attempts to locate the archaeological evidence for this story.

Repeated excavations by various expeditions at Jericho and Ai, the two cities whose conquest is described in the greatest detail in the Book of Joshua, have proved very disappointing. Despite the excavators' efforts, it emerged that in the late part of the 13th century BCE, at the end of the Late Bronze Age, which is the agreed period for the conquest, there were **no cities** in either tell (hill) and of course no walls that could have been toppled. Naturally, explanations were offered for these anomalies. Some claimed that the walls around Jericho were washed away by rain, while others suggested that earlier walls had been used; and, as for Ai, it was claimed that the original story actually referred to the conquest of nearby Beit El and was transferred to Ai by later redactors.

Biblical scholars suggested a quarter of a century ago that the conquest stories be viewed as **etiological legends** and no more. But as more and more sites were uncovered and it emerged that the places in question died out or were simply abandoned at different times, the conclusion was bolstered that there is no factual basis for the biblical story about the conquest by Israelite tribes in a military campaign led by Joshua.

The Canaanite cities: The Bible magnifies the strength and the fortifications of the Canaanite cities that were conquered by the Israelites: "great cities with walls sky-high" (Deuteronomy 9:1). In practice, all the sites that have been uncovered turned up remains of **unfortified settlements**, which in most cases consisted of a few structures or the ruler's palace rather than a genuine city. The

66

urban culture of Palestine in the Late Bronze Age disintegrated in a process that lasted hundreds of years and did not stem from military conquest. Moreover, the biblical description is inconsistent with the geopolitical reality in Palestine. Palestine was under **Egyptian rule** until the middle of the 12th century BCE. The Egyptians' administrative centers were located in Gaza, Yaffo and Beit She'an. **Egyptian findings** have also been discovered in many locations on both sides of the Jordan River. This striking presence is not mentioned in the biblical account, and it is clear that it was unknown to the author and his editors.

The archaeological findings blatantly contradict the biblical picture: the Canaanite cities were not "great," were not fortified and did not have "sky-high walls." The heroism of the conquerors, the few versus the many and the assistance of the God who fought for his people are a theological reconstruction lacking any factual basis.

Origin of the Israelites: The fusion of the conclusions drawn from the episodes relating to the stages in which the people of Israel emerged gave rise to a discussion of the bedrock question: the identity of the Israelites. If there is no evidence for the exodus from Egypt and the desert journey, and if the story of the military conquest of fortified cities has been refuted by archaeology, who, then, were these Israelites? The archaeological findings did corroborate one important fact: in the early Iron Age (beginning some time after 1200 BCE), the stage that is identified with the "settlement period," hundreds of small settlements were established in the area of the central hill region of the Land of Israel, inhabited by farmers who worked the land or raised sheep. If they did not come from Egypt, what is the origin of these settlers? Israel Finkelstein, professor of archaeology at Tel Aviv University, has proposed that these settlers were the **pastoral shepherds** who wandered in this hill area throughout the Late Bronze Age (graves of these people have been found, without settlements). According to his reconstruction, in the Late Bronze Age (which preceded the Iron Age) the **shepherds** maintained a barter economy of meat in exchange for grains with the inhabitants of the valleys. With the disintegration of the urban and agricultural system in the lowland, the nomads were forced to produce their own grains, and hence the incentive for fixed settlements arose.

The name "Israel" is mentioned in a single Egyptian document from the period of Merneptah, king of Egypt, dating from 1208 BCE: "Plundered is Canaan with every evil, Ascalon is taken, Gezer is seized, Yenoam has become as though it never was, Israel is desolated, its seed is not." Merneptah refers to the country by its Canaanite name and mentions several cities of the kingdom, along with a non-urban ethnic group. According to this evidence, the term **"Israel"** was given to one of the population groups that resided in Canaan toward the end of the Late Bronze Age, apparently in the **central hill** region, in the area where the Kingdom of Israel would later be established.

A kingdom with no name

The united monarchy: Archaeology was also the source that brought about the shift regarding the reconstruction of the reality in the period known as the "united monarchy" of David and Solomon. The Bible describes this period as the zenith of the political, military and economic power of the people of Israel in ancient times. In the wake of David's conquests, the empire of David and Solomon stretched from the **Euphrates River to Gaza** ("For *he controlled the whole region west of the Euphrates, from Tiphsah to Gaza, all the kings west of the Euphrates," 1 Kings 5:4). The archaeological findings at many sites show that the construction projects attributed to this period were* **meager** *in scope and power.*

The three cities of Hazor, Megiddo and Gezer, which are mentioned among Solomon's construction enterprises, have been excavated extensively at the appropriate layers. Only about half of Hazor's upper section was fortified, covering an area of only 30 dunams (7.5 acres), out of a total area of 700 dunams which was settled in the Bronze Age. At Gezer there was apparently only a citadel surrounded by a casemate wall covering a small area, while Megiddo was not fortified with a wall.

The picture becomes even more complicated in the light of the excavations conducted in Jerusalem, the capital of the united monarchy. Large sections of the city have been excavated over the past 150 years. The digs have turned up impressive remnants of the cities from the Middle Bronze Age and from Iron Age II (the period of the Kingdom of Judea). **No remains** *of buildings have been found from the period of the* **united monarchy** *(even according to the agreed chronology), only a few pottery shards. Given the preservation of the remains from earlier and later periods, it is clear that Jerusalem in the time of David and Solomon was a* **small city***, perhaps with a small citadel for the king, but in any event it was not the capital of an empire as described in the Bible. This small chiefdom is the source of the "Beth David" title mentioned in later Aramean and Moabite inscriptions. The authors of the biblical account* **knew Jerusalem in the 8th century BCE***, with its wall and the rich culture of which remains have* been found in various parts of the city, and **projected** this picture back to the age of the united monarchy. Presumably Jerusalem acquired its central status after the destruction of Samaria, its northern rival, in 722 BCE.

The archaeological findings dovetail well with the conclusions of the critical school of biblical scholarship. David and Solomon were the rulers of **tribal kingdoms** that controlled small areas: the former in Hebron and the latter in Jerusalem. Concurrently, a separate kingdom began to form in the Samaria hills, which finds expression in the stories about Saul's kingdom. Israel and Judea were from the outset **two separate**, independent kingdoms, and at times were in an adversarial relationship. Thus, the great united monarchy is an **imaginary** historiosophic creation, which was composed during the period of the Kingdom of Judea at the earliest. Perhaps the most decisive proof of this is the fact that we do not know the name of this kingdom.

Jehovah and his consort: How many gods, exactly, did Israel have? Together with the historical and political aspects, there are also doubts as to the credibility of the information about belief and worship. The question about the date at which **monotheism** was adopted by the kingdoms of Israel and Judea arose with the discovery of inscriptions in ancient Hebrew that mention a pair of gods: Jehovah and **his Asherah**. At two sites, Kuntiliet Ajrud in the southwestern part of the Negev hill region, and at Khirbet el-Kom in the Judea piedmont, Hebrew inscriptions have been found that mention "**Jehovah and his Asherah**," "Jehovah Shomron and his Asherah, "**Jehovah Teman and his Asherah**." The authors were familiar with a pair of gods, Jehovah and his consort Asherah, and send blessings in the couple's name. These inscriptions, from the 8th century BCE, raise the possibility that monotheism, as a state religion, is actually an **innovation** of the period of the Kingdom of Judea, following the destruction of the Kingdom of Israel.

The archaeology of the Land of Israel is completing a process that amounts to a scientific revolution in its field. It is ready to confront the findings of biblical scholarship and of ancient history. But at the same time, we are witnessing a fascinating phenomenon in which all this is simply **ignored** by the Israeli public. Many of the findings mentioned here have been known for **decades**. The professional literature in the spheres of archaeology, Bible and the history of the Jewish people has addressed them in dozens of books and hundreds of articles. Even if not all the scholars accept the individual arguments that inform the examples I cited, the majority have adopted their main points.

Nevertheless, these revolutionary views are not penetrating the public consciousness. About a year ago, my colleague, the historian Prof. Nadav Ne'eman, published an article in the Culture and Literature section of Ha'aretz entitled "To Remove the Bible from the Jewish Bookshelf," but there was **no public outcry**. Any attempt to question the reliability of the biblical descriptions is perceived as an attempt to undermine "our **historic right to the land**" and as shattering the myth of the nation that is renewing the ancient Kingdom of Israel. These symbolic elements constitute such a critical component of the construction of the Israeli **identity** that any attempt to call their veracity into question encounters **hostility or silence**. It is of some interest that such tendencies within the Israeli secular society go hand-in-hand with the outlook among educated Christian groups. I have

*found a similar hostility in reaction to lectures I
have delivered abroad to groups of Christian bible
lovers, though what upset them was the **challenge**
to the foundations of their **fundamentalist**
religious belief.*

*It turns out that part of Israeli society is ready to
recognize the injustice that was done to the Arab
inhabitants of the country and is willing to accept
the principle of equal rights for women - but is not
up to adopting the archaeological facts that shatter
the **biblical myth**. The blow to the mythical
foundations of the Israeli **identity** is apparently too
threatening, and it is more convenient to turn a
blind eye.*

Israel won a war that exposed her lie

Surah 31: Luqman of the Holy Qur'an verse 16 reads:

*"Oh my son, even if it be the weight of a grain of
mustard-seed, even though it be in a rock, or in the
heaven or in the earth, Allah will bring it forth.
Surely Allah is Knower of subtilities, Aware."*

We chose this verse from the Holy Qur'an to point out a fact
that is more than an irony. Israel won what is called the "Six Days
War" in 1967. It was held as proof of God's benevolence towards
the state of Israel and gave great moral strength to the Jewish people
who were taking Palestinian's land based on their belief that the God
of the Bible had promised this land to them on their Exodus from
Egypt 3,500 years ago.

However, as luck would have it the winning of that war,
according to Professor Shlomo Sand in his 2009 book *The Invention
of the Jewish People*, opened up Arab land for Israeli archaeologists
bent on proving the historical accuracy of the Bible stories in
particular the Exodus. When leading scholars such as Israel
Finkelstein and Neil Asher Silberman reviewed the archaeological
evidence which they published in their 2002 book, *The Bible*

Unearthed, they concluded that the wanderings of the patriarchs, the Exodus from Egypt, Joshua's conquest of Canaan, and David and Solomon's vast kingdom was not backed up by the archaeological evidence. They went on to try to explain when and why the Bible was written to fulfill a need for Jewish identity.

However, Sand, Finkelstein and Silberman could not explain why the Jews needed to fabricate a new identity. The Honorable Elijah Muhammad and Minister Farrakhan are exposing a "well dressed lie" which has stolen the identity and suffering of the "Real Children of Israel", the tribe of Shabazz, the Black man and woman of America. We will get deeper into this identity theft in Chapter 4 of this book.

The 1967 "Six Days War" also had an effect on the Civil Rights Movement in America. The younger members of SNCC/SCLC took up the cause of the Palestinians whose land was taken, while the older members stuck with their friends and financial backers, the Jews. History has proven that the young Blacks picked the correct moral issue, because the Israeli's claim on the Palestinians' land is a hoax.

Not only is their claim a hoax, but the accepted story line behind the "Six Days War" has been revealed as bogus as well. In 2012 Miko Peled the son of Israeli Major General Matti Peled wrote a book called *The General's Son.* In this book he wrote on pages 42 and 43:

> "In the late spring of 1967, Egypt's President Nasser expelled the United Nations peacekeeping forces that had been monitoring the ceasefire between the two countries from the Sinai Peninsula. He sent Egyptian troops across the Suez Canal and into the demilitarized Sinai Peninsula, and he threatened to blockade the straits of Tiran and not permit Israeli ships to proceed toward the Israeli port city of Eilat. These were acts that blatantly violated the terms of the ceasefire that was signed between Egypt and Israel. The army was calling it a plausible *casus belli,* or justification for war.
>
> According to documents I found in the IDF (Israeli Defense Forces) archives and other sources, the Soviet

73

government fed misinformation to the Egyptians, claiming that Israel was planning a surprise attack against Syria. The Soviets claimed that Israel had amassed troops on the border with Syria. Syria and Egypt had a mutual security pact, and President Nasser had to act in defense of his Syrian allies. As the Israeli cabinet was considering its options, on May 26, 1967, the Russian prime minister sent the Israeli prime minister, Levi Eshkol, a letter through the Soviet ambassador in Tel Aviv, calling for a peaceful resolution to the conflict. When the Russian ambassador presented Prime Minister Eshkol with the letter, Eshkol invited the ambassador to see with his own eyes that the claim had no merit and that Israeli troops were not amassed at the Syrian border.

The army was recommending that Israel initiate a preemptive strike against Egypt. The cabinet was hesitant and wanted time to explore other options before committing to a full-scale war. Things came to a head in a stormy meeting of the IDF General Staff and the Israeli cabinet that took place on June 2, 1967. After opening remarks, my father told the cabinet in no uncertain terms that the Egyptians needed a year and a half to two years in order to be ready for a full-scale war. The other generals agreed that the Israeli army was prepared and that this was the time to strike another devastating blow." (Paled 2012: 42,43)

After further debate the Israeli cabinet decided to follow the advice of the military generals and Israel launched a devastating attack on an ill-prepared Egyptian army that was lured into a fight by their supposed friends, the Russians. There are three lessons to be learned from this episode in history: 1. Don't trust white people no matter what they call themselves, 2. The Jews and Israel are wicked and ruthless warmongers and 3. They hid their lies for over 40 years but to no avail; they have been exposed.

Walking out of the 6,000 year old grave of Bible Interpretation

As the above article by Ze'ev Herzog demonstrates the Exodus story as presented in the Bible and so popularly promoted by such movies as "The Ten Commandments" did not happen at the time and place that the Zionist occupiers of Palestine would have the world to believe. However, is there some historical basis to this Exodus story that provided the Bible writers with the raw material from which they weaved their story?

The Honorable Elijah Muhammad in his great book *Message to the Black Man* explains this Exodus story by writing:

"America has fulfilled this to the very letter and spirit with her slaves (the so-called Negroes) under the type of Israel. The Egyptians did nothing of the kind to Israel when they were in bondage to them. In fact, and as God taught me, the Bible is not referring to those people as His People, it is referring to the so-called Negro and his enemy (the white race)." (Muhammad 1965: 268)

So, The Messenger sees the Exodus story in the Bible as a prophecy which the Black people of America have fulfilled. However, he admits that at one time the Egyptians did have white people, Israel, in some type of bondage, but did not afflict them the way the Bible describes their captivity in Egypt. So when and what was the nature of this "bondage"?

The story of Moses, Pharaoh and the Exodus is an integral part of the Holy Qur'an as well and therefore to deny that story would be to deny that the Holy Qur'an is indeed a holy book without blemish. However, I would ask any Qur'anic scholar to point out any reference to a date of this story in the Holy Qur'an. One is lead to assume that the time frame in the Holy Qur'an is the same as the story in the Bible. However, removing the commentary and Arab scholars' attempts at reading the Holy Qur'an as chronological history, could it be possible that the events described did indeed happen, but long before 4,000 years ago and maybe even long before there was a white race on our planet? Have the Arab scholars tried to interpret a book dedicated for spiritual enlightenment and scriptural correction as though it was a book of history to be approved by Jewish scholars? Could it just be possible that the Holy Qur'an's story of Moses, a Pharaoh and an Exodus happened, say, 6,000 years ago or even earlier and not 3,500 years ago as previously believed by Jewish and Christian scholars?

Once we remove the mental shackles of the interpretation of the Bible as a 6,000 year history of the human being, we can intelligently evaluate previously unexplained archaeological findings and oral traditions of the indigenous people of the areas in and close to the Holy Land. For instance archaeologists have been trying to explain the "Memorial Tablet of Narmer" which was discovered 100 years ago and now is housed in the Cairo museum. This stone tablet, which archaeologists believe to be 6,000 years old, seems to portray a war going on in the delta region of Ancient Egypt which culminated in the losers being put on ships in exile. The dates for this battle fall around 6,000 years ago and according to Sir Arthur Evans, the people on those boats were destined for the island of Crete in the Aegean Sea and developed the Minoan Civilization. Could this be the Exodus? And if this is the real Exodus, could the Jewish writers of the Bible have changed the place and time to give a justification for coming back into the Holy Land without revealing the real reasons for their exile?

The Honorable Elijah Muhammad teaches us that after the white people were expelled from the Holy Land for causing trouble, they were placed behind the Caucasus Mountains 6,000 years ago and guards were placed at the foot of those mountains to insure that they could not get out and move south again. The Black people did not oppress them, but denied them access to the rest of the civilized world. In that isolation they went savage and oppressed themselves

76

with their own wickedness. Musa (Moses) was a half-original man and a prophet and was sent to those white people 2,000 years later. He gave them law, as was written in the Torah, and taught them how to build homes for themselves and walk upright once again.

In another context there is an Arab fable about a prince who destroyed a mountain that stood between modern day Yemen (Arabia) and Djibouti (Africa). This mountain was a barrier between the Indian Ocean and a great valley civilization. When this mountain was destroyed, that civilization was drowned in what became the Red Sea; and that strait between Arabia and Africa is called the "Gate of Tears" (Bab el Mandeb), because of the thousands of people that died there. Could this be Moses parting the Red Sea and drowning Pharaoh's army?

Black people in America were stripped of their name, history, language, way of life and religion. However, the whole world may have been stripped of its true history and is living in a 6,000 year old box, grave, invented by the new race on our planet; white people, Jacob, Israel. The Teachings of The Honorable Elijah Muhammad carry us back to at least 50,000 years ago as the ancestor of America's once black slave, Father Shabazz, took us into the jungles of Africa to tame the wilderness. He was one of the scientists of his era, but had to leave the Holy Land with his tribe and find a new home. Could this be the Exodus? Could the great kingdom of Ancient Egypt (Kemit) be the "Promised Land"? However, Egypt is just one of the African civilizations produced by this legendary Tribe of Shabazz. Many are still hidden underneath the sands of the desert and the jungles of the rain forests according to The Honorable Elijah Muhammad.

Now that many Biblical scholars admit that the "Exodus" story in the Bible is probably a composite of different events and stories, we must take a second look at what The Honorable Elijah Muhammad taught us and walk out of the 6,000 year old grave that Biblical theologians have buried us in. The white race has destroyed every library of the ancient world that they could get their bloody hands on to annihilate any records of events before 6,000 years ago so as to hide the trail of the great usurper, Jacob (Israel, Yakub's genetically modified human). Israel had to rewrite history to place the white race at the center of human history and nullify Black people's role as the original producers of civilization and keepers of the Faith and Holy Land. They, the white race, have taken the written history that they found among the indigenous people which stretched for hundreds of thousands of years and compressed them to fit their 6,000 years of existence as a race.

With the new light given to us by The Honorable Elijah Muhammad and the strength of faith and will exemplified by the Honorable Minister Louis Farrakhan we can dig to find the facts that will straighten out this crooked path of an arch-deceiver. Do not be afraid of this journey, because every truth that you will find will bear witness to the Teachings of The Most Honorable Elijah Muhammad and bear witness to the Honorable Minister Louis Farrakhan's assertion that the Black people in America are the "Real Children of Israel" whose time for deliverance has arrived.

(*Deconstructing the walls of Jericho: Who are the Jews*)*continued...*

(http://www.hiddenmysteries.org/mysteries/history/jehovah.html)

The Hyksos, an Aryan Invasion

*Like Herzog, the historian Josephus (c. 37CE - c. 100CE) denied the account of the Hebrews being held in captivity in Egypt, but he went a drastic step further about the racial origins of the Jews, whom he identified with the Hyksos. He further claimed they did not flee from Egypt but were **evicted** due to them being leprous.*

It must be said that Josephus has been vilified over the ages as a Roman collaborator by both Jewish and Christian scholars who have argued that the dating of the exodus of the "Hebrews" from

Egypt in the Bible positively rules out their identification as Hyksos.

However, Jan Assmann, a prominent Egyptologist at Heidelberg University, is quite positive in his writings that the Exodus story is an **inversion of the Hyksos expulsion** and furthermore that **Moses** was an **Egyptian**.

Likewise, Donald P. Redford, of Toronto University, presents striking evidence that the **Expulsion of the Hyksos** from Egypt was **inverted** to construct the exodus of the Hebrew slaves story in the Torah and Old Testament. His book, which argued this theory, Egypt, Canaan, and Israel in Ancient Times was Winner of the 1993 Best Scholarly Book in Archaeology Award of the Biblical Archaeological Society.

There is irrefutable evidence that the Hyksos, a mixed Semitic-Asiatic group who infiltrated the Nile valley, seized power in Lower Egypt in the 17th Century BCE. They ruled there from c. 1674 BCE until expelled when their capital, **Avaris**, fell **to Ahmose** around 1567 BCE. The Hyksos in Egypt worshipped **Set**, who like ISH.KUR they identified as a storm deity.

Under the "inversion theory", Jewish scholars in the 7th Century BCE changed the story from "expelled" to "escaped" and as a further insult to their enemy, Ahmose, changed and miss-spelled his name to Moses, presenting him as leader of a Hebrew revolt. But there is also a strong possibility of two separate origins to the "Moses" character being merged into one, which I will come to later.

Ahmose's success in 1567 BCE led to the establishment of the 18th Dynasty in Egypt. ThotMoses III overthrew the transvestite Pharaoh Hatchepsut, and under ThotMoses IV Egyptian conquests extended beyond the Sinai into Palestine, Syria, reaching Babylonia and included Canaan.

*By the end of this expansion, Amenophis III (1380BCE) ruled an Egyptian empire whose provinces and colonies bordered what is now known as Turkey. This empire would have included the regions in which most of the **expelled Hyksos** now lived.*

*Amenophis IV succeeded the throne in 1353BCE. He established a new monotheism cult establishing "Aten" as the one supreme god and he changed his name to **Akhenaton**. Married to the mysterious Nefertiti, Akhenaton declared himself a god on earth, intermediary between the one-god Aten (Ra) and humanity, with his spouse as partner, effectively displacing Isis and Osiris in the Egyptian Ennead.*

*Declaring all men to be the children of Aten, historians suspect Akhenaten planned an empire-wide religion. He banned all idolatry, the use of images to represent god, and **banned** the idea that there was more than one supreme god.*

It is alongside Akhenaten and his father Amenophis III that we find the second Moses. An important figure during this period was confusingly called Amenophis son of Hapu. He was First Minister (Vizier) to both kings. He is generally depicted as a scribe, crouching and holding on his knees a roll of papyrus. He more than anyone was responsible for authoring the religion in which the old gods were merged into one living god, Aten, who had been responsible for the creation of the Earth and of humanity.

The symbol of this god, the sun disk, represented Ra, Horus and the other gods in one. The sun disk, in symbolism, was supported between the horns of a bull. The Son of Hapu says this about creation: "I have come to you who reigns over the gods oh Amon, Lord of the Two Lands, for you are Re (Ra) who appears in the sky, who illuminates the earth with a brilliantly shining eye, who came out of the Nou, who appeared above the primitive water, who created everything, who generated the great Ennead of the gods,

80

who created his own flesh and gave birth to his own form."

The king's overseer of the land of Nubia was a certain Mermose (spelled both Mermose and Merymose on his sarcophagus in the British Museum). According to modern historians, in Amenhotep's third year as king, Mermose took his army far up the Nile, supposedly to quell a minor rebellion, but actually to secure gold mining territories which would supply his king with the greatest wealth of any ruler of Egypt.

*Recent scholarship has indicated Mermose took his army to the neighborhood of the confluence of the **Nile and Atbara Rivers** and beyond. But who was this Mermose? According to historian Dawn Breasted, the Greek translation of this name was Moses. Does Jewish tradition support this identification?*

*According to Jewish history not included in the Bible, Moses led the army of Pharaoh to the South, into the land of Kush, and reached the vicinity of the Atbara River. There he attracted the love of the princess of the fortress city of Saba, later Meroe. She gave up the city in exchange for marriage. Biblical confirmation of such a marriage is to be found in Numbers 12:1. "And Miriam and Aaron spoke against Moses because of the **Ethiopian woman** whom he had married: for he had married an Ethiopian woman."*

Who are the "circumcised"?

The so-called Jews claimed that the mark of circumcision was a sign of God's covenant with them **only**. However, Herodotus points out that the Egyptians, Ethiopians and Colchians were circumcised **first**.

As you will read in the following quotes, these Colchians are very interesting. They were the remnants of army left by an Egyptian King from at least the 12th dynasty of Egypt placing them at the foot of the Caucasus mountains before the Hyksos invasion. Could these soldiers be the "guards with fiery swords" that the Messenger said were placed at the foot of the Caucasus to keep the white race bottled up in Europe? Could these same Colchians have instituted a white slave trade of women stolen from behind the Caucasus and sold into Egypt? Could this miscegenation be where the half-breeds or Semites began?

http://realhistoryww.com/world_history/ancient/Anatol ia_Turkey_2a

Ancient Man and His First Civilizations

Anatolia-3

Modern Turkey

Herodotus on Colchis

Passing over these monarchs, therefore, I shall speak of the king who reigned next, whose name was Sesostris. He, the priests said, first of all proceeded in a fleet of ships of war from the Arabian gulf along the shores of the Erythraean sea, subduing the nations as he went, until he finally reached a sea which could not be navigated by reason of the shoals. Hence he returned to Egypt, where, they told me, he collected a vast armament, and made a progress by land across the continent, conquering every people which fell in his way.

In the countries where the natives withstood his attack, and fought gallantly for their liberties, he erected pillars, on which he inscribed his own name and country, and how that he had here reduced the inhabitants to subjection by the might of his arms: where, on the contrary, they submitted readily and without a struggle, he inscribed on the pillars, in addition to these particulars, an emblem to mark that they were a nation of women, that is, unwarlike and effeminate.

[2.103] In this way he traversed the whole continent of Asia, whence he passed on into Europe, and made himself master of **Scythia** and of Thrace, beyond which countries I do not think that his army extended its march. For thus far the pillars which he erected are still visible, but in the remoter regions they are no longer found. Returning to Egypt from Thrace, he came, on his way, to the banks of the river Phasis. Here I cannot say with any certainty what took place. Either he of his own accord **detached** a body of **troops** from his main army and left them to **colonize** the country, or else a certain number of his soldiers, wearied with their long wanderings, deserted, and established themselves on the banks of this stream.

[2.104] There can be no doubt that the Colchians are an Egyptian race. Before I heard any mention of the fact from others, I had remarked it myself. After the thought had struck me, I made inquiries on the subject both in Colchis and in Egypt, and I found that the Colchians had a more distinct recollection of the Egyptians, than the Egyptians had of them. Still the Egyptians said that they believed the Colchians to be descended from the army of Sesostris. My own conjectures were founded, first, on the fact that they are **black-skinned** and have **woolly hair**, which certainly amounts to but little, since several other nations are so too; but further and more especially, on the circumstance that the **Colchians**, the **Egyptians**, and the **Ethiopians** (Nubians), are the **only nations** who have practiced **circumcision** from the **earliest times**.

The Phoenicians and the Syrians of Palestine themselves confess that they **learned** the custom of the Egyptians; and the Syrians who dwell about the rivers Thermodon and Parthenius, as well as their neighbours the Macronians, say that they have recently

83

adopted it from the Colchians. Now these are the only nations who use circumcision, and it is plain that they all imitate herein the Egyptians. With respect to the Ethiopians, indeed, I cannot decide whether they learnt the practice of the Egyptians, or the Egyptians of them - it is undoubtedly of very ancient date in Ethiopia - but that the others derived their knowledge of it from Egypt is clear to me from the fact that the Phoenicians, when they come to have commerce with the Greeks, cease to follow the Egyptians in this custom, and allow their children to remain uncircumcised.

[2.105] I will add a further proof to the identity of the Egyptians and the Colchians. These two nations **weave** their linen in **exactly** the same way, and this is a way entirely **unknown** to the rest of the world; they also in their whole mode of life and in their language resemble one another. The Colchian linen is called by the Greeks Sardinian, while that which comes from Egypt is known as Egyptian.

[2.106] **The pillars** which Sesostris erected in the conquered countries have for the most part disappeared; but in the part of Syria called **Palestine**, I myself saw **them still standing**, with the writing above-mentioned, and the emblem distinctly visible. In Ionia also, there are two representations of this prince engraved upon rocks, one on the road from Ephesus to Phocaea, the other between Sardis and Smyrna. In each case the figure is that of a man, four cubits and a span high, with a spear in his right hand and a bow in his left, the rest of his costume being likewise half **Egyptian, half Ethiopian**. There is an inscription across the breast from shoulder to shoulder, in the sacred character of Egypt, which says, "With my own shoulders I conquered this land." The conqueror does not tell who he is, or whence he comes, though elsewhere Sesostris records these facts. Hence it has been imagined by some of those who have seen these forms, that they are figures of Memnon; but such as think so err *very widely from the truth.*

===

http://www.ucg.org/brp/materials/throne/appendices/ap4.html

The Colchis Connection

*Besides Cecrops of Athens, some have identified Zerah's descendant Calcol or Chalcol with the land of Colchis, a "nearly triangular region at the eastern end of the Black Sea south of the Caucasus, in the western part of the modern [former] Georgian S.S.R." ("Colchis," Encyclopaedia Britannica, Micropaedia, 1985, Vol. 3, p. 443). This location makes it contiguous with ancient **Iberia—the land of the Hebrews**!*

Continuing on: "In Greek mythology Colchis was the home of Medea [daughter of King Aeetes and possessor of the famous golden fleece] and the destination of [Jason and] the Argonauts [sailors of Argos of the Danoi, who were likely Danites], a land of fabulous wealth and the domain of sorcery" (p. 443)—which any land of superior technological ability and perhaps prophets (be they true or false) might seem.

*First-century-B.C. historian Diodorus of Sicily has identified Argos and **Colchis with the Israelites who emigrated from Egypt**—and relates the same origin for Athens.*

===

http://www.theoi.com/Ther/DrakonKholkikos.html

THE DRAKON KHOLKIKOS (or Colchian Dragon)

Diodorus Siculus, Library of History 4. 47. 3 :

*"He [Aeetes] also threw a wall about the precinct [where the **Golden Fleece** was kept] and stationed there many **guardians**, these being men of the Tauric Chersonese, and it is because of these guards that the Greeks invented monstrous myths. For instance, the report was spread abroad that there were fire-breathing Tauroi (Bulls) round about the precinct and that a **sleepless Drakon** (Dragon) guarded the fleece, the identity of the names having led to the transfer from the men who were Taurians to the cattle because of their strength and the cruelty shown in the **murder of strangers** having been made into the myth of the bulls breathing fire; and similarly the name of the guardian who watched over the sacred precinct, which was Drakon, has been transferred by the poets to the monstrous and fear-inspiring beast, the drakon."*

The Sign of God's Covenant with Abraham

Now let us deal with the implications of the above information on "circumcision."

Genesis 17 King James Version (KJV)

17 And when Abram was ninety years old and nine, the LORD appeared to Abram, and said unto him, I am the Almighty God; walk before me, and be thou perfect.

2 And I will make my covenant between me and thee, and will multiply thee exceedingly.

3 And Abram fell on his face: and God talked with him, saying,

4 As for me, behold, my covenant is with thee, and thou shalt be a father of many nations.

⁵ *Neither shall thy name any more be called Abram, but thy name shall be Abraham; for a father of many nations have I made thee.*

⁶ *And I will make thee exceeding fruitful, and I will make nations of thee, and kings shall come out of thee.*

⁷ *And I will establish my covenant between me and thee and thy seed after thee in their generations for an everlasting covenant, to be a God unto thee, and to thy seed after thee.*

⁸ *And I will give unto thee, and to thy seed after thee, the land wherein thou art a stranger, all the land of Canaan, for an everlasting possession; and I will be their God.*

⁹ *And God said unto Abraham, Thou shalt keep my covenant therefore, thou, and thy seed after thee in their generations.*

¹⁰ *This is my covenant, which ye shall keep, between me and you and thy seed after thee; Every man child among you shall be **circumcised**.*

¹¹ *And ye shall **circumcise** the flesh of your foreskin; and it shall be a token of the **covenant** betwixt me and you.*

¹² *And he that is eight days old shall be circumcised among you, every man child in your generations, he that is born in the house, or bought with money of any stranger, which is not of thy seed.*

¹³ *He that is born in thy house, and he that is bought with thy money, must needs be circumcised: and my covenant shall be in your flesh for an everlasting covenant.*

[14] *And the uncircumcised man child whose flesh of his*
foreskin is not circumcised, that soul shall be cut off from
his people; he hath broken my covenant.

So the Bible makes a big deal behind this circumcision thing. However, it seems that Egyptians and Ethiopians were also circumcised and practiced this operation long before these so-called Jews. The Colchians who were the remnants of an Egyptian army stationed at the foot of the Caucasus Mountains seemingly to keep the white folks bottled in Europe were also circumcised. Now let us take into consideration that Musa (Moses) the lawgiver, according to The Messenger, did not lead the Children of Israel out of Egypt, but went up into the caves and hillsides of Europe and raised white people back into civilization.

Let us mix in this pot of facts how "Israel" got its, his, name. According to the Bible, Jacob wrestled with an angel or God all night long. The next morning Jacob's name was changed to Israel. All this adds up to a more plausible explanation of how white folk got circumcised and civilized by Moses so that they could return from their exile, not slavery. It seems that they learned civilization and how to mix with the civilized people of the known world at that time. However, they have not given the world a true history of themselves being civilized by black or mixed black people. Instead, they have made up a story of how God directly taught them and gave them a right to return to as close to the Holy Land of Egypt and Mecca as they could get, i.e. Palestine.

I noticed that Herodotus never mentioned "Israel", "Judea", "Hebrews" or "Jews" in this above passage nor in the rest of the book. Why? He definitely traveled in Palestine because he mentions the pillar that Sesostris left "*...in the part of Syria called **Palestine.***"

Then Herodotus states about those countries that adopted circumcision, *"The Phoenicians and the Syrians of Palestine themselves confess that they learned the custom of the Egyptians…"* Again, no mention of Jews or Israel being in Palestine. If there were Jews in Palestine, then they were the circumcised Phoenicians and Syrians who learned circumcision from the Egyptians. This further indicates that as late as the times of Herodotus 484- 424 BC, there was no great nation of Israel covering Palestine, so present day claims by the Jews on that territory is completely bogus and their story is fake.

Searching for the Messiah

Why is the world waiting for a "Messiah"? More specifically why must the Messiah be "King of the Jews" from the line of David? There is one way to answer these questions within the Biblical paradigm and then there is another way to attack these questions within the new historical paradigm taught by The Most Honorable Elijah Muhammad

The Biblical reason for waiting on the Messiah is that Jesus was coming back to finish what he started 2,000 years ago. However, what Jesus was offering the Jews at that time was a little different from what they were expecting. They were expecting someone to take the yoke of Rome off of their backs and reinstate the great kingdom of David and Solomon. Research has shown that there was no great kingdom of David or Solomon and there was no great nation of Israel running from the borders of Egypt to Mesopotamia.

Let us revisit the words of The Honorable Elijah Muhammad as he discusses Jesus and his mission. In *Our Saviour Has Arrived* (chap 31, 166), The Messenger wrote these weighty words **about** the **historical Jesus**:

89

"Jesus came to the Jews and not to us and then he got disappointed that he was ahead of the time of the Jews to preach the doctrine of the destruction or judgment and the setting up of a New Kingdom of Heaven after the destruction of the Jew's civilization. Jesus was born two thousand years ahead of the judgment of the Jews. "(Muhammad 1992: 166)

Jesus' mission was not and is not to put the Jews on top of civilization but to judge the civilization that they brought in. What was or is the "Jews civilization" and when was it established? According to Webster's Dictionary, civilization is the "culture characteristic of a particular time or place." If we look at the behavior of Jacob and his sons, according to the Bible, the Jews' civilization is based on lies, stealing and murder. In the beginning their way of life was confined to a small area in the Middle East, but today their way of life is the way of life of our planet. Christianity itself is really the continuation of the themes developed in the Old Testament. If we take an overall analysis of the Old Testament, we could say that it is a story of a villain. If we then capsulate the mindset produced by the New Testament, it is a mindset of a willing victim who sacrifices himself to the evil mob and does not say a mumbling word.

However, in the book of Revelations the "Son of Man" described there is less like the suffering servant, Jesus, and more like a conquering hero, Christ, who does not forgive the wicked but slays them with a two edged sword. The Son of Man prophesied to come is more like the Jesus that The Most Honorable Elijah Muhammad talks about coming at the end of the Jew's civilization to judge and destroy it. The "Messiah" that this world is worried about showing up is more like the one that the FBI has been searching for and why they killed Malcolm X in 1965 and why they "resurrected" him in 1991.

Why was Malcolm Resurrected?

In the spring of 1991 at a Chicago Bulls practice Michael Jordan came to the gym wearing an "X" cap. "X" paraphernalia was popping up everywhere as Spike Lee began his promotional campaign for his soon-to-be-released movie *Malcolm X*. The movie was scheduled to be released in 1992, but caps and T-shirts were being sold everywhere by the summer of 1991.

Minister Louis Farrakhan was growing in strength and popularity, even though members of the Jewish community wanted him dead. He had been touring Black America and Black college campuses on a "Stop the Killing" campaign to stop Black-on-Black violence. The youth were becoming more politicized with the release of anti-apartheid leader Nelson Mandela in 1990. The system had to put a stop to this activism before it got out of hand. Why was Malcolm being "resurrected" at this time? Who would benefit?

In his book *Racial Matters: The FBI's Secret File on Black America, 1960–1972* (1989), Kenneth O'Reilly describes the purpose of a special division of the FBI: "Division Five also worked to 'prevent the rise of a "**messiah**"—someone 'who could unify, and electrify, the militant black nationalist movement.' **Malcolm X** had been the most likely candidate, but his assassination removed that threat. Malcolm was simply 'the martyr of the movement today.'" Notice that the FBI did not specify *Black* "messiah," because the wise Whites of this world know that the real "Children of Israel" are Black. They have always known that the Jesus of history was Black and the Christ to come would be "Black." (See *Final Call* articles "Was Jesus Black?" and "Color Struck: America's White Jesus Is a Global Export.")

Malcolm X, considered a "threat" to the established white

order, was "removed" in 1965, but he had to be brought back to life at a later time to be used to stop the rise of Farrakhan, "who could unify, and electrify, the militant black nationalist movement." At the time of his assassination Malcolm was not liked by white journalists, but after his death he was used by white journalists to cause mischief. The *New York Times* is America's "newspaper of record" and this quote is from an editorial published February 22, 1965, the day after Malcolm's murder:

> "Malcolm X had the ingredients for leadership, but his ruthless and fanatical belief in violence not only set him apart from the responsible leaders of the civil rights movement and the overwhelming majority of Negroes. It also marked him for notoriety, and for a violent end."

This, from a 1963 *Playboy* interview, is what Malcolm thought about the Jews:

> "Anybody that gives even a just criticism of the Jew is instantly labeled anti-Semite. The Jew cries louder than anybody else if anybody criticizes him. You can tell the truth about any minority in America, but make a true observation about the Jew, and if it doesn't pat him on the back, then he uses his grip on the news media to label you anti-Semite. Let me say just a word about the Jew and the black man. The Jew is always anxious to advise the black man. But they never advise him how to solve his problem the way the Jews solved their problem. The Jew never went sitting-in and crawling-in and freedom-riding, like he teaches and helps Negroes to do. The Jews stood up, and stood together, and they used their ultimate power, the economic weapon. That's exactly what the Honorable Elijah Muhammad is trying to teach black men to do."
> (http://www.malcolm-x.org/docs/int_playb.htm)

Not a loved fellah by either white Gentiles or Jews, but by 1999 he was on a U.S. postage stamp. Why was his image cleaned up? The Honorable Minister Louis Farrakhan related an encounter with a leading Jewish religious leader, Rabbi Marx, who told him: *"You're a very talented person. You could go a long way and nobody in history that has been an enemy of the Jewish people has ever been written of well in history, and we want you to be written of in history as a friend of the Jewish community."* And then he, along with Rabbi Shalman, *Chicago Sun-Times* columnist Irv Kupcinet, George O'Hare (an Irish Catholic), and a few other rabbis, said: *"If you do all these ... things [on a list of demands], we will clean up your image."*
(http://v1.noi.org/statements/rift/interview_3.htm)

When Malcolm died, he was considered "an enemy of the Jewish people." So why did they "clean up" his image? Manning Marable, in *Black Routes to Islam* (2009), described how *The Autobiography of Malcolm X* was put together by Alex Haley:

"In late 1963, Haley was particularly worried about what he viewed as Malcolm X's anti-Semitism. He therefore rewrote material to eliminate a number of negative statements about Jews in the book manuscript, with the explicit covert goal of 'getting them past Malcolm X,' without his coauthor's knowledge or consent. Thus, the censorship of Malcolm X had begun well prior to his assassination."(Marable 2009 :312)

After he was killed they even tried to make Malcolm a "civil rights leader" instead of a "black nationalist."

In 1994 Minister Farrakhan announced plans to stage a Million Man March to the Capitol in Washington, D.C., and began a "Men's Only" tour of the country promoting the March. By the end of 1994 a documentary was produced called "Brother Minister: The Assassination of Malcolm X," which was used by Gabe

Pressman to lure Betty Shabazz into a trap and confrontation with Minister Farrakhan that they hoped would stir up division and break the spirit of the 1995 Million Man March. Not only was the March successful—2 million men showed up—but **Betty Shabazz** even **spoke at the March** to further the process of reconciliation.

Okay, resurrecting Malcolm in 1991 and 1994 did not stop the rise of a "messiah," so they put Malcolm away, only to be resurrected again as Minister Farrakhan starts a campaign to prove that Black people are "The Real Children of Israel" and white so-called Jews are imposters. In 2012 Minister Farrakhan brings in scientists at the Nation of Islam's Saviours' Day Convention that prove that "9/11 was an inside job." Also in 2012, Minister Farrakhan went back to the streets to stop Black-on-Black crime and began touring college campuses to prevent the mental genocide of Black students. He has a major presence on Twitter and has produced a 52-week lecture series (actually 58 weeks) on the Internet called **"The Time and What Must Be Done,"** where he is speaking directly to Black and white people alike.

This time they don't just resurrect Malcolm and put words in *his* mouth, they resurrect Betty Shabazz, who passed away in 1997, and manipulate *her* words to try once more to stop the rise of a "messiah" for Black people. They did this act through the Lifetime movie called "Betty and Coretta." However, there is an antidote for this poison. Please continue to read *The Final Call* and go to www.NOI.org to view Minister Ava Muhammad's definitive defense of Minister Farrakhan and let us allow our brother Malcolm X to rest in peace.

The Assassination of the Master Architect

White people have always feared the rise of the Messiah. Unlike us, the inner circle of white people always knew that God's Chosen People were and are black people and therefore the Messiah would be Black. Now let's deal with the assassination and resurrection of the Master Architect, Hiram Abif.

White people have a stratified society. They are first and foremost racist, but within white supremacy is a hierarchy based on lineage, wealth and acceptance into secret societies where supposedly great secrets are revealed that are not taught in the regular educational institutions. One of the best known of these secret societies is the "Freemasons."

A very interesting book was published in 2001 by Christopher Knight and Robert Lomas entitled, *The Hiram Key: Pharaohs, Freemasonry, and the Discovery of the Secret.* According to their book, a group of Asiatic people led by rulers called the "Hyksos", which most have recorded as **"Shepherd Kings**," took over Lower Egypt from 1782-1570 BC. However, the authors say that the name means "desert princes." "Hyksos" has also been translated to mean "rulers of foreign lands," "rulers of the lands of the nomads" and "rulers of the **hill country**."

According to Knight and Lomas, they were a mixed group of Asiatic peoples, mainly Semites, who appeared out of Syria and Palestine (Knight 2001: 123). From this group came what is known today as "Jews", but at that time the tribe of Judah did not exist. The Hyksos were kicked out of Egypt and the group that resettled in Jerusalem later became the Jews. The authors link the Hyksos invasion to the arrival of Abraham into Egypt seeking food and water from the drought in the Middle East.

The Hyksos worshipped the god, Set or Seth, which was the enemy of Egypt's most cherished god, Osiris. The Hyksos set up their capital in the Delta at a place called Avaris, but also extended their power to the old Egyptian capital of Memphis. The indigenous Egyptian rulers kept control of Thebes which was about 300 miles south of Memphis.

The Hyksos kings took on the customs and paraphernalia of

their conquered hosts, but were not initiated into the rituals which made a king into a god. This led to what the authors identify as the killing of Theban king, **Seqenenre Tao**, because he would not give up the **"secrets of Osiris"** (Ibid.133) He died before he could pass on these secrets to his legitimate successors as well and therefore the secrets of "king-making" were lost.

The authors then tie this to the story of Hiram Abif, the Master Architect in Masonry, who would not divulge the secret **"name of God"**. "In Masonic legend the killers of Hiram Abif are named as Jubelo, Jubela and Jubelum, together described as **'the Juwes'"**. (Ibid.: 136)

The Hyksos were finally driven out of Egypt by the two successors to Seqenenre Tao, **Kamose and Ahmose** (Ibid.:147), and driven back to Jerusalem. (Comment: In this battle of liberation the Theban princes were betrayed by leaders in Nubia who had formed an alliance with the Hyksos. This connection between the Asiatics and the Nubians against Egypt will pop up many times in this search for the real history of the "Jews".)

My argument is this: The "name" and the "secret" that the Hyksos were looking for was the **name** of the **"Messiah"** which was to come at the end of Yakub's rule. It seems that the Asiatic "Jews" and the Nubian "Jews" are both awaiting the return of the Messiah and want to control that event. Now we will go to the evidence that the "Ark of the Covenant" of Moses may be in Ethiopia.

In *The sign and the seal: the quest for the lost Ark of the Covenant* by Graham Hancock (1992) the author points out that when Nebuchadnezzar captured Jerusalem, there is no mention that he took away the Ark. This has led to the great search for the Ark of the Covenant. The author argues that the Ark reached Ethiopia in the fifth century BC after staying in a Jewish Temple on **Elephantine** for 200 years (Hancock 1992: 444).

In 525 BC a Persian king, Cambyses, knocked down all the temples of Egypt accept the Jewish Temple at **Elephantine**. This temple remained intact until the Persians were kicked out around

410 BC after which it was destroyed by the Egyptian who believed that the Jews had **collaborated** with the Persians on the invasion of Egypt. The author then argues that the Falasha Jews took the Ark of the Covenant with them to Ethiopia. The author further relates the Ancient Egyptian celebration of **Apet or Opet** to the yearly **procession of the Ark** in Ethiopia as seen below.

Commentary: I argue that the Ark of the Covenant was the Ark of Amun-Re stolen by the Jews of Elephantine when Cambyses destroyed the temple of Karnak. The Falashas Jews of Elephantine then took their prize with them to Ethiopia once the Egyptian had run the Persians out. The Egyptian artifact was a composite symbolism of "Noah's Ark", the boat, and the Ark or box that held the sacred tablet or **Tabot** that was found by the son of Menkaure at Khemennu or Axum described in the Book of the Dead. Therefore the Jews who went to Ethiopia from Elephantine felt justified in returning the Ark which held the tablet (Tabot) that originated in Ethiopia before Egypt was settled: http://www.sacred-texts.com/egy/ebod/ebod16.htm

(As you notice there is a "box" inside of the boat.)

> *"This chapter was found in Khemennu. written upon a slab of steel of the South, in the writing of the god himself, under the feet of the majesty of the god, in the time of the majesty of Men-kau-Ra, the king of the North and of the South, triumphant, by the royal son Heru-tata-f who found it while he was journeying to inspect the temples.*

Jesus was not the first "Messiah"

I have moved the "Babylonian Captivity" to the next chapter because the time around what is put forward as the "Babylonian Captivity" may prove to be exactly when the "babies were switched in the cradle." The modern understanding of the idea of the "Messiah" and a messianic priesthood awaiting the return or advent of the Messiah is all tied up into this issue of stolen identity which we will tackle next. But now let us deal with the concept of "messiah."

I argue that the word "messiah" has as its root "**messi**" which is an Egyptian hieroglyphic word which means "**birth**." And since the Egyptian did not write with the vowels "e" or "o", the consonants, "mss", could be pronounced "messes", such as in **Ramesses or Moses**. "Ramesses" is a composite word "Ra" plus "messes". Ahmoses and his brother Kamoses are made up of two Egyptian words each: **Ah+moses** and **Ka+moses**. Now it gets interesting. Add to your thoughts that the word "Ra" or really "Ray" was the Egyptian sun god. "Ah" was the moon god and "Ka" was the divine "Will."

The phonetic connections between Ancient Egyptian hieroglyphic words and Semitic dialects is thoroughly explored by Dr. Wesley Muhammad in his book *Black Arabia and the African Origin of Islam (2009)*. He makes the parallel between "Ra" or "Rah" and "Allah" and states: "Rah's name thus possesses the same two phonemes as does the name of the Semitic solar deity, '*l*'. Underneath the hieroglyphic Rah is no doubt the Semitic *(a)lah*." (W. Muhammad 2009: 116)

Take the time to go back over the sections dealing with the Hyksos invasion and their subsequent expulsion by Ahmoses and Kamoses who established the 18th Dynasty of Egypt. Also in this dynasty we have a string of kings with "Moses" attached to their names: Thutmoses I, II, III and IV. "Thut" was really "Tehuti", the god of wisdom. These great kings all had something in common. They were major players in the **redemption** of the Egyptian kingdom and civilization from the evil control of the Hyksos. So these kings were saviors or **messiahs** to their people.

Each one of them carried the name meaning "birth" or "rebirth." So Ramesses saw himself as being the rebirth of "Ra", while Ahmoses saw himself as being the rebirth of "Ah." At this time the Egyptian felt that they had been restored to their former greatness and that they were rid of these devils forever. Unfortunately, like Jesus, Ramesses, Ahmoses, Kamoses, Thutmoses were ahead of time to judge the Jews' civilization and put the Black man back on top of civilization for good. Now since we know that the Exodus did not happen the way the Bible portrays, Ramesses **could not** have been the "Pharaoh" of the Exodus. However, the so-called Jews hatred for him as one of the kings that pushed them back out of the

Holy Land can be understood. Also according to what is written in stone on the walls of Egypt, this strong Black man, Ramesses, along with his pet lion, **killed 10,000** of these white enemies at the battle of Kadesh near the Orontes River in modern day Syria. So, the enemies of the Black man have been waiting on the advent of that final Messiah so that they can kill him as they failed to kill Ramesses. This is why Minister Farrakhan is having a hard time with the Jews of today who want him dead. But he is on time and is backed by the God who has a big weapon, the **Mother Plane.**

Who enslaved who?

The "Poison Book" is an interesting document that contradicts itself on many occasions. For instance although the major them of the Bible centers around the children of Jacob being enslaved and afflicted by the Egyptians, if one carefully reads the account of Jacob and his sons entering Egypt another story emerges. We will highlight the book of Genesis chapter 47:

Genesis 47:11King James Version (KJV)

11 And Joseph placed his father and his brethren, and gave them a possession in the land of Egypt, in the best of the land, in the land of Rameses, as Pharaoh had commanded.

Genesis 47:20-27King James Version (KJV)
20 And Joseph bought all the land of Egypt for Pharaoh; for the Egyptians sold every man his field, because the famine prevailed over them: so the land became Pharaoh's.

21 And as for the people, he removed them to cities from one end of the borders of Egypt even to the other end thereof.

22 Only the land of the priests bought he not; for the priests had a portion assigned them of Pharaoh, and did eat their portion which Pharaoh gave them: wherefore they sold not their lands.

23 Then Joseph said unto the people, Behold, I have bought you this day and your land for Pharaoh: lo, here is seed for you, and ye shall sow the land.

24 And it shall come to pass in the increase, that ye shall give the fifth part unto Pharaoh, and four parts shall be your own, for seed of the field, and for your food, and for them of your households, and for food for your little ones.

25 And they said, Thou hast saved our lives: let us find grace in the sight of my lord, and we will be Pharaoh's servants.

26 And Joseph made it a law over the land of Egypt unto this day, that Pharaoh should have the fifth part, except the land of the priests only, which became not Pharaoh's.

27 And Israel dwelt in the land of Egypt, in the country of Goshen; and they had possessions therein, and grew, and multiplied exceedingly.

Let us now dissect these passages. First of all verse 11 indicates that Joseph gave his father and brothers land in the "land of Rameses." Well according to Exodus 1:11, Rameses was built by the children of Israel under bondage to Pharaoh. How can you give someone something that does not yet exist?

According to Genesis 47:20, *"Joseph bought all the land of Egypt for Pharaoh."* Now this is quite strange. Why would the King of Egypt have to buy "his" land from "his" own people? He was king over all the land or at least he should have been, unless he was a usurper or invader. Then after Joseph bought the Egyptians' land for Pharaoh, the people in the countryside were taken to the cities. Sounds like captives of a foreign power to me.

But somehow the "priests" escaped getting their land confiscated by Pharaoh. These priests look like "collaborators" with an invader. Then Joseph just told the Egyptian people right out: *"I have **bought you** this day and your land for Pharaoh..."* In other words the **Egyptian people** became the **slaves** of "Pharaoh" at the hands of Joseph, the son of a foreigner, Jacob.

Then the Egyptian people bowed down to this "Pharaoh": *"...Thou hast saved our lives: let us find grace in the sight of my lord, and we will be Pharaoh's servants."* Wow, the Egyptian feel that "Pharaoh" has saved their lives and therefore they decided to be his servants. So what was the relationship between "Pharaoh" and the people of Egypt before these events?

This whole story makes one suspicious of the term "Pharaoh" as even the title of an indigenous, legitimate king of Egypt. In fact "Pharaoh" was not one of the five titles given to the king of Egypt. According to http://www.britannica.com/EBchecked/topic/455117/pharaoh,

> *pharaoh, (from Egyptian per ʿaa, "great house"), originally, the royal palace in ancient Egypt; the word came to be used as a synonym for the Egyptian king under the New Kingdom (starting in the 18th dynasty, 1539–1292 BCE), and by the 22nd dynasty (c. 945–c. 730 BCE) it had been adopted as an epithet of respect. The term has since evolved into a generic name for all ancient Egyptian kings, although it was **never** formally the king's title. In official documents, the full title of the Egyptian king consisted of **five names**, each preceded by one of the following titles: Horus, Two Ladies, Golden Horus, King of **Upper and Lower Egypt**, and Son of Re. The last name was given to him at birth, the others at coronation.*

This definition is important because the 18th dynasty began on the expulsion of the Hyksos in 1539 BCE or so. Therefore the title "Pharaoh" must have come with the Hyksos. Furthermore, according to Sir Wallace Budge's *Egyptian Dictionary,* the only kings of Egypt who had the official title of "Pharaoh" were foreigners: Persian usurpers Xerxes, Khabbasha and Artaxerxes, then the Macedonian usurper, Alexander II.

Now what is telling about the use of this term "Pharaoh" is that Alexander I who first conquered Egypt by running the Persians out, did not take the title "Pharaoh", however his successor Alexander II did. When Alexander I ran the Persians out of Egypt and took over the throne he had not as yet conquered Persia in its home base of Mesopotamia and Iran (Aryan). This clue leads me to believe that the term "Pharaoh" is only applied to someone who controls both Egypt (Africa) and Mesopotamia (Asia). At one time there seems to have been an empire that included both Africa and Asia, with the "Pharaoh" as its head. Only when the two continents are combined together in one kingdom can one claim to be "Pharaoh." We have been limited to look at history through the eyes of a six thousand year old child instead of one that stretches hundreds of thousands of years into the past. These new white children have taken great pains to hide traces of that history and are still afraid that some of it will pop out of the sand, the jungle or the ocean to bite at their made up lie, the "Poison Book." Well I should not call it a total lie, but even worse, some truth mixed with falsehood. The truth makes you want to read, while the lies poison your soul.

Going back to the title of the king, **Horus** is one of the oldest and most significant deities in ancient Egyptian religion, who was worshipped from at least the late Predynastic period through to Greco-Roman times. In Egyptian his name was Heru from which we get our English "Hero."

The **Two Ladies** are Wadjet (cobra) and Nekhbet,(vulture); the deities who were the patrons of the Ancient Egyptians and worshiped by all after the unification of its two parts, Lower Egypt, and Upper Egypt. Sometimes It is called the "nebti" or the "two ladies title."

Golden Horus was represented by a falcon perched on the

103

glyph for gold (nub) hence, Heru-nub. Since gold lasts forever, this name is associated with eternity.

*King of **Upper and Lower Egypt*** in hieroglyphic language this was "nesu-bit". "Nesu" was the "papyrus reed" and represented Upper Egypt and "bit" was the "bee" and represented Lower Egypt.

Son of Re in Egyptian was Sa-Re or Sa-Ra which meant the son of Ra. The SaRa name was the name given at birth or the family name.

This idea of the double crown is expressed in both the "Nebti" title and the "Nesu-bit" title which goes back to "Dhu-l-Qarnain" talked about earlier. However this SaRa name is too close to "Sarah" of the Bible to be ignored. She was the wife of Abraham and her son was Isaac who was the father of Jacob which is the central figure in this Biblical lineage, "rightful heir," game.

Let us now look at the name "Abraham" itself and break it apart, then interpret it according to Ancient Egyptian as translated in Budge's *Hieroglyphic Dictionary*. Ab-Ra-Ham: Ab means father, pure, priest and to love. Ra is the Sun God and Ham means "his majesty", servant or priest. So we can see where Abraham is called the beloved or "friend of God" in the Bible and Holy Qur'an. The covenant was given to Abraham's seed. Plus "Ham" was not a bad name or title until the Rabbis of Babylon made up the "curse of Ham."

While we are dealing with alternative interpretations of names, we might as well throw in "Israel". Is-Ra-El could be "Is" meaning the man from as in the name Judas Is-cariot which means the man from "Kerioth." Ra is the Sun God and El means god. So we have Israel meaning "the man from where the God is Ra." We will get more into this identity theft and name changing in the next chapter.

Chapter 4

Stolen Identity: Who, where, why and when?

Farrakhan and the Real Children of Israel

The Honorable Minister Louis Farrakhan caused a controversy in the Jewish community with his announcement that the Real Chosen People of God written of in the Old Testament are the Black people of America. He further stated that the Jewish people who currently hold sway in Israel and throughout the world do not fit the clear Biblical description. The Minister reasons that the Jewish people have never fit the criteria established in the Bible for the people that would wear that divine title.

The Honorable Minister Louis Farrakhan has boldly challenged twenty-five hundred years of traditional Judeo-Christian interpretation of Old Testament scripture by declaring that there is no way to prove biologically, anthropologically, historically, scientifically or scripturally that those who today are called Jews fit the category such a designation requires, and he has offered his life if anyone could disprove his controversial claim. It is this claim that is stirring up a major furor on college campuses across the nation as The Minister seeks to stimulate the thought process of the future leaders of America and the world.

At the root of this controversy is whether or not such a claim can be proved. Based on the accepted interpretation of Old Testament theology, the Jews were slaves in Egypt for four centuries. After suffering unspeakably harsh treatment God sent Moses to demand that the Pharaoh of Egypt release the captured

Israelites or God would send plague after plague until the people were set free. Pharaoh relented and upon being set free they wandered in the Sinai Desert for 40 years before being led to their new "Promised Land."

The only problem is that no evidence exists to corroborate such claims. And this is conceded by some of the most respected Israeli historians as we have shown above. There is no evidence of housing units having been built to accommodate a million and a half people, no toilets, no farming, no cattle; no transportation system uncovered, no utensils, no nothing. What has been traditionally presented to us as history is largely mythology as we demonstrated in the previous chapter.

This Biblical episode is actually prophecy, not history. No ancient nation in the world has as meticulously detailed a written history as has Egypt. It speaks of the cuisine the average Egyptian enjoyed thousands of years ago, what its population was, and the intimate details of almost every aspect of their daily lives. And yet they have no history of a Jewish nation living inside of Egypt for over 400 years. None.

Another aspect of the biblical relationship between Blacks and Jews is the story of the dueling twins in Genesis. Isaac has two sons named Jacob and Esau. The character, nature and behavior of each son are polar opposites. Jacob, the younger son is stealthy, cunning, an oppressor, cleaver, and dishonest. Jacob, in collaboration with his mother Rebekah trick his dying father to give Jacob his older brother's (Esau's) birthright.

Jacob the imposter then wrestles with God and he prevails. The King James version uses the word God, but some scholars use angel. In either case, this Jacob fellow seems to be a pretty audacious guy. In the battle *"When the man saw that he could not overpower him, he touched the socket of Jacob's hip so that his hip was wrenched as he wrestled with the man;*(Genesis 32:25) leaving Jacob with a permanent limp, so he could never walk a straight path. Joseph otherwise prevailed in this struggle and was given the new name of "Israel."

Esau, on the other hand, his birthright stolen, is made a slave by Jacob. However, the Bible promises Esau that one day he will break the yoke of his younger brother and he, Esau, will be the winner in the end. God tells Esau of his future in Genesis (27:40) in these words:

"By thy sword shalt thou live, and shalt serve your brother; and it shall come to pass when thou shalt have the dominion, that thou (Esau) shalt break his (Jacob's) yoke from off thy neck."

Farrakhan has been singled out by the white Jewish establishment (Israel) because he has the audacity to remind the world what has been done to us, and by whom. Their fear is that he will influence the thinking of untold millions who are unaware of the damage that has been done to us by our Jewish "friends." Their fear is that Black youth will be inspired by the truth of Minister Farrakhan's teaching and "Esau" will break free of Israel's control.

So, we ask today, "Who are the legitimate heirs of God's covenant? Is it the children of the Black slave, or the children of the White slave master?"

Black people have had their identity stolen. We want to show how it was done, where it was done, when it was done and by whom. The first clue in this puzzle or crime is the fact that the first five books of the Bible supposedly written by Moses were not written by him. Instead they were put together by scribes during the supposed "Babylonian Captivity." Judaism, as we know it, was formed in **Babylon** not Jerusalem using writings probably borrowed from Egypt. Gerald Massey in his *Book of the Beginning* reprinted in 1987 argues that the original Bible was written in Egyptian Hieroglyphs not Hebrew. This corresponds to what The Most Honorable Elijah Muhammad writes in *Message to the Blackman* that Musa spoke "**Ancient Egyptian Arabic**" and therefore not Hebrew (Muhammad 1965: 93). Massey writes:

> "Terru denotes the roll of papyrus, drawing and colours with the symbol of the hieroglyphic scribe. The Hebrew form of the word, Taroth, does but add the plural terminal which is Egyptian as well as Hebrew, and we have the Teruu, the hieroglyphic rolls of papyrus, whilst Haphtaroth denotes either the hidden papyrus rolls or the papyrus rolls of the law. It thus appears on this showing, that the Hebrews were still in possession of the papyri and possibly of the hieroglyphic writing which were preserved and read by the learned when the better known copies of the law were **destroyed**. Ezra is credited with founding the Great Synagogue, or men of the Assembly, which succeeded in establishing the regular reading of the Sacred Records, and with **rewriting** the law after the books had been burnt. 'For thy Law is burnt, therefore no man knoweth the things that are done of thee, or the works that shall begin.'(2 Esdras 14:21)
>
> This burning of the books is the destruction during the persecution when the Haphtaroth come into notice. The Haphtaroth being the secret papyrus rolls written in the sacred, that is hieroglyphical language, we now see that the work of Ezra, described with supernatural accompaniments, was that of re-translating the Law from the hieroglyphical or Ibri writing into the Chaldee of Ashurith, or the square letter.
>
> Ezra dictated the translation during forty days and nights, and the five scribes wrote down what they were told by him. Which they knew not, as they did not understand the original characters." (Massey 1987: 119)

Other scholars allude to the same conclusions as Massey, but they beat around the bushes instead of going to the bottom line. For instance Israel Finkelstein and Neil Silberman in *The Bible Unearthed* first gave King Josiah credit for finding the "Law" during renovations to the Jerusalem Temple in 622 B.C. (Sounds like Heru-tata-f who found a chapter of the Egyptian Book of the Dead in a temple.) However, after further analysis they write: "To sum up, there is little doubt that an original version of Deuteronomy is the book of the Law mentioned in 2 Kings. Rather than being an old book that was suddenly discovered, it seems safe to conclude that it was written in the seventh century BCE, just before or during Josiah's reign." (Finkelstein 2002: 281)

There is no mention in the Bible or in Babylonian writings that the Ark of the Covenant or the Torah was brought to Babylon. So if the "Book of the Law" was destroyed in 586 B.C., then what Josiah supposedly found was destroyed and not rewritten until Ezra did so in 458 BC. (Ibid: 300). The "Second Temple" was supposedly finished in 516 B.C. But if there was no "Book of the Law" between 586 and 458 B.C., then what was in the Temple from 516 to 458 B.C.? You had a Temple with no Book until the Hebrew Bible was **produced.**

Therefore, the Hebrew Bible was born in "captivity" and authorized by the foreign kings of that "captivity." According to the Bible (Ezra 7:6, 10): "He was a scribe skilled in the law of Moses which the Lord the God of Israel had given...For Ezra had set his heart to study the law of the Lord." Then "Ezra was sent to make inquiries 'about Judah and Jerusalem' by Artaxerxes king of Persia, who authorized him to take with him an additional group of Jewish 'exiles' from Babylon who wanted to go there. The Persian king provided Ezra with funds and **judicial authority**."(Ibid: 300) This sounds a lot like a Persian colony being sent to Palestine to establish Judaism as authorized by Cyrus, a follower of Zoroaster.

The efforts of Ezra and the cupbearer of king Artaxerxes, Nehemiah, "...and the efforts of other Judean priests and scribes which took place over the one hundred and fifty years of exile (597-445 B.C), suffering, soul-searching, and political rehabilitation— led to the birth of the Hebrew Bible in its substantially final form."(Ibid: 301)

I like that phrase **"political rehabilitation"**. That means "brainwashing" and the establishment of a Persian/Babylonian civilization in the name of Judaism. We have here the **switching** of the babies in the cradle. We will go further into this identity theft and fabrication as we dig into this so-called "Babylonian Captivity" and "Return."

Deportation and Return???

In the ancient Near East deportation and return just was **not done**. It was not state policy at that time for Aryan and half-breed conquerors to take people from one area then later allow them to return to the same area. Let us read from the *Bible Unearthed* to see how it was really done: "Conquest and deportation were not the end of the story. After exiling the Israelites from their land to Mesopotamia in 721 BC, the Assyrians brought new settlers to Israel. "And the king of Assyria brought people from Babylon, Cuthah, Avva, Hamath, and Sepharvaim, and placed them in the cities of Samaria instead of the people of Israel; and they took possession of Samaria, and dwelt in the cities." (2 Kings 17:24) ...The ten northern tribes of Israel were now lost among the distant nations."(Ibid: 199)

> *"Thus the Assyrians deployed a policy of deportation and repopulation on a grand scale. This policy had many objectives, which all served the goals of continuing imperial development. From a military point of view, the capture and removal of native villages had the effect of terrorizing and demoralizing the population and splitting them up to prevent further organized resistance. ...And finally, the systematic resettling of new populations in empty or recently conquered territories was intended to expand the overall agricultural output of the*

empire." (Ibid: 216)

In other words there was no "return" of the children of exiled Israel back to their homeland. That just was not done. According to the Bible, the leadership class was taken into captivity, leaving the peasants and farmers behind. If Babylon or Persia sent back the children of that leadership class, those children would easily be able to unite with the peasant class with whom they had kinship, and produce a force that could compete with "headquarters" again.

Just as the Assyrians brought in people from outside Palestine to repopulate Palestine in the past, Persia would have done the same thing. One might say that Persia and Assyria were not the same country. Each wolf in a wolf pack is different, but all follow the same leader until that lead wolf is challenged and a new one becomes the pack leader. However, they all are wolves in the same wolf pack and they all eat sheep. The Assyrians, Babylonians and Persians were all different tribes who were off springs from the invading Scythians or Aryans who took over these lands after their escape from the Caucasus Mountains after being trained by Musa (Moses). The Aryans, like lions after taking over a "pride", killed the males of the indigenous peoples, took the women and made half-breed babies which they trained to be warriors in their armies of conquest.

The people who were sent to Palestine after the Nebuchadnezzar conquest were no more "Israelites" or "Judeans" as were the half-breeds produced by the Christianized-Jews to infiltrate Africa in the 15th century A.D., "Africans." White folk like to throw up in Black folk faces that it was "Africans who sold each other into slavery." But let us look at a practice that white folks have used over and over again to gain access to forbidden territories.

111

The Sao Tome Enterprise

The Most Honorable Elijah Muhammad taught us that the new white race came to live with the original people 6,000 years ago. Evidently at that time the people allowed these new white folk to live among them until they found out that they were devils. After which they ran them from among them. The white man had to invent another tactic and that tactic was to raid and steal black woman, rape them to produce mulatto children, then raise those children, like a new breed of cattle, to go in among the original people to trick them into doing business with their white fathers. Take the island of Sao Tome as an example.

In a new book, *Jews and Judaism in African History*, author Richard Hull describes how Portuguese in 1470 found an "uninhabited" island 120 miles off the coast of the kingdom of the Kongo. In the 1480s the Portuguese began capturing slaves in the "slave rivers" of the Bight of Benin. After they captured Kongolese female slaves they would bring them back to this island and breed them with white Jewish castoffs (lancandos) and conversos (Jewish converts to Christianity) until they had produced a mixed population of "mesticos". Some of these mesticos became rich and powerful on the island and laid the foundations, not only of the trans-Atlantic slave trade, but of the modern plantation system of agriculture that further evolved in the New World (Hull 2009: 91).

So how would you categorize these "mesticos"? If you asked them, they would call themselves "Portuguese." If you ask modern historians who want to blame the indigenous Africans for the slave trade, they would classify them as "Africans."

We should look at what happened in Palestine 2,500 years ago in the same manner. Were the "returnees" the Children of Israel or the "Children of the Babylonian/Persian" rapists?

According to the Bible, the male children that were captured by the Babylonians were castrated and made eunuchs to be (bell-wether) servants to the Babylonian leadership. After King Hezekiah, king of Jerusalem, had entertained emissaries from Babylon, Isaiah the prophet declared: 2 Kings 20:17, 18

> *"17 Behold, the days come, that all that is in thine house, and that which your fathers have laid up in store until this day, shall be carried into Babylon: nothing shall be left, saith the Lord.*
>
> *18 And of thy sons that shall issue from thee, which thou shalt beget, shall they take away; and they shall be **eunuchs** in the palace of the king of Babylon."*

A "eunuch" is a castrated male.

Included among them was Daniel who according to the Bible served Nebuchadnezzar, Cyrus and Darius, but was never recorded to have married or fathered children. And since descent or lineage is passed down through the father in a patriarchal society, the dignitaries and royal families of Jerusalem could **never** have off springs to be "returnees". Therefore, the only candidates for "return" were **children of the raped women** who had been brought up in the house of Babylon and Persia to **serve** the aims, wishes and gods of **their masters**.

According to the Bible these "returnees" were not supposed to marry people who lived in Judea although these were supposed relatives. The invaders, Pharisees (sheepdogs), kept themselves separate from the indigenous masses (sheep) and ruled over them for Persia (Magi, evil shepherds).

I had accepted this false idea of "captivity and return" until I read one line in a book by Okasha El-Daly called *Egyptology: The Missing Millennium (2005)*. It reads, "…it was suggested that a Babylonian king, Nebuchadnezzar, conquered Egypt and killed her lame pharaoh, then took back with him thousands of Egyptians who settled in Babylon" (El-Daly 2005: 16). However, other historians argue that Nebuchadnezzar never entered Egypt. Now before I bring more evidence on this point, I must refer us back to our introduction and the statement that The Messenger wrote about Jesus going to Jerusalem looking for the "lost sheep." We asked the question, "Who were these 'lost sheep' and how did they end up in Israel?" Also remember from your Bible studies that Jesus was taken to Egypt when he was a little boy by his parents. Did he learn about these "lost sheep" while he lived in Egypt?

The Most Honorable Elijah Muhammad has warned us about the "Poison Book." Now let's show how it has been manipulated in the hands of a snake. According to the book of Ezekiel, the "Sovereign Lord" gave him a prophecy about Nebuchadnezzar conquering Egypt. Bible scholars understood the problem this would bring to their whole Jerusalem/captivity/return model if indeed Nebuchadnezzar had conquered a **real prize** or kingdom (**Egypt**) instead of just a city, Jerusalem. However, to deny the fact that Nebuchadnezzar actually conquered Egypt and even built a huge fort there would make Ezekiel a false prophet and the Bible suspect. These passages from the 29th chapter of Ezekiel are illuminating from a number of perspectives.

Ezekiel 29:8-21 **New International Version (NIV)**:

8 Therefore this is what the Sovereign LORD says: I will bring a sword against you and kill both man and beast. 9 Egypt will become a desolate wasteland. Then they will know that I am the LORD.

Because you said, "The Nile is mine; I made it," 10 therefore I am against you and against your streams, and I will make the land of Egypt a ruin and a desolate waste from Migdol to Aswan, as far as the border of Cush. 11 The foot of neither man nor beast will *pass through it; no one will live there for **forty years**. ¹² I will make the land of Egypt desolate among devastated lands, and her cities will lie desolate forty years among ruined cities. And I will disperse the Egyptians among the nations and scatter them through the countries.*

*¹³ Yet this is what the Sovereign LORD says: At the end of forty years I will gather the Egyptians from the nations where they were scattered. ¹⁴ I will bring them back from captivity and return them to **Upper Egypt**, the land of their ancestry. There they will be a lowly kingdom. ¹⁵ It will be the lowliest of kingdoms and will never again exalt itself above the other nations. I will make it so weak that it will never again rule over the nations. ¹⁶ Egypt will no longer be a source of confidence for the people of Israel but will be a reminder of their sin in turning to her for help. Then they will know that I am the Sovereign LORD.'*

*¹⁷ In the twenty-seventh year, in the first month on the first day, the word of the LORD came to me: ¹⁸ "Son of man, Nebuchadnezzar king of Babylon drove his army in a hard campaign against Tyre; every head was rubbed bare and every shoulder made raw. Yet he and his army got no reward from the campaign he led against Tyre. ¹⁹ Therefore this is what the Sovereign LORD says: I am going to give Egypt to Nebuchadnezzar king of Babylon, and he will carry off its wealth. He will loot and plunder the land as pay for his army. ²⁰ I have given him **Egypt as a reward** for his efforts because he and his army did it for me, declares the Sovereign LORD.*

Now let us dissect these passages. First of all this is some pretty specific stuff. The "Sovereign Lord" was angry with Egypt because the people of Egypt claimed to have "made" the Nile River. Well this is **true.** The Ancient Egyptians did indeed **build** the **Nile River**

115

as an engineer would build a road. You can see my proofs in *I will not apologize: The resurrection of the Master Architect.* But this "Sovereign Lord" is a real jealous fellow.

Then in verses 13 and 14 the Egyptians would be taken away from Egypt for 40 years and then returned to "Upper Egypt." Well Upper Egypt would be Aswan or Elephantine where a Jewish colony was indeed established by the Persians at about the same time that the Persians sent their colony of half-breeds into Palestine. Since I don't accept this exile and return to the same land, I will latter give a more realistic view of what happened.

In verse 19 the Sovereign Lord promises to pay Nebuchadnezzar for taking Tyre by giving him the **"wealth"** of **Egypt**. So evidently what was taken by Nebuchadnezzar from the Jerusalem Temple was **not enough** payment. If a sane mind would compare the wealth of the Jerusalem Temple to the wealth of Egypt at that time, that sane mind would say that the "Sovereign Lord" could not have "bought" Nebuchadnezzar with the Jerusalem Temple's wealth. There is no comparison. Egypt had at least **42 temples** that were all bigger and had more gold in **each of them** than did the **one** temple in Jerusalem.

I find it most interesting that the writers of the Bible had knowledge of Egypt up to "Aswan" at the first cataract in Upper Egypt. However, there is no mention in the Bible of the **pyramids or the Sphinx** which were near modern Cairo where the Nile branches out into the Delta which is considered Lower Egypt, because the Nile runs South to North. At first I thought that the pyramids and Sphinx were not mentioned in the Bible because its authors never made it that far up into Egypt. The Great Pyramid still stands and was 481 feet high, hard to miss. However, the Bible talks about the great Tower of Babel or Babylon, which is yet to be archaeologically verified.

So now we see that the authors of the Bible were **jealous** of the greatness of Egypt. And this was why Egypt was such a great "prize" that the Sovereign Lord "gave it" to Nebuchadnezzar as payment for a job well done. He used the wealth and slaves from Egypt to build his own "tower" of Babylon and her great walls. The Bible begins to look more like **propaganda** produced by enemies of Egypt in Mesopotamia.

Fort Babylon in Egypt

As I studied Ancient Egypt and the pyramids I always wondered why was there a town or precinct called "Babylon" within the present city of Cairo. A 2010 book by Peter Sheehan, *Babylon of Egypt,* presents a history of Old Cairo based on new archaeological evidence gathered between 2000 and 2006 during a major project to lower the groundwater level affecting the churches and monuments of this area of Cairo known by the Romans as "Babylon."

In his book Sheehan reprints a seventh-century account of John, the Coptic Bishop of Nikiu, of the conquering of Egypt by Nebuchadnezzar in 568 BC and the building of the fortress of Babylon:

> "...Nebuchadnezzar the king of the Magi and Persians was the first to build its foundations and to name it the fortress of Babylon...Nebuchadnezzar came to Egypt with a numerous army and made a conquest of Egypt, because the Jews had revolted against him, and he named [the fortress] Babylon after the name of his own city..."(Sheehan 2010: 38)

The location of this fortress was strategic. Not only was it at the apex of the Delta, but was connected to a canal which Necho II had errantly dug in his attempt to connect the Nile with the Red Sea.

After Necho II was defeated by Nebuchadnezzar at Carchemish in Northern Syria in 605 BC, Necho thought of digging a canal not far from the capital of Egypt, Memphis, to the Red Sea which would allow him to mount a naval attack against Nebuchadnezzar via the Red Sea, the Arabian Sea and the Persian Gulf. When warned about the danger of making such a canal that could be used in the reverse against Egypt, Necho halted the construction even after 120,000 men had died in the undertaking.

However, the Nile itself after an exceptional flood level could have made its on channel through the unfinished canal. This connection to the Red Sea then could allow Nebuchadnezzar to enter Egypt at this very strategic point and conquer her. Even though some modern historians do not want to accept the fact that Nebuchadnezzar accomplished this victory, the 200 meter by 400 meter fort named after his city is pretty solid evidence.

According to what we read in Ezekiel 29, Egypt lay desolate under the control of Babylon/Persia for 40 years bringing us to 528 BC. Cambyses enters Egypt and destroys temples of all the gods except the Jewish god at Elephantine in 525 BC. He tried to reach Ethiopia but failed.

Chronology of major events (see Appendix C):

605 BC – A. Nebuchadnezzar's reign begins, B. Nebuchadnezzar defeats Necho, C. Daniel captured

597 BC – Jerusalem attacked by Nebuchadnezzar and first deportation

586 BC – Jerusalem destroyed and second deportation

568 BC – A. Nebuchadnezzar enters Egypt builds Fort Babylon and B. Massive African deportation

556 BC – A. Nebuchadnezzar's reign ends, B. Belshazzar's reign or Nabonidus' reign begins

539 BC – A. Cyrus' reign begins and B. First "returnees" to Jerusalem

530 BC - A. Cyrus' reign ends, B. Daniel dies and Cambyses' reign begins

118

525 BC – Cambyses destroys all Egyptian temples except Jewish temple
   at Elephantine
522 BC – A. Cambyses' reign ends and B. Darius' reign begins
519 BC – Darius authorizes the building of a Jewish Temple in Jerusalem
518 BC – Darius orders codification of Egyptian Laws
502 BC – Codification completed
458 BC – Ezra writes Pentateuch and Judaism is born

Where did Ezra get the material to write the Pentateuch or Torah?

Now we know that the Pentateuch, first five books of the Bible, also called the Torah, was not in the possession of the Jews until their sojourn in Babylon. According to Jeremiah 8:8 **New International Version (NIV):**

> 8 *"'How can you say, "We are wise,*
> *for we have the law of the LORD,"*
> *when actually the lying pen of the scribes*
> *has handled it falsely?"*

So "Jeremiah" agrees with The Most Honorable Elijah Muhammad that the Bible has been tampered with, however the question remains is where did Ezra and the other "scribes" get the raw material from which to translate and change? If you remember, Gerald Massey wrote that Ezra had rolls of papyrus written in Egyptian hieroglyphics: "…Ezra dictated the translation during forty days and nights, and the five scribes wrote down what they were told by him. Which they knew not, as they did not understand the original characters." (Massey 1987:119)

Ezra himself is an enigmatic figure according to the *Bible Unearthed*. He shows up from nowhere, dictates the five books of

119

Moses to a number of scribes, takes his new Torah to Jerusalem, then disappears. Since he came to Babylon under the rule of Darius, we can now see where he may have gotten the raw materials from which to extract what he needed to please his patron, Darius. Darius had **all** the scribes and learned men of Egypt to spend **16 years** transcribing what they saw on the walls of the temples in Egypt and their libraries, then place that information on **papyrus rolls**. (Remember what Gerald Massey wrote about these papyrus rolls.)

Sixteen years is a lot of time, therefore the volume of writings must have been immense. I visited Egypt in 1989 and the amount of writings on the walls of the few restored temples that I visited was tremendous.

Darius was a lot wiser than the Assyrians who conquered Egypt and took her capital, Memphis, in 667 BC, only to see Egyptians return from their original home, Ethiopia, kick them out and run them back to Turkey. Cambyses tried to get to Ethiopia but almost died in the deserts of Nubia before he could reach Ethiopia (see Appendix). Darius took a different route. The Persians put half-breeds at the two gates of Egypt, Jerusalem and Elephantine, then they destroyed the temples, took all the books, then fabricated a new Book of history and a new religion for these new Jews, giving everybody a new identity based on the political and theological framework of Persia/Babylonia/Iran. It worked.

Ben Ezra Synagogue

The Jews love to brag on their history and do all they can to control anything that they believe once belonged to them. A case in point is the decision by Abraham ibn Ezra of Jerusalem in 882 AD to purchase land within Fort Babylon for the erection of a synagogue which is called the Ben Ezra Synagogue or the El-**Geniza** Synagogue. This was the synagogue whose **genizah** or store room was found in the 19th century to contain a treasure of abandoned Hebrew secular and sacred manuscripts. The collection, known as the Cairo Geniza, was brought to Cambridge, England at the instigation of Solomon Schechter and is now divided between several academic libraries (http://en.wikipedia.org/wiki/Ben_Ezra_Synagogue).

It may just be a coincidence that a synagogue set up by a Rabbi named after Ezra, who is credited with restoring the Torah and probably had volumes of Egyptian manuscripts to work from, also was a storage house in the Babylon of Egypt for ancient Hebrew manuscripts. Could this be the place where Ezra actually did his work in the service of Darius who had the law of Egypt codified? Could this be a case of a criminal returning to the scene of the crime?

Your father, the devil

John 8:33, 44

> *33 They answered him, "We are Abraham's descendants and have never been slaves of anyone. How can you say that we shall be set free?"*
>
> *44 You belong to your father, the devil, and you want to carry out your father's desires. He was a murderer from the beginning, not holding to the truth, for there is no truth in him. When he lies, he speaks his native language, for he is a liar and the father of lies.*

Now let us go back to these words ascribed to Jesus in the Book of John. How can a people be Abraham's seed, but never being a slave and whose father is "the devil"? Jesus was arguing with the Pharisees, so let us look at them from the perspective of the paradigm that I have presented above; the so-called "returnees" to Jerusalem were the products from the rape of African/Egyptian women by the Babylonians/Persians. Therefore, through the female

121

they may have the seed of Abraham, but through rape, the seed of the devil, white man, was forcibly placed in them and that seed of the devil is what is arguing with Jesus.

Another clue to this paradigm is the name of the first governor of Judea after the "Captivity," Zerubbabel which means "seed of Babylon." Zerubbabel was put in charge of collecting taxes for Persia and given the charge by Darius of building the Temple in Jerusalem. Since Zerubbabel had no Hebrew Bible, his main function must have been tax collection for Persia. The "seed of Babylon" takes on a new skin and shrouds itself in "mystery" as it passes from generation to generation, chapter to chapter up to Revelations and "Mystery Babylon."

Return of the Khazarians (Scythians)

In the 2003 book *I Will Not Apologize: Resurrection of the Master Architect* I wrote: "According to Arthur Koestler in his book, *The Thirteenth Tribe*, those of European descent who call themselves Jews were a tribe north of the Black Sea who converted to Judaism during the Dark Ages. Therefore they were not descendants of Abraham or Shem, but Japhet. Since Western Jews are only Jews by faith and not lineage, how can they be Jews yet not follow Judaism? Therefore, I call them so-called Jews." (Mu'min 2003: 151)

In appendix "F" of this chapter we have printed portions of an article reporting the DNA research findings of Eran Elhaik, a Jew, where he verified the "Khazarian Hypotheses" as being the best explanation of the origins of European Jews. This Khazarian Hypotheses suggests that Eastern European Jews are descendants of ancient and late Judeans who joined the Khazars, a confederation of Slavic, Scythian, Sabirs, Finno-Ugrian, Alan, Avars, Iranian, and Turkish tribes who formed in the northern Caucasus one of most powerful and pluralistic empires during the late Iron Age and converted to Judaism in the 8th century CE (http://arxiv.org/ftp/arxiv/papers/1208/1208.1092.pdf).

Now based on the information presented in this book let us try to piece together the history of the European white Jews, Ashkenazim. First of all, white people were made on the Island of Pelan or Patmos in the Aegean Sea 6,000 years ago. They moved into the Holy Land and started mischief, causing the original people to fight and kill one another. They were kicked out and driven across the desert and placed in the Caucasus Mountains. The Egyptians built walls and iron gates to keep them in. Soldiers were left to guard the walls. We now know that the Colchians, as highlighted by Herodotus, were once among those Egyptian soldiers.

Research by archaeologists and anthropologists now bear witness to The Most Honorable Elijah Muhammad and say that a new white race appeared in the Caucasus Mountains about 4,000 BC or 6,000 years ago which they called the "Kurgan culture." These whites killed or enslaved the indigenous darker peoples who lived north of the Caucasus Mountains between the Volga River and Black Sea 6,000 years ago. Musa (Moses), a half-original, came 2,000 years later and civilized some of these whites then called Scythians. The Whites that he civilized first conquered Mesopotamia then Egypt. They were kicked out of Egypt, but they stayed and mixed with the indigenous peoples in Mesopotamia producing the Persian and Babylonian Semites. We know that Moses gave them a book, but we now know that we do not have the original book that he wrote. Instead we have the Bible (Old Testament) that the priests in Babylon, Ezra and company, produced using pieces from the original scriptures in 458 BC and after. With this "Bible" and Babylonian Talmud the Rabbis developed what we know today as Rabbinical Judaism.

Over time the Persians through Darius and the Greeks through Alexander the Great defeated the Scythians and again bottled them up behind the Caucasus Mountains. However, in 740 CE (almost 1200 years later) Jews from Babylon went up behind the Caucasus Mountains and converted the Khazarians (Scythians) to Judaism which looked a lot like what Moses (Musa) taught to their ancestors 2,800 years previous (2000 BC). So in one sense when the Khazarians accepted Judaism, they were accepting something similar to what they were taught by Moses. But the book and the religion had been tampered with by their ancestors, Scythians, who had conquered the indigenous people in Mesopotamia and made a mixed race, Semites, called the Jews which they relocated to Jerusalem, Palestine and Elephantine, Egypt.

So white European Jews, Khazarians, Ashkenazim, have accepted a corrupted version of what Musa (Moses) had taught their ancestors and they, the Khazarians (Ashkenazim), had all but forgotten. But now they had, thanks to the Hebrew Bible, Jacob, the usurper, liar and crook (evil shepherd) to study all over again, so that they could finally establish the "Jewish Civilization" which now rules the world through "money and banking." They have made their headquarters in Israel, not because God gave them Palestine as the "Promised Land", but because England and America wants them lodged in the Middle East to be a counterweight to Islam and control the oil. They will not have full hegemony until they conquer Egypt, "The Prize."

As a shepherd studies sheep, the evil shepherd (Jews), studies human nature so as to better fleece them. Chapter 5 will go into the details of how the Jews have built their civilization through control of the money supply. The Jews (Evil Shepherd) now control the sheep (the original people) and the sheepdog (non-Jewish whites) with their crook (Poison Book) and their money (green pastures).

Conclusions to Part I

The Most Honorable Elijah Muhammad said that we as a people were "buried" in this "poison" book. He writes on the back of Muhammad Speaks and now on the inside cover of The Final Call under "What The Muslims Believe": *"4. WE BELIEVE in the truth of the Bible, but we believe that it has been tampered with and must be reinterpreted so that mankind will not be snared by the falsehoods that have been added to it."*

The Teachings of The Most Honorable Elijah Muhammad breaks through the clouds of confusion produced by the Bible and gives us a proper lens to see through and evaluate that book. With this lens and keys we can then go to libraries and find the morsels of truth that bear witness to The Messenger's Teachings and allows us to piece together the real history of the world using the road markers provided in our Lessons. We can essentially fill in the gaps between firm historical markers given to us by The Messenger's Teachings.

At the same time we must realize that even though the Bible has been tampered with, it was put together from scripture given to Moses and copied from writings on the walls of Ancient Egypt. When the enemy tampered with these writings, his intent was to place themselves in the place of the Real Children of Israel or Chosen People. However, what they did was to actually preserve and pass on to God's Chosen People the information waiting for the Messiah to come and reinterpret these scriptures. What the enemy messed up or stunk up as "history", he passed on as "prophecy" by mistake. It was his mistake but Allah's plan. Just as he made the mistake of bringing Black people from Africa to be made slaves and suffer for 400 years, Allah used his own hands as an instrument of his undoing

As stated earlier in this chapter, our Scientists wrote history 25,000 years in advance. They saw Mr. Yakub 8,400 years before he was born. They knew what he would make and they knew how his made man would think. They had already prepared a way for our redemption. They knew that the grafted man would change scripture and steal our identity. They knew that our enemies would take us to a strange land and take away our religion and language. How could the Scientists 15,000 years ago figure out a way to teach these blind, deaf and dumb people who would be in the grips of a new man with a new language?

In Ancient Egypt there was a "neter" or scientific principle represented by a scarab or beetle called "khepera". The beetle insect was very important to the Egyptians because a specie known as the "dung beetle" feed exclusively on dung. They would transform this dung into fertilizer. So they cleaned the sewers as well and provided nutriment for plants. The way they reproduced themselves was by rolling their eggs in dung. The dung would provide heat for incubation and hatching. Then this dung would be used as food for the new beetles.

In the same way the knowledge needed for rebirth or resurrection was hidden in an unpleasant (confusing) form to be passed on to a new generation awaiting The Messiah to clear up the confusion. At first, the enemy would not allow his slaves to read the Bible. However, after Nat Turner used it to start a rebellion, the enemy decided to train a few Negro preachers (bell-wether sheep) the "proper" interpretation of the Bible that would not resurrect the deadened mind of the slave. Now this book that had been made into a poison was in the hands of his former slaves. But now 400 years after our captivity this same book under the Messianic interpretation can be used for the Resurrection of a mentally dead people.

We must always remember what The Most Honorable Elijah Muhammad taught: **"As the Holy Qur'an teaches, they planned against us, but Allah also has plans, and He is the best of planners."** (Muhammad 1965: 296)

126

Appendix to Chapter 4

Commentary:

Mind you that the historians write that Darius' predecessor, Cambyses, destroyed all the Egyptian temples except the Jewish temple at Elephantine. Later these same "Jews" were used as spies against Ethiopia. Evidently they were spies against Egypt for Cambyses and the Persians before they invaded Egypt.

So they tried to destroy the Egyptian records while preserving them for themselves and later Ezra comes out with a new Torah from Babylon with a colony of Jews to resettle Jerusalem. This new set of Jews, according to the Bible, would not accept those that were not deported to Babylon, the Samaritans. Jacob has now successfully stolen the birthright of Esau, the first born, i.e., Egypt, the older civilization and civilizer.

A. Jewish Temple at Elephantine

http://www.kchanson.com/ancdocs/westsem/templeau th.html

Petition to Authorize Elephantine Temple Reconstruction

Now, our ancestors built this temple in the fortress of Yeb in the days of the kingdom of Egypt; and when Cambyses came to Egypt he found it (already) constructed. They (the Persians) knocked down all the temples of the Egyptian gods; but no one damaged this temple.

==

Herodotus on Cambyses

When Cambyses determined to send the spies, he sent for those Fish-eaters from the city of Elephantine who understood the Ethiopian language. [3.19.2] While they were fetching them, he ordered his fleet to sail against Carthage. But the Phoenicians said they would not do it; for they were bound, they said, by strong oaths, and if they sailed against their own progeny they would be doing an impious thing; and the Phoenicians being unwilling, the rest were inadequate fighters. [3.19.3] Thus the Carthaginians escaped being enslaved by the Persians; for Cambyses would not use force with the Phoenicians, seeing that they had willingly surrendered to the Persians, and the whole fleet drew its strength from them. The Cyprians too had come of their own accord to aid the Persians against Egypt.

[3.20.1] When the Fish-eaters arrived from Elephantine at Cambyses' summons, he sent them to Ethiopia, with orders what to say, and bearing as gifts a red cloak and a twisted gold necklace and bracelets and an alabaster box of incense and an earthenware jar of palm wine. These Ethiopians, to whom Cambyses sent them, are said to be the tallest and most handsome of all men. [3.20.2] Their way of choosing kings is different from that of all others, as (it is said) are all their laws; they consider that man worthy to be their king whom they judge to be tallest and to have strength proportional to his stature.

[3.21.1] When the Fish-eaters arrived among these men, they gave the gifts to their king and said: "Cambyses, the king of the Persians, wishing to become your friend and ally, sent us with orders to address ourselves to you; and he offers you as gifts these things which he enjoys using himself." [3.21.2] But the Ethiopian, perceiving that they had come as

128

spies, spoke thus to them: "It is not because he values my friendship that the Persian King sends you with gifts, nor do you speak the truth (for you have come to spy on my realm), nor is that man just; for were he just, he would not have coveted a land other than his own, nor would he try to lead into slavery men by whom he has not been injured. Now, give him this bow, and this message: [3.21.3] 'The King of the Ethiopians advises the King of the Persians to bring overwhelming odds to attack the long-lived Ethiopians when the Persians can draw a bow of this length as easily as I do; but until then, to thank the gods who do not incite the sons of the Ethiopians to add other land to their own.'"

==

B. Yahweh and U<u>a</u>

Commentary: The following is taken from Budge's translation of the "Book of the Dead" whose proper name is "Pert-en-ru" or "Coming forth by Day." "The One" which he refers to is represented in the hieroglyphic language according to Budge's "Hieroglyphic Dictionary" as a "U" or "W" followed by a long "A" which would be vocalized as "Ooh-yeh" or "Ooh-Wa-Yeh". I say that this is where the Jews got "Yahweh". The following is taken directly from Budge's book with no additions from myself.

Attached are two files which are pages from Budge's Hieroglyphic Dictionary which shows that "Ua" really meant the "One God".

THE BOOK OF THE DEAD

The Papyrus of Ani

By E. A. WALLIS BUDGE [1895]

http://www.sacred-texts.com/egy/ebod/ebod09.htm

129

We have seen above[1] that among other titles the god Amen was called the "only One", but the addition of the words "who hast no second" is remarkable as showing that the Egyptians had already conceived the existence of a god who had no like or equal, which they hesitated not to proclaim side by side with their descriptions of his manifestations. Looking at the Egyptian words in their simple meaning, it is pretty certain that when the Egyptians declared that their god was One and that he had no second, they had the same ideas as the Jews and Muhammadans when they proclaimed their God to be "One"[1] and alone. It has been urged that the Egyptians never advanced to pure monotheism because they never succeeded in freeing themselves from the belief in the existence of other gods, but when they say that a god has "no second," even though they mention other "gods," it is quite evident that like the Jews, they conceived him to be an entirely different being from the existences which, for the want of a better word, or because these possessed superhuman attributes, they named "gods."

http://www.sacred-texts.com/egy/ebod/ebod26.htm

Plate XI

"Thou sendest forth the word, and the earth is flooded with silence, O thou only One, who livedst in heaven before ever the earth and the mountains were made. (12) O Runner, Lord, only One, thou maker of things which are, thou hast molded the tongue of the company of the gods, thou hast drawn forth whatsoever cometh from the waters, and thou springest up from them over the flooded land of the Lake of Horus (13)."

http://www.sacred-texts.com/egy/ebod/ebod32.htm

Plate XXVI

"I am the One among the worms which the eye of the Lord, the only One, hath created."

http://www.sacred-texts.com/egy/ebod/ebod37.htm

Plate XXXII

I am the only One born of an only One, who goeth round about in his course; (18) I am within the eye of the Sun.

I am he who riseth and shineth; the wall of walls; the only One, [son] of an only One.

http://www.sacred-texts.com/egy/ebod/ebod40.htm

Plate XXXV

"Homage to thee, (2) O thou lord, thou lord of right and truth, the One, the lord of eternity and creator (3) of everlastingness.

C. Timeline of history:
http://www.aboutbibleprophecy.com/p345.htm

Necho was a Pharaoh of Egypt. He was the second king of Egypt's 26th dynasty. He ruled from 610 to 595 B.C. As Necho and his army marched north to fight the Babylonians at Carchemish, Josiah, the King of Judah, went out to intercept him.

Necho warned Josiah not to interfere saying "What quarrel is between us, King of Judah? I have not come against you this day, for my war is with another kingdom, and God has told me to hasten" (2 Chronicles 35:20-24).

Josiah did not listen and was killed in the battle. Necho later lost the battle of Carchemish, to Nebuchadnezzar and the Babylonians in 605 B.C. Necho withdrew back to Egypt, and stopped a Babylonian army on Egypt's frontier, with heavy losses on both sides, in 601 B.C. He died six years later.

The Greek historian Herodotus writes that Necho sent a Phoenician crew on a three-year voyage around Africa to construct a canal from the Nile to the Red Sea, a project that cost the lives of 120,000 Egyptians.

===

http://www.concordialutheranchurch.com/b2006/20060305.pdf

605 BC - Daniel captured
586 BC - Jerusalem destroyed
556 BC - Nebuchadnezzar's reign ends, Belshazzar's reign is happening
539 BC - Belshazzar's reign ends, Cyrus' begins (Medo-Persian)
530 BC - Cyrus' reign ends (Daniel's death? at 85-90 yrs-old?

The Academy, Volume 11 (Google eBook) by J. Murray 1877

http://books.google.com/books?id=bVk8AQAAIAAJ&pg=PA440&lpg=PA
440&dq=Nebuchadnezzar+cyrus+Cambyses&source=bl&ots=0Lvrljq87T
&sig=xhl02xSwUfhcRzqYVoJ5fzzC_Ng&hl=en&sa=X&ei=4H4YVPmmGOn
E8AG56ICIAg&ved=0CDIQ6AEwBA#v=onepage&q=Nebuchadnezzar%20
cyrus%20Cambyses&f=false

Reign begins

605 BC – Nebuchadnezzar
562 " - Evil Merodach
560 " - Neriglisaar
556 " - Nabonidus
539 " - Cyrus
530 " - Cambyses
522 " - Darius

132

D. Canal to Red Sea

http://www.moellerhaus.com/Persian/Hist01.html

The first circumnavigation
of Africa

by Jona Lendering

Herodotus, *The Histories* **4.42: The first circumnavigation of Africa**
Libya is washed on all sides by the sea except where it joins Asia, as was first demonstrated, so far as our knowledge goes, by the Egyptian king Necho, who, after calling off the construction of the canal between the Nile and the Arabian gulf, sent out a fleet manned by a Phoenician crew with orders to sail west about and return to Egypt and the Mediterranean by way of the Straits of Gibraltar. The Phoenicians sailed from the Arabian gulf into the southern ocean, and every autumn put in at some convenient spot on the Libyan coast, sowed a patch of ground, and waited for next year's harvest. Then, having got in their grain, they put to sea again, and after two full years rounded the Pillars of Heracles in the course of the third, and returned to Egypt. These men made a statement which I do not myself believe, though others may, to the effect that as they sailed on a westerly course round the southern end of Libya, they had the sun on their right - to northward of them. This is how Libya was first discovered by sea.

The Egyptian pharaoh Necho, or -more properly- Wehimbre Necho, was the ruler of the old kingdom along the Nile from 610 to 595. When he started his reign, there were some serious problems on Egypt's northeastern border. The old kingdom of Assyria had succumbed to Babylonian aggression, and the Babylonian king wanted to punish Egypt for its support to the Assyrian cause (cf. the biblical book *2 Kings* 23.29). From a Babylonian chronicle, we know that Necho was campaigning in

133

Syria from 609 until 605, when the Babylonian king Nebuchadnezzar decisively defeated the Egyptians at Carchemish and proceeded along the Mediterranean coast. It is not entirely clear where the border was drawn: *2 Kings* 24.7 implies that Egypt retired to the Sinai desert and left the Palestine coast in Babylonian hands; Herodotus 2.159 suggests that Gaza remained Egyptian.

However this may be, it is obvious that Necho was in big trouble, and he seems to have considered the possibility to attack southern Babylonia by sea. He ordered a canal to be made between the Nile and the Red Sea; however, he learned from an oracle that he was giving free access to his enemies too, and therefore, the canal remained uncompleted until the Persians had taken over Egypt in the last quarter of the sixth century.

E. Darius codifying Egyptian Law

He empowered the Egyptians to reestablish the medical school of the temple of Sais, and he ordered his satrap to codify the Egyptian laws in consultation with the native priests. In 519 BC he authorized the Jews to rebuild the Temple at Jerusalem, in accordance with the earlier decree of Cyrus. In the opinion of some authorities, the religious beliefs of Darius himself, as reflected in his inscriptions, show the influence of the teachings of Zoroaster, and the introduction of Zoroastrianism as the state religion of Persia is probably to be attributed to him.

============================

Persia

Darius as an administrator.

Author: Grote, George "While measures were thus taken to unite the diverse peoples of the empire by a uniform administration, Darius followed the example of Cyrus in respecting native religious institutions. In Egypt he assumed an Egyptian titulary and gave active support to the cult. He built a temple to the god Amon in the Kharga oasis, endowed the temple at Edfu, and carried out restoration work in other sanctuaries. He empowered the Egyptians to reestablish the medical school of the temple of Sais, and he ordered his satrap to codify the Egyptian laws in consultation with the native priests. In the Egyptian traditions he was considered as one of the great lawgivers and benefactors of the country. In 519 BC he authorized the Jews to rebuild the Temple at Jerusalem, in accordance with the earlier decree of Cyrus. In the opinion of some authorities, the religious beliefs of Darius himself, as reflected in his inscriptions, show the influence of the teachings of Zoroaster, and the introduction of Zoroastrianism as the state religion of Persia is probably to be attributed to him."

http://history-world.org/darius_as_an_administrator.htm

==============================

ARYANDES, Achaemenid satrap of Egypt. The name is of uncertain etymology (R. Schmitt, "Medisches und persisches Sprachgut bei Herodot," *ZDMG* 117, 1967, pp. 119-45 esp. p. 134 n.106). He was appointed by Cambyses in 522 B.C. (Herodotus 4.166). Soon after, a rebellion forced the imperial officials out (DB 2.5-8 with Polyaenus 7.11.7), but Darius traveled to Egypt in the summer of 518, pacified the people, and reinstated Aryandes (Polyaenus, loc. cit., with G. Posener, *La première domination perse en Egypte*, Cairo, 1936, pp. 36ff.; R. A. Parker, "Darius and his Egyptian Campaign," *AJSL* 58, 1951, pp. 373ff.; G. G. Cameron, "Darius, Egypt and "the Land beyond the Sea"," *JNES* 2, 1943, pp. 307-13, esp. p. 310). Desiring to codify the Egyptian laws (Diodorus 1.95.4-5), Darius wrote "to his satrap" before December, 518: "Let them bring to me the wise men among the warriors, priests, and scribes of Egypt, who have assembled from the temples, and let them write down the former law of Egypt until year XLIV of Pharaoh Amasis.

135

The law of Pharaoh, temple and people let them bring here" (W. Spiegelberg, *Die sogennante demotische Chronik*, Paris, 1914, pp. 30ff.; A. T. Olmstead, *History of the Persian Empire*, Chicago, 1948, p. 142).

http://www.iranica.com/newsite/index.isc?Article=http://www.iranica.com/newsite/articles/unicode/v2f7/v2f7a009.html

======================

For Cambyses' policy in Egypt, there's the Udjahorresne inscription (he said that Cambyses restored the Temple of Neith at Sais and provided it with revenues). For Cyrus there's the Cyrus cylinder as well as the Babylonian documents such as the Nabonidus Chronicle, Verse Account of Nabonidus, Sippar Cylinder, the pillar inscription in Parsagardae. Also, the Bible gives some account of Cyrus II, Darius I, Xerxes I and Artaxerxes I, though (like always) not very reliable. For Darius I there's the Naqshi-Rustam inscription, letter to Gadatas to codify existing Egyptian laws, Book of Ezra (from the Bible), Wage lists in Persepolis, Fortification texts, Wadi Hammamat Inscription, Book of Esther (from Bible, again), Udjahorresne Inscription and, for an interesting note, a letter from Darius I (found in Persepolis) telling an official (exact ranking I've forgotten... have to look it up again) something about a present for his daughter. For Artaxerxes I aside from the Biblical texts (Book of Ezra and Nehemiah) there's also the Nippar documents which is a financial record of the Marshu family- a wealthy, banking family in Artaxerxes I's time in Babylon (yes, it's Babylonian).

"Julia Poon" <ira_poon@...>

http://groups.yahoo.com/group/AncientTactics/message/3566

======================

ASSYRIANS, MEDES, AND PERSIANS:

The Struggle for Power in the Ancient Near East

"Darius codified the laws that would govern the empire in a document called the Ordinances of Good Regulations. Though no copy of the document has been uncovered as yet by archaeologists references to the document have been found in Assyrian and Babylonian inscriptions, as well as in several royal documents. In the Biblical book of Daniel there are references to the "Law of the Medes and Persians, which alters not." The law was extreme, but it was consistent, and it applied to the king himself as well as to any commoner."

http://worldhistory1a.homestead.com/PERSIA.html

==================================

So Cook, *The Persian Empire*, 71. Plato refers to Darius I as the great lawgiver, and Olmstead (*History*, 119-34) credits him with the establishment of a penal law code. In Egypt, Darius ordered Aryandes to set up a commission to collect and codify laws, and within sixteen years they were codified on papyrus and published in Egyptian demotic and Aramaic. It is likely that Darius's efforts in the provinces in this area also touched Yehud, where we can imagine that the Primary History underwent further refinement and that other sacred writings, notably the prophets, were collected and organized.

http://personal.centenary.edu/~sbrayfor/meyersnotes.htm

F. Khazarian Hypotheses

http://arxiv.org/ftp/arxiv/papers/1208/1208.1092.pdf

The Missing Link of Jewish European Ancestry:

Contrasting the Rhineland and the Khazarian Hypotheses

Eran Israeli-Elhaik (Dec. 2012)

Abstract

The question of Jewish ancestry has been the subject of controversy for over two centuries and has yet to be resolved. The "Rhineland Hypothesis" proposes that Eastern European Jews emerged from a small group of German Jews who migrated eastward and expanded rapidly. Alternatively, the "Khazarian Hypothesis" suggests that Eastern European descended from Judean tribes who joined the Khazars, an amalgam of Turkic clans that settled the Caucasus in the early centuries CE and converted to Judaism in the 8th century. The Judaized Empire was continuously reinforced with Mesopotamian and Greco-Roman Jews until the 13th century. Following the collapse of their empire, the Judeo-Khazars fled to Eastern Europe. The rise of European Jewry is therefore explained by the contribution of the Judeo-Khazars. Thus far, however, their contribution has been estimated only empirically; the absence of genome-wide data from Caucasus populations precluded testing the Khazarian Hypothesis. Recent sequencing of modern Caucasus populations prompted us to revisit the Khazarian Hypothesis and compare it with the Rhineland Hypothesis. We applied a wide range of population genetic analyses — including principal component, biogeographical origin, admixture, identity by descent, allele sharing distance, and uniparental analyses — to compare these two hypotheses. Our findings support the Khazarian Hypothesis and portray the European Jewish genome as a mosaic of Caucasus, European, and Semitic ancestries, thereby consolidating previous contradictory reports of Jewish ancestry.

Introduction

Contemporary Eastern European Jews comprise the largest ethno-religious aggregate of modern Jewish communities, accounting for nearly 90% of over 13 million Jews worldwide (United Jewish Communities 2003). Speculated to have emerged from a small Central European founder group and maintained high endogamy, Eastern European Jews are considered invaluable subjects in disease studies (Carmeli 2004), although their ancestry remains debatable among geneticists, historians, and linguists (Wexler 1993; Brook 2006). Because correcting for population structure and using suitable controls are critical in medical studies, it is vital to test the different hypotheses pertaining to explain the ancestry of Eastern European Jews. One of the major challenges for any hypothesis is to explain the massive presence of Jews in Eastern Europe, estimated at eight million people at the beginning of the 20th century. The two dominant hypotheses depict either a sole Middle Eastern ancestry or a mixed Middle Eastern-Caucasus-European ancestry.

The "Rhineland Hypothesis" envisions modern European Jews to be the descendants of the Judeans – an assortment of Israelite-Canaanite tribes of Semitic origin. It proposes two mass migratory waves: the first occurred over the next two hundred years after the Muslim conquest Palestine (638 CE) and consisted of devoted Judeans who left Muslim Palestine for Europe (Dinur 1961; Sand 2009). It is unclear whether these migrants joined the existing Judaized Greco-Roman communities and the extent of their contribution to the Southern European gene pool. The second wave occurred at the beginning of the 15th century by a group of 50,000 German Jews who migrated eastward and ushered an apparent hyper-baby-boom era for half a millennia affecting only Eastern Europe Jews (Atzmon et al. 2010). The annual growth rate that accounted for the populations' rapid expansion from this small group was estimated at 1.7-2% (Straten 2007), twice the rate of any documented baby boom period and lasting 20 times longer. This growth rate is also one order of magnitude larger than that of Eastern European non-Jews in the 15th-17th centuries. The Rhineland Hypothesis predicts a Middle Easter ancestry to European Jews and high genetic similarity among European Jews (Ostrer 2001; Atzmon et al.

139

2010; Behar et al. 2010).

The competing "Khazarian Hypothesis" considers Eastern European Jews the descendants of ancient and late Judeans who joined the Khazars, a confederation of Slavic, Scythian, Sabirs, Finno-Ugrian, Alan, Avars, Iranian, and Turkish tribes who formed in the northern Caucasus one of most powerful and pluralistic empires during the late Iron Age and converted to Judaism in the 8th century CE (Figures 1-2) (Polak 1951; Brook 2006; Sand 2009). The Khazarian, Armenian, and Georgian populations forged from this amalgamation of tribes (Polak 1951), followed by high levels of isolation, differentiation, and genetic drift in situ (Balanovsky et al. 2011). The population structure of the Judeo-Khazars was further reshaped by multiple migrations of Jews from the Byzantine Empire and Caliphate to the Khazarian Empire. The collapse of the Khazar Empire followed by the Black Death (1347-1348) accelerated the progressive depopulation of Khazaria (Baron 1993) in favor of the rising Polish Kingdom and Hungary (Polak 1951). The newcomers mixed with the existing Jewish communities established during the uprise of Khazaria and spread to Central and Western Europe. The Khazarian Hypothesis predicts that European Jews comprise of Caucasus, European, and Middle Eastern ancestries and is distinct from the Rhineland Hypothesis in the existence of a large genetic signature of Caucasus populations. Because some Eastern European Jews migrated west and admixed with the neighboring Jewish and non-Jewish populations they became distinct from the remaining Eastern European Jews. Therefore, different European Jewish communities are expected to be heterogeneous. Alternative hypotheses, such as the "Greco-Roman Hypothesis" (Zoossmann-Diskin 2010), were also proposed to explain the origins of European Jews; however, they do not explain the massive presence of Eastern Europeans Jews in the 20th century and therefore were not tested here.

Conclusions

We compared two genetic models for European Jewish ancestry depicting a mixed Khazarian-European-Middle Eastern and sole Middle Eastern origins. Contemporary populations were used as surrogate to

140

the ancient Khazars and Judeans, and their relatedness to European Jews was compared over a comprehensive set of genetic analyses. Our findings support the Khazarian Hypothesis depicting a large Caucasus ancestry along with Southern European, Middle Eastern, and Eastern European ancestries, in agreement with recent studies and oral and written traditions. We conclude that the genome of European Jews is a tapestry of ancient populations including Judaized Khazars, Greco-Romans and Mesopotamian Jews, and Judeans and that their structure was formed in the Caucasus and the banks of the Volga with roots stretching to Canaan and the banks of the Jordan.

Part II
Money and Cycles

Part I of this book dealt with clearing up the history of the white man and the identity theft by the so-called Jews. We were able to show our major points using scripture and pieces of history from many different sources guided by the historical paradigm taught to us by the Most Honorable Elijah Muhammad.

Now we will focus on "money" and "cycles." For these we will need to use both history and some mathematical tools to uncover hidden "patterns" within that history which will reveal how the Jews got so rich at the expense of everybody else. Brother Allan X. has written a very helpful book entitled *Mathematical Theology and the Physics of God (2012)*. In it he gives a definition of and usefulness for mathematics from Keith Delvin's book, *The Language of Mathematics: Making the Invisible, Visible (1998)*: **"...mathematics is the science of patterns..."** (Allan X.: 46) which **"...makes the invisible visible."** (Ibid.: 49) This describes our task undertaken in Part II: "Money and Cycles."

Chapter 5

Money and Banking

Where does "money and banking" fit into our paradigm of "sheep, sheepdog and evil shepherd"? In our previous chapters we have highlighted one of the control mechanisms of the "evil shepherd," the "Poison Book." The Poison Book is like the shepherd's crook or stick which keeps the sheep and the sheepdog in line so that everyone knows his place and role. The "Poison Book" is the "Law" that produces "order" and gives legitimacy to the authorities (sheepdogs) as the sheep try to graze and survive in the "Jews' Civilization."

"Money" represents the "green pastures" for the sheep. Scientists have analyzed why domesticated animals allow themselves to be ruled by humans. The humans take the place of the mother, nourisher and sustainer of the infant. A child does not want to stray far from his mother. The sheep follow the shepherd because he provides nourishment for them. He who controls the economics of a people essentially has ultimate power over that people. A saying attributed to Amsel B. M. Rothschild in 1838 is how the bankers of the world think and they are right: "Let me issue and control a Nation's money and I care not who makes its laws." (http://www.rense.com/general79/tril.htm)

One of the main problems with returning a domesticated animal into the wild is to teach that animal how to find its own food and defend itself. The Honorable Elijah Muhammad teaches us that economics and military science are two of the sciences that the slave master's children did not want their former slaves to learn. It is most interesting that Jews who have claimed to be the friends of black people in America never taught us about economics and money, even though they were the masters of both. Indeed, "economics" is the Jews' real religion and they never invited us to join.

In this chapter we will give you some background information on how economics shapes our lives and how black people are kept out of the loop. We also demonstrate how even the "sheepdog", non-Jewish Whites are reduced to a form of economic slavery through the banking system and usury.

Business is Warfare: Freedom or Non-economic liberalism

The poor Black man and woman in America have been forced to explain their lack of economic development without being allowed to point the finger at the forces aborting that development. We Blacks are asked to forget about the past and to stop making excuses for our poverty, lack of wealth and absence of industry. It seems like Blacks just can't get it together either in America, the Caribbean or in Africa.

The Honorable Minister Louis Farrakhan has declared that "We are at war" and "Business is Warfare." However, Black people are expected to participate in these war games without the knowledge of our past or the knowledge of those we have to compete against. Unlike other races such as the Jews, Japanese, Chinese and others who pass on their collective history and knowledge base to each generation of would-be entrepreneurs, we Blacks are forced to enter the cutthroat world of business from scratch as inexperienced, naïve babes. It's as if we are physically disabled, mentally challenged beginner Little Leaguers thrown into a major league football game (that's rigged) without being taught the rules of the game, the offensive or defensive strategy, the goal we are to defend, or the role those guys with the striped shirts and whistles are supposed to play.

However, The Most Honorable Elijah Muhammad teaches us, **"History is above all our studies. The most attractive and best qualified to reward our research."**

So now we find in *The Secret Relationship Between Blacks and Jews, Volume 2* (TSRv2) that the Jews did not suffer persecution in the South before or after the Civil War. In fact, they were active not only in the slave trade but also in their family businesses as traders, middlemen and financiers. They loaned money to individual slave plantations and to the Confederacy itself in its war against the Union. And it was Judah P. Benjamin, the Jewish former Secretary of State for the Confederacy, who bankrolled the Ku Klux Klan. After the Civil War the Jews became the heirs to the slave barons in the South and set up a new form of slavery for the ex-slaves called "sharecropping." They used their gold accumulated over decades and stored in the vaults of Jewish bankers in Europe and America to finance cotton production and the distribution of that cotton through their extensive networks and trading outlets all over the world.

Now let us compare the Jewish businessman who retained his capital from generation to generation and maintained family connections in Europe, Africa, Asia and the New World with the African slave who was cut off from his homeland, cut off from inherited wealth, cut off from his craft and livelihood, cut off from his history and heritage, cut off from access to business opportunities and cut off from leaving the confines of the plantation even after slavery. The Black Codes were established after slavery to make what was legal for Whites against the law for Blacks: it was illegal for Blacks to own farm land, set up retail stores, peddle or even sell their own farm-produced commodities in the open market. A Black person found walking the streets of any town in the South could be picked up and put on a plantation to work as a virtual slave, if he could not show papers that he or she was working for a White person.

Enemies of the rise of Black people today would have you to believe that Blacks never understood what was in our best interest and never organized to accomplish those goals. However, according to TSRv2, Black farmers organized the Colored Farmers Alliance

145

(CFA) in 1886 to set up independent cooperatives through which they could market their products. The CFA spread to every state in the South, reaching a total membership of 1.2 million. Whites responded to this legitimate attempt of Blacks to do "white folk business" by bringing in three national guard units, which, along with local Whites, marched through the Mississippi countryside lynching 20 Blacks and aborting the movement.

Seeing the futility in trying to exercise their rights of citizenship in the general population, groups of ex-slaves all across the South went into hiding in the woods, swamps and uninhabited wildernesses and set up independent communities. In a book called **Freedom Colonies** by Thad Sitton and James H. Conrad the stories of some of these settlements in Texas were explored for the first time. Much of the history of these communities were not written down or found in the courthouse records of these different counties because the Blacks purposely stayed to themselves. However, between 1870 and the early 1890s many of these wise "isolationists" Black Texans had accumulated thousands of acres of land right underneath the noses of their white oppressors using "squatter's rights" or "the law of adverse possession". Using these methods Blacks sued for tracts of land from 160 acres to 640 acres at a time until the "authorities" in different states found out what the Blacks were up to.

When the first national census was taken that counted Black land ownership, the country was surprised and alarmed to find that Blacks owned nearly 10 million acres of land. But by 1910 that acreage had increased to 16 million acres, so the white folks got busy. The Whites in the South increased their terroristic war against Blacks with more atrocious and publicized lynching, while the Blacks' so-called Jewish friends were financing the KKK down South and luring black people up North with promises of "non-economic liberalism" where they could feel safe against the lynch man's noose, but not the moneylender's grip.

Whites throughout the South continued their terroristic war

against Black "citizens," a war spearheaded by the Jewish-financed KKK. These wholesale killings of Blacks occurred across the South in response to attempts by Blacks to assert their citizenship rights, such as voting or seeking political office or acquiring land or education or participating in business, as well as other unwelcomed manifestations of Black progress. But usually it was just pure race hate that drove these open racial slaughters. As one scholar wrote of postwar Whites: "They loathed the Negro and…were ready to hunt him like an animal." And Jews were just as active in aiding in the persecution of Blacks as any other class of White people. It was a Jew—in Springfield, Illinois—that led a mob in the commission of at least seven murders and the destruction of 40 homes and 24 businesses.

While one set of Jews were financing and engaging in this war against Blacks down South, their Jewish northern cousins lured Blacks to northern cities with promises of "non-economic liberalism," where they could feel safe against the lynch-man's rope but not the moneylender's noose. However, Jews in the North aborted every legitimate effort made by Blacks for economic development: Sufi Hamid, the Honorable Marcus Garvey, The Most Honorable Elijah Muhammad, the Honorable Louis Farrakhan and others advocating for Black economic development and independence were all targeted by Jews. History teaches that we Blacks have been hunted and hated and cut off from kindred and kind by the very people who claim to be "God's Chosen People," but who have demonstrated throughout history that they are in fact the enemies of the Real Children of Israel.

The NAACP and "Non-Economic Liberalism"

"Non-economic liberalism" was the philosophy guiding the activities of the early NAACP (National Association for the

Advancement of Colored People), which sought the social acceptance of Blacks instead of building an independent business economy. The Honorable Elijah Muhammad warned Black people that Whites would never teach us "the science of business," so "non-economic liberalism" was a philosophy developed by the longtime white Jewish president of the NAACP, Joel Spingarn, for Black people's social and political advancement without economic empowerment.

This philosophy was in direct contrast to the economic and political empowerment goals of the Niagara Movement, which was supplanted by the NAACP. When historians write about the NAACP, they make you think that it was the direct outgrowth of the Niagara Movement, which was secretly started by 29 Black men, who stated in their 1905 *Declaration of Principles* that they "especially complain against the denial of equal opportunities to us in **economic** life; in the rural districts of the South this amounts to peonage and virtual slavery; all over the South it tends to crush labor and small business enterprises…" These Black men demonstrated that Black people in the South strove toward The Most Honorable Elijah Muhammad's brand of economic independence. In fact, by 1910 Black people had acquired over 16 million acres of land, mostly in the South, but Black landownership steadily declined after the advent of the NAACP, as this organization made the northern cities appear safer for Black people, thus facilitating the Great Migration(s) out of the South. They herded us into the cities as Joseph herded the Egyptians into the cities for the Pharaoh of that time.

When W. E.B. Du Bois brought a white woman, Mary White Ovington, into the Niagara Movement, founding members like William Monroe Trotter broke away and set up the all-Black National Equal Rights League (NERL). Now this William Trotter was a brother who had received a bachelor's degree in international banking from Harvard University, graduating Magna Cum Laude in 1895, and went on to earn his Masters from Harvard in 1896. However, he could never get a career started in the banking industry.

Now, this same white woman, Mary White Ovington, a New York City news reporter, tracked Du Bois down in 1906, and later introduced him to 300 other white "liberals" in New York City, who then founded the NAACP in 1910. Du Bois was the only member of the original 29 founders of the Niagara Movement to join the white-dominated NAACP. Du Bois had been recently traumatized by the race riot or massacre of Blacks in Atlanta in 1906 which effectively castrated his belief in an independent economic solution for Black people. He became a castrated ram or bell-wether leader of the flock, but only responding to white folks' directives. These early white leaders of the NAACP included wealthy Jewish merchants, rabbis, economists, scholars and journalists and others such as **Jacob Schiff**, Julius Rosenwald, Joel Spingarn, Rabbi Stephen Wise, all of whom hypocritically pushed "non-economic liberalism."

For instance, one of these Jewish board members of the NAACP, Jacob Schiff, was a senior partner in the Wall Street banking house of Kuhn, Loeb and Company. Schiff also became the director of many other important corporations, including the National City Bank of New York, Equitable Life Assurance Society, Wells Fargo & Company, and the Union Pacific Railroad. He was one of the big bankers behind the establishment of the Federal Reserve System and is credited with getting Pres. Woodrow Wilson elected and to sign it into law.

He could have hired and mentored William Monroe Trotter, who had two degrees in international banking from Harvard, but instead, Schiff (evil shepherd) watched over the shoulder of Du Bois as he edited the *Crisis Magazine*. Schiff decided not to help the man who could have led Black people to economic independence and power, but decided instead to shepherd another Black man toward being the most eloquent **complainer** about Black people's condition.

W.E.B. Du Bois was one of our great Black writers who travelled through the South and wrote *The Souls of Black Folk* in 1903, which got the attention of the Jews. The book was very radical for the time and even pointed out the great influx of European Jews into the South, where they exploited the Blacks through the system of "sharecropping" cotton, while selling back to them cheap manufactured goods from their cousins up North. According to *The Secret Relationship Between Blacks and Jews, Volume 2* (TSRv2),

149

Du Bois made his way to Dougherty County, Georgia, a farming region and home to ten thousand Blacks, who outnumbered whites by five to one. However, according to the U.S. government's report of the Industrial Commission on Immigration (1901), "Nine-tenths of the storekeepers in Dougherty County are Jewish merchants—some Russian and German Jews, but most of them Polish Jews."

His observations and facts led W.E.B. Du Bois to state, "The Jew is the heir of the slave-baron in Dougherty [County]," for Blacks all over the South fell victim to a system of debt peonage called "sharecropping," which Southern so-called Jews set up and used to their advantage to make the Blacks the poorest of the poor, while at the same time making a class of Jewish cotton merchants the richest of the rich. These Jews used "sharecropped" cotton to advance from peddler to store owner to banker to international financiers. These Jews kept this economic blue print to obtain wealth to and for themselves, while they led Black people to a strategy of "non-economic liberalism."

According to TSRv2, after the publication of *Souls of Black Folk* in 1903, NAACP board members Jacob Schiff and Rabbi Stephen Wise hired Du Bois to be the editor of the NAACP's **Crisis Magazine** and later pressured him to alter several passages of his book that referred to this nefarious Jewish economic activity. It took fifty years of pressure at close quarters from these so-called Jews to finally tame Du Bois and made him change "Jew" to "foreigner" and "immigrant" in the 1952 edition of his book, thus concealing the Jewish presence in the post-slavery Southern economy, a fact that they never wanted exposed. Du Bois was a writer who had a firsthand view of what the Jews were doing in the South, but now his pen had been compromised, as the original voices of the Niagara Movement had been marginalized. How, and through what means, they "pressured" him is a study in how a people with a plan and hidden agenda can manipulate unsuspecting and trusting souls away from their best self-interests.

Why would financier Jacob Schiff and Rabbi Stephen Wise

spend so much time and effort to sway the mind of one Black man, Du Bois, while ignoring and marginalizing another Black man, Trotter? Jacob Schiff was one of the most important men behind getting Pres. Woodrow Wilson elected in 1912, and then he lobbied him to sign the legislation in 1913 that set up the Federal Reserve System. Jacob Schiff was also instrumental in setting up the Anti-Defamation League (ADL) also in 1913. This ADL has been a watchman at the gate of the Federal Reserve System, who would point a finger of Anti-Semitism at anyone who would dare question the Federal Reserve and try to find out who were its private owners.

Another prominent Jew and NAACP board member Rabbi Steven Wise, who founded the Federation of American Zionists in 1897, became one of Wilson's most trusted advisors. This is the same Wilson who initiated the wholesale firing of Blacks from government positions, and established segregation for those who remained, continuing the employment of Blacks only where whites did not find them "objectionable."

While Jewish board members of the NAACP were changing the economic destiny and banking system of Gentile America, TSRv2 exposed that they were also promoting and cheering the advancement of white supremacists who dedicated their lives to ensuring that Blacks would never rise in any capacity above servant and menial labor. They supported newspapers in the South such as the *Raleigh News and Observer*, which became a "malicious and vindictive negro-baiting organ" of white supremacy. While these Jewish NAACP board members courted white supremacists, they at the same time controlled the direction of Black people's struggle against these same white supremacists, carefully herding Blacks away from economic development, which is a human right, toward some type of "social liberation."

Powerful Jewish forces used the NAACP to effectively change the social climate in the northern cities, which were opened up to the Blacks from the South who in the "great migration" to the North left their farms behind, to be the servants for the northern elite and their immigrant white factory workers from Europe. Southern white Jews had made their fortune off "sharecropped" cotton and a captured Black market in the South, and having moved to the northern cities to set up their clothing factories, they brought their Black "virtual slaves" with them.

Therefore, "non-economic liberalism" was a product of white hypocrites and deceivers masquerading as friends to the Black man, who saw us coming down the intelligent road of economic development, but championed the enemies of our economic rise and herded us off into the wilderness and dead end of social liberation with their lower class of Whites.

The Great Bank Heist of 2008

As the Jews were guiding Black people to non-economic liberalism they were busy ripping off the white American sheepdog with their Federal Reserve System. Sen. Bernie Sanders revealed the 2012 report of the Government Accountability Office, which stated that more than $4 trillion in near zero-interest Federal Reserve loans and other financial assistance went to the banks and businesses of at least 18 current and former Federal Reserve regional bank directors in the aftermath of the 2008 financial collapse (http://www.sanders.senate.gov/newsroom/press-releases/fed-board-member-conflicts-detailed-by-gao-banks-and-businesses-took-4-trillion-in-bailouts). This $4 trillion dollars that went to bail out banks using money printed by the Federal Reserve was in addition to the $700 billion bailout money "stolen" from the Treasury Department at the end of the George W. Bush administration.

However, **seven years** earlier in September of 2001, there was another great theft that went unnoticed because of the bombing of the World Trade Center and the Pentagon on September 11, 2001 (9/11). Then Defense Secretary Donald Rumsfeld announced on

September 10, 2001 that $2.3 **trillion** of the defense budget could not be accounted for. Donald Rumsfeld declared war—but not on foreign terrorists but on "…the adversary's closer to home. It's the Pentagon bureaucracy," he said. This money wasted by the military posed a serious threat. "In fact, it could be said it's a matter of life and death," he said. (http://www.defense.gov/speeches/speech.aspx?speechid=430). Of course all was forgotten after the next day's great calamities.

With these great inside-job thefts are we witnessing the "Fall of America"? The Most Honorable Elijah Muhammad published a book in 1973 with this ominous title, which included such chapters as "'Mystery Babylon, The Great,'" "The Judgment of America," "America surrounded with The Judgment of Allah," "Four Great Judgments of America," "The Fall of America Foretold, Separation Is the Answer," "The House Doomed to Fall," "The Destruction and Fall," "The Day of America's Downfall" and "Modern Babylon Is Falling." When The Messenger delivered these warnings, he was **mocked** because America was the greatest super power both militarily and economically. But now as we read these stories of America being financially raped from within, we thank the Honorable Minister Louis Farrakhan for keeping the words of The Messenger alive and current. We can put what we see in perspective—prophecy is being fulfilled right before our eyes. In the chapter "**Modern Babylon Is Falling**," The Messenger writes:

In the Bible, Rev. 18:4,5 in the Revelation of John, a people are warned to flee out of her. Here, we get the name Babylon to become a modern day people. The voice of an angel warns the people of a certain class to fly out of Babylon. "…Come out of her, my people, that ye be not partakers of her sins, and that ye receive not of her plagues. For her sins have reached unto heaven, and God hath remembered her iniquities" (as being an evil people). So the angel notifies us saying, "Babylon the great is fallen." Today, we see this same thing.

153

There is no people to be warned to come out of another
people that answers to the description of this warning so
clearly as the so-called Negro in America of lost-found
people of our own Black kind does.

Here, the so-called Negro is warned to fly out of her and not
to be partakers of her judgment—her torment. The angel says,
so much evil has she done to thee Rev. 18:6, "Reward her
even as she rewarded you, and double unto her double
according to her works: in the cup which she hath filled fill to
her double." (Muhammad 1973 :142)

When Bernie Sanders revealed that 18 present or former board members of the Federal Reserve had their hands in the cookie jar, the cry was **"conflicts of interest,"** not **"get the thief,"** which is cried when someone sees a Black person rob a liquor or convenience store. And when that Black "crook" is caught, he will get substantial time in prison because he stole maybe $864, which is the average amount stolen in grand larceny cases. And if his face is caught on a surveillance camera, you will be sure to see it on the 11:00 news.

How many Americans knew about this $4 trillion that was heisted from the Federal Reserve? A Google search of the news in the week of June 16, 2012 reveals that there were only 85 news articles written nationwide on this story, while in this same week there were 12,200 news articles on store robberies and 109,000 news articles on the rumor that Kim Kardashian and Kanye West might get married. As the sports commentators might say, "C'mon man," are we being taken for a ride as these bums hide? Is the news media's job to fake the public out with trivia, while their cousins or brothers fleece the wealth of America? Of course 9/11 was not trivia, but it has been proven to be a diversionary inside job that blamed the bombing on Arabs while shifting attention away from the Pentagon's hands in the taxpayers' "cookie jar."

While the crooks were backing the "getaway van" to the back door of the Federal Reserve and Treasury in October of 2008, America was drunk with the anticipation of electing her first Black president, who promised "change that we can believe in." However, one of the first things that he did after his inauguration was to exonerate President George W. Bush and Vice-President Dick Chaney of any wrong doing while they were in office.

And what does $4 trillion dollars look like anyway? Many of us have never had more than $10,000 cash money that we could put our hands on. The average American family in 2010 only made $45,800. At that rate it would take the average family 82.5 **million** years to earn $4 trillion. And you remember Bernie Madoff who made off with $18 billion of his investors' money? It would take this same average American family 371.1 thousand years to make that kind of money that Bernie stole in about 40 years.

When a Black man robs a convenience store for the average take of $864, what can he buy: a few loaves of bread or pay down some type of debt? It would take 4.7 billion people to steal this average $864 to equal the $4 trillion stolen by these sophisticated financial raiders. What can people like Madoff or those 18 Federal Reserve board members—whose average take in this heist was **$222.2 billion**—do with such wealth? After they buy some more mansions, boats and hookers, they would still have more money than we could ever imagine spending. They could gamble a part of this wealth on the stock market to raise the value of stocks so as to sucker more small investors into their financial traps, as they prepare the "sheep" to be fleeced yet another time. But what could a sociopath do with $222.2 billion? In America he could buy a governor, as in the case of Wisconsin in 2012, where the opposition candidate's campaign budget was dwarfed by the out-of-state influence peddlers. Such a sophisticated crook could outfit an army with surplus military weapons—guns, boats, planes, tanks, missiles and ships—and start wars to control the resources all over the world, as many international bankers have in fact done.

These great bank and treasury heists have also had a great economic impact on the average American. The Federal Reserve released figures on June 11, 2012 that the net worth of the typical American family fell by 40% between 2007 and 2009. In fact, the typical American family was robbed to the point that their net worth is what it was in the 1990s—just like the American military bombed Iraq back into the "stone ages" in their "Shock and Awe" display in 2003. The Bush administration used 9/11 as the pretext for destroying Iraq, while somebody in his administration had walked

155

off with $2.3 trillion in 2001 from the Defense Department, $700 billion in 2008 from the Treasury Department and $4 trillion from 2008 to 2009 from the Federal Reserve.

The Mystery of Money Revealed

Out of ignorance the people worship "money". Out of deceit a set of people produce and control "money". Through the control of "money" a small set of wickedly wise people depicted as "beasts" or "snakes" in the Bible, which we call the "Evil Shepherds", control the world. We want to break the bonds of the illusion of money to free our people's minds so they can set up a better economic system and world. We also need to show our people how those who they look up to and fear, the sheepdogs, are just as gullible as they are when it comes to money.

In our Teachings we are asked the question: "Why does the devil keep our people illiterate? ANS. - So that he can use them for a tool and, also, a slave. He keeps them blind to themselves so that he can master them. Illiterate means ignorant." (F. Muhammad 1992: 12) The Honorable Elijah Muhammad has given us "An Economic Blueprint", which we described in detail in *Commonomics: Developing a Post Yakub Economy*. Now we must remove the veil of mystery or ignorance concerning "money" to give our people the confidence to help the Honorable Minister Louis Farrakhan manifest the economics of that blueprint.

We wrote our first book on *"Commonomics..."* immediately after the latest failure of the capitalist system at the end of 2008 and into 2009. There have been a plethora of books written to try to explain why the economic system fell apart. Now the general public can, if they desire, learn a lot about the inner-workings of Wall Street and the moneychangers. The masses of white people can now learn how they have been tricked out of their nest eggs and retirement savings. However, the pundits agree that the system will recover because they do not see anything on the horizon to replace it. This is where we come in to explain the past and chart a future for our people and the world based on the sound principals taught to us by The Most Honorable Elijah Muhammad. We understand that these raids on the people's wealth is a periodic act of economic warfare by a group of sophisticated devils whose major weapon is the ignorance of the people of money and economics. We live in the greatest capitalist country in the world, but an American citizen can go all the way through high school, college and graduate school without taking one course in economics. They don't even know who is in charge of their money supply. In fact they don't even know what "money" is.

"Money" has been variously defined as "a medium that can be exchanged for goods and services," and "assets and property considered in terms of monetary value; wealth." However, what falls under those definitions keep changing and this is a source of confusion. A simple way to understand "money" is that it is a store of "labor" that can be exchanged for other goods and services. Money has no value unless it can get someone to do something for it or give up something to get it. Without two or more people willing to work or trade, money has no value. Most things traded have required some level of labor to produce them. Air is free and is everywhere. However, water must be caught or moved or stored by someone for it to be useful. Manufactured products usually cost more than the sum of the individual raw products from which they are made, because labor must be used to transform the raw products into a finished form.

mon·ey : (http://www.thefreedictionary.com/money)
n. pl. **mon·eys** or **mon·ies**
1. A medium that can be exchanged for goods and services and is used as a measure of their values on the market, including among its forms a commodity such as gold, an officially issued coin or note, or a deposit in a checking account or other readily liquefiable account.
2. The official currency, coins, and negotiable paper notes issued

by a government.
3. Assets and property considered in terms of monetary value; wealth.

Economic Definition of Money

What is **money**? Money is any good that is widely used and accepted in transactions involving the transfer of goods and services from one person to another. Economists differentiate among three different types of money: **commodity money, fiat money**, and **bank money.** Commodity money is a good whose value serves as the value of money. Gold coins are an example of commodity money. In most countries, commodity money has been replaced with fiat money. Fiat money is a good, the value of which is less than the value it represents as money. Dollar bills are an example of fiat money because their value as slips of printed paper is less than their value as "money." Bank money consists of the **book credit** that banks extend to their depositors. Transactions made using **checks** drawn on deposits held at banks involve the use of bank money. (http://www.cliffsnotes.com/more-subjects/economics/money-and-banking/definition-of-money)

Money is any object or record that is generally accepted as payment for goods and services and repayment of debts in a given socio-economic context or country. The main functions of money are distinguished as: a medium of exchange; a unit of account; a store of value; and, occasionally in the past, a standard of deferred payment. Any kind of object or secure verifiable record that fulfills these functions can be considered money.

Money is historically an emergent market phenomenon establishing the commodity, money, but nearly all contemporary money systems are based on fiat money. Fiat money, like any check or note of debt, is without intrinsic use value as a physical commodity. It derives its value by being declared by a government to be legal tender; that is, it must be accepted as a form of payment within the boundaries of the country, for "all debts, public and private". Such laws in practice cause fiat money to acquire the value of any of the goods and services that it may be traded for within the nation that issues it.

The money supply of a country consists of currency (banknotes and coins) and bank money (the balance held in checking accounts and savings accounts). Bank money, which consists only of records (mostly computerized in modern banking), forms by far the largest part of the money supply in developed nations. (http://en.wikipedia.org/wiki/Money)

This book is not designed to get anyone to do physical harm to anyone else. We just want our Black people to finally realize that The Most Honorable Elijah Muhammad was 100% correct when he taught us that the best and only solution to our problems is to separate from our open enemies and their ways. The proven enemy, past and present, to black people are the people who call themselves "white". Skin color is a good beginning point to determine who "white" people are, but there are many people with pale skin who are black albinos and Blacks "passing" as "white". One of the surest ways of determining who are "white people" is to ask them, "Who are you?" If they answer "white", then they are enemies to black people who we can truthfully call "devils". However, if they say "black" or "human", then we have to give them the benefit of the doubt, but observe their activities the same way that a prudent black person would even observe other Blacks.

A person who labels him or herself as "white" immediately has taken a position of an assumed superiority. History shows that people who call themselves "white" think that they have a right to oppress all non-white people and take their resources. In the past Whites just used physical force to take what they wanted. In fact Jewish mathematician and historian of science, Jacob Bronowski, stated, "[War], organized war, is not a human instinct. It is a highly planned and cooperative form of theft. And that form of theft began ten-thousand years ago when the harvesters of wheat accumulated a surplus and the nomads rose out of the desert to rob them of what they themselves could not provide." Even though, Bronowski, like other white so-called Jews puts the beginning of "war" about 4,000

159

years too early to hide the fact that these "nomads" were a race of white people who were not here until 6,000 years ago. Today these "nomads", better known as white people and in particular the lead tribe of white people, the so-called Jews, has developed a more sophisticated way of robbing the people, called "usury". "Usury" is loaning money with an interest charge, even 1 percent or less.

Usury: http://www.jewishencyclopedia.com

In modern language this term denotes a rate of interest greater than that which the law or public opinion permits; but the Biblical law, in all dealings among Israelites, forbids all "increase" of the debt by reason of lapse of time or forbearance, be the rate of interest high or low, while it does not impose any limit in dealings between Israelites and Gentiles. Hence in discussing Jewish law the words "interest" and "usury" may be used indiscriminately.

There are three Biblical passages which forbid the taking of interest in the case of "brothers," but which permit, or seemingly enjoin, it when the borrower is a Gentile, namely, Ex. xxii. 24; Lev. xxv. 36, 37; Deut. xxiii. 20, 21.

The Hebrew word for "usury" is "neshek," meaning literally "a bite," from its painfulness to the debtor; while in Lev. xxv. 36, 37 "increase" is the rendering of the Hebrew "marbit" or "tarbit" which denotes the gain on the creditor's side, and which in the later Hebrew becomes "ribbit." Lending on usury or increase is classed by Ezekiel (xviii. 13, 17) among the worst of sins. See also Ps. xv, in which among the attributes of the righteous man is reckoned the fact that he does not lend on usury.

The Talmud (B. M. 61b) dwells on Ezek. xviii. 13 (Hebr.): "He has lent on usury; he has taken interest; he shall surely not live, having done all these

160

abominations"; on the words with which the prohibition of usury in Lev. xxv. 36 closes: "Thou shalt be afraid of thy God"; and on the further words in which Ezekiel (*l.c.*) refers to the usurer: "He shall surely suffer death; his blood is upon him"; hence the lender on interest is compared to the shedder of blood.

Case of a Gentile:

When an Israelite lends money to a Gentile or to an "indwelling stranger" (a half-convert of foreign blood), he may and should charge him interest; and when he borrows from such a person he should allow him interest. It is the opinion of Maimonides that for Jews to charge Gentiles interest is a positive command of the written law. [The reason for the non-prohibition of the receipt by a Jew of interest from a Gentile, and vice versa, is held by modern rabbis to lie in the fact that the Gentiles had at that time no law forbidding them to practice usury; and that as they took interest from Jews, the Torah considered it equitable that Jews should take interest from Gentiles. Conditions changed when Gentile laws were enacted forbidding usury; and the modern Jew is not allowed by the Jewish religion to charge a Gentile a higher rate of interest than that fixed by the law of the land.—E. C.]

The Miracle of Compound Interest

"The most powerful force in the universe is compound interest."
Albert Einstein
(http://www.datagenetics.com/blog/april22014/index.html)

This science of "compound interest" is a great robber of the people and was understood in Ancient Babylon and taught to the Jews. On a clay tablet from Mesopotamia, dated to about 1,700 BCE and now in the Louvre, poses the following problem: "How long will it take for a sum of money to double if invested at 20 percent interest rate compounded annually?" The answer is 4 years.

The compound interest formula is $FV=PV \times (1+r)^n$ where FV is the future value of an amount of money whose PV (present value) is multiplied by $1 + r$ (interest rate) raised to the nth power. Let us ask "What will be the sum of money generated (FV) at 20% (r) compound interest for 100 years (n) if we start with $100 as the principle (PV)?" The answer is $8,280,000,000. Can you say $8.2 billion? Well one could argue that this is indeed "usury." However, let us use an interest rate that is considered not usurious like 6%. Below we present a graph which shows that at 6% interest, $100 grows to $33,930 in 100 years. For the first couple of years one does not feel the "bite" of compound interest, but once you get past 50 years, the graph shoots to the sky. Even after 50 years you are at $1,842 even though it started out as $100. That $100 even doubles after 12 years. Most of our homes are mortgaged for 30 years.

The Federal Reserve has been lending money to the U.S. government for over 100 years from 1913 to 2014. Even though they have moved the interest rate up and down, they have milked the American people like a dairy farmer would milk a cow.

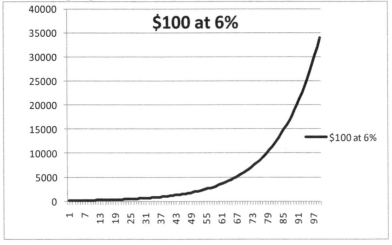

$100 at 6%

162

Appendix to Chapter 5

A. It's the Interest, Stupid! Why Bankers Rule the World

*Thursday, 08 November 2012 10:10 By Ellen Brown,
Truthout |*

*Interest charges are a strongly regressive tax that the poor
pay to the rich. A public banking system could realize
savings up to 40 percent - allowing taxes to be cut, services
increased and market stability created - with banks feeding
the economy rather than feeding off it.*

In the 2012 edition of Occupy Money *released last week,
Professor Margrit Kennedy writes that a stunning 35
percent to 40 percent of everything we buy goes to interest.
This interest goes to bankers, financiers, and bondholders,
who take a 35 percent to 40 percent cut of our GDP. That
helps explain how wealth is systematically transferred from
Main Street to Wall Street. The rich get progressively
richer at the expense of the poor, not just because of "Wall
Street greed," but because of the inexorable mathematics of
our private banking system.*

*This hidden tribute to the banks will come as a surprise to
most people, who think that if they pay their credit card
bills on time and don't take out loans, they aren't paying
interest. This, says Dr. Kennedy, is not true.*

*Tradesmen, suppliers, wholesalers and retailers all along
the chain of production rely on credit to pay their bills.
They must pay for labor and materials before they have a
product to sell, and before the end-buyer pays for the
product 90 days later. Each supplier in the chain adds*

interest to its production costs, which are passed on to the ultimate consumer. Dr. Kennedy cites interest charges ranging from 12 percent for garbage collection, to 38 percent for drinking water, to 77 percent for rent in public housing in her native Germany.

Her figures are drawn from the research of economist Helmut Creutz, writing in German and interpreting Bundesbank publications. They apply to the expenditures of German households for everyday goods and services in 2006; but similar figures are seen in financial sector profits in the United States, where they composed a whopping 40 percent of US business profits in 2006. That's more than *five times* the 7 percent made by the banking sector in 1980. Bank assets, financial profits, interest and debt have all been growing exponentially.

Exponential growth in financial sector profits has occurred at the expense of the non-financial sectors, where incomes have at best grown **linearly**.

By 2010, 1 percent of the population owned 42 percent of financial wealth, while **80 percent** of the population owned only **5 percent** of financial wealth. Dr. Kennedy observes that the bottom **80 percent** pay the hidden interest charges that the **top 10 percent** collect, making interest a strongly regressive tax that the poor pay to the rich.

Exponential growth is unsustainable. In nature, sustainable growth progresses in a logarithmic curve that grows increasingly more slowly until it levels off... Exponential growth does the reverse: It begins slowly and increases over time, until the curve shoots up vertically (the chart above). Exponential growth is seen in **parasites, cancers - and compound interest**. When the parasite runs out of its food source, the growth curve suddenly collapses.

People generally assume that if they pay their bills on time, they aren't paying compound interest; but again, this isn't true. Compound interest is baked into the formula for most mortgages, which comprises 80 percent of US loans.

If credit cards aren't paid within the one-month grace period, interest charges are compounded daily; and even if you pay within the grace period, you are paying 2 percent to 3 percent for the use of the card, since merchants pass their merchant fees on to the consumer. Debit cards, which are the equivalent of writing checks, also involve fees. Visa-MasterCard and the banks at both ends of these interchange transactions charge an average fee of 44 cents per transaction - though the cost to them is about 4 cents.

Even if you pay cash, you are liable to be paying an additional 2 percent to 3 percent, since, until recently, merchants were not allowed to give discounts for cash payments. A July 2012 settlement with Visa and MasterCard, however, allowed merchants in the settlement to add a surcharge for credit card use.

How to Recapture the Interest: Own the Bank

The implications of all this are stunning. If we had a financial system that returned the interest collected from the public directly to the public, 35 percent could be lopped off the price of everything we buy. That means we could buy three items for the current price of two, and that our paychecks could go 50 percent farther than they go today.

Direct reimbursement to the people is a hard system to work out, but there is a way we could collectively recover the interest paid to banks. We could do it by turning the banks into public utilities and their profits into public assets. Profits would return to the public, either reducing taxes or increasing the availability of public services and infrastructure.

165

By borrowing from their own publicly-owned banks, governments could eliminate their interest burden altogether. This has been demonstrated elsewhere with stellar results, including in Canada, Australia, and Argentina, among other countries.

In 2011, the US federal government paid $454 billion in interest on the federal debt - nearly one-third the total $1.1 trillion ($1,100 billion) paid in personal income taxes that year. If the government had been borrowing directly from the Federal Reserve - which has the power to create credit on its books and now rebates its profits directly to the government - personal income taxes could have been cut by a third.

Borrowing from its own central bank interest-free might allow a government to eliminate its national debt altogether. In Money and Sustainability: The Missing Link, Bernard Lietaer and Christian Asperger, et al., cite the example of France. The treasury borrowed interest-free from the nationalized Banque de France from 1946 to 1973. The law then changed to forbid this practice, requiring the treasury to borrow instead from the private sector. The authors include a chart showing what would have happened if the French government had continued to borrow interest-free, versus what did happen. Rather than dropping from 21 percent to 8.6 percent of GDP, the debt shot up from 21 percent to 78 percent of GDP.

> *"No 'spendthrift government' can be blamed in this case," write the authors. "Compound interest explains it all!"*

It is not just federal governments that could eliminate their interest charges in this way. State and local governments could do it too.

Consider California. At the end of 2010, it had general obligation and revenue bond debt of $158 billion. Of this, $70 billion, or 44 percent, was owed for interest. If the state had incurred that debt to its own bank - which then returned the profits to the state - California could be $70 billion richer today. Instead of slashing services, selling off public assets, and laying off employees, it could be adding services and repairing its decaying infrastructure.

The only US state to own its own depository bank today is North Dakota. North Dakota is also the only state to have escaped the 2008 banking crisis, sporting a sizable budget surplus every year since then. It has the lowest unemployment rate in the country, the lowest foreclosure rate, and the lowest default rate on credit card debt.

Globally, 40 percent of banks are publicly owned, and they are concentrated in countries that also escaped the 2008 banking crisis. These are the BRIC countries - Brazil, Russia, India, and China - which are home to 40 percent of the global population. The BRICs grew economically by 92 percent in the last decade, while Western economies were floundering.

B. The History of Jews and Banking

The words "Jews" and "banking" are almost redundant. So as not to be labeled anti-Semitic I will reproduce for you the history of the Jews in banking from their own hands from a Jewish website: www.jewishvirtuallibrary.org

http://www.jewishvirtuallibrary.org/jsource/judaica/ejud_0002_0003_0_01978.html

BANKING AND BANKERS

Antiquity

There is little likelihood that financial transactions played a prominent role in the **pre-Exilic** epoch in Erez Israel; according to the ethos of Jewish society, then founded on a pronounced agrarian structure, lending was part of the assistance a man owed to his neighbor or brother in need (cf. Deut. 23:21). During the Babylonian era Jews had greater opportunities to come into contact with a highly developed banking tradition and to participate in credit operations. **After** the Exile, commerce and **credit** certainly had a place in Erez Israel. Though the society remained predominantly agrarian, Jerusalem had a number of wealthy families, including **tax agents** and landowners, who speculated and deposited their gains in the **Temple**, which had in some ways the function of a **national bank** (see *Heliodorus). Organized banking probably arose in connection with Ma'aserot ("tithes"), in particular Ma'aser sheni, and the pilgrimages to Jerusalem, through the activities of the *money changers. The use of Greek terms indicates a strong Hellenistic influence on the establishment of banking. Meanwhile, the Jewish communities forming in the Diaspora, the most important at first being that of *Babylonia, were given an impulse toward a new way of life by the longstanding traditions of a **capitalist** type of economy existing around them (see Nippur and*Murashu's sons). In Babylonia, Jews engaged in financial transactions: some were **farmers of taxes** and customs, and the wealthiest of them were landowners; among the latter were *Huna, the head of the academy of Surah, and Rav *Ashi. However, talmudic references show that the standards of an agrarian economy were still dominant and therefore gamblers and **usurers** were not thought trustworthy witnesses (see e.g., Sanh. 3:3).

168

Commentary: Question: If Jews were enslaved by the Babylonians, why would their slave masters teach them banking? Our slave masters never wanted us to even have any money much less be moneylenders. This passage indicates that the people who call themselves Jews were more than likely a colony trained and empowered by first Babylon, then later Persia, to rule over the indigenous people of Palestine.

*Another important Jewish colony was to be found at Alexandria, center of the trade between the Mediterranean and the Arabian and Indian world, where Jews were engaged not only in commerce and international trade but in moneylending too. According to Josephus, a Jewish **tax agent**[1] was able to make a loan of 3,000 talents. The alabarch Alexander Lysimachus, who loaned King Agrippa I 200,000 drachmas (Jos., Ant., 18:159–160), was also the steward of Antonia, mother of Emperor Claudius. Another Alexandrian Jew was treasurer to Candace, queen of Ethiopia.*

1. *http://encyclopedia2.thefreedictionary.com/Tax+Farming*
   ### Tax Farming
   a system for collecting taxes and other state revenues from the population. Under this system, the state transfers the right of collection to private individuals called tax farmers in exchange for a certain fee. Tax farmers accumulated great wealth since the taxes and charges they collected exceeded by two or three times the amount deposited in the treasury.

   Tax farming is characteristic of precapitalist systems in which a natural economy is predominant, credit is not developed, the state is in financial difficulties, and communications are poor. Three forms of tax farming existed: (1) general, which encompassed a country or the entire tax system; (2) regional, which encompassed a single city or region; and (3) special, which dealt with individual taxes, such as customs duties or revenues from the liquor monopoly. **Tax farming** first became widespread in **Iran in the sixth century B.C.** and in Greece and Rome in the fourth century B.C. In the Middle Ages, it was widespread in France from the 13th century and was also practiced widely in Holland, Spain, and England. It was one of the most important sources for the primitive accumulation of capital. As capitalism developed, tax farming was preserved in a distinctive form in 20th-century Italy, where private and savings banks collected certain taxes. In the late 19th and early 20th centuries, forms of tax farming were used for collecting tax arrears in the USA. Tax farming was widely used in the Ottoman Empire beginning in the late 16th or early 17th century; it was abolished in 1925. It was also widely practiced in Iran from approximately the tenth century to the 1930's and in India from the 13th or 14th century to the 19th century.

Middle Ages

THE CALIPHATE

*With the rapid development of city life and commerce in the caliphate of Baghdad from the late eighth century and the transition of the majority of Jews under caliphate rule from agriculture and a village environment to the cities, banking became one of the occupations of some upper-class Jews, especially in **Baghdad** and later under the Fatimids (from 968) in Egypt. This Jahbadhiyya, as it was called, was a form of banking based on the savings and economic activities of the whole Jewish merchant class and not only on the fortunes of the very*

170

rich: the bankers loaned to the state and its officers money deposited with them as well as from their own fortunes. The vast sums at the disposal of these Jewish bankers and their relative immunity from confiscation by the autocratic authorities both tend to confirm that these Jewish *"court bankers"* from the beginning of the tenth century onward were well-known to their Muslim debtors as a kind of *"deposit banker"* for Jewish merchants. Under the Fatimid caliph al-Mustanṣir the brothers Abu Saʿd al-Tustarī and Abu Naṣr Ḥesed b. Sahl al-Tustarī (both died in 1048) were influential in the finances of Egypt. With the rise of Saladin and the foundation of the Ayyubid dynasty in Egypt (1169), the position of the Jews deteriorated but they were able to continue their *moneychanging* activities at least. Toward the end of the Mamluk period (1517), Samuel, a *moneychanger* in Cairo, must have possessed considerable wealth, for the Arab chronicler Ibn Iyās tells that the sultan extorted from him more than 500,000 dinars. During the Muslim rule on the Iberian peninsula, Córdoba Jews were active in the financial administration in the tenth and eleventh centuries. The responsa of this period show a highly developed money economy existing before the First and Second Crusades.

EARLY MERCHANTS IN EUROPE

Persecution, such as occurred in Alexandria in **414** or the oppressive measures promulgated in the Byzantine Empire beginning with Constantine and intensified under Justinian, may have contributed to the fact that from the fifth century Jewish merchants followed their Greek and Syrian counterparts to Gaul and not only traded in luxury goods but also loaned money. With the disappearance of the Syrians and Greeks from Europe in the seventh century, the Jewish merchants were able to expand. Within the administration of the Merovingian kings (from 481) Jews possibly farmed taxes or advanced money on

171

revenues to high officials; according to Gregory of Tours (c. 538–94), the count of Tours and his vicar were indebted to the Jew Armentarius. During the Carolingian period (from the mid-eighth century), Jews settled in the Rhineland again as they had done during the Roman Empire – some of them **lending money on pledges** or giving money to merchants in a kind of commenda partnership. Archbishop Anno of Cologne (d. 1075), as well as Emperor Henry IV (1056–1106), borrowed money from Jews.

THE MONEYLENDERS IN EUROPE

After the First Crusade **(1096)** the Jewish merchant, in his necessarily long journeys, no longer enjoyed even **minimal physical security**. In Western and Central Europe, especially in Spain, the crystallization of the essentially Christian nature of the rising city communes combined with this insecurity to drive out the Jews from commerce and prohibit them from engaging in crafts. In France, England (up to **1290**), Germany, Austria, Bohemia, Moravia, and northern and central Italy, Jews had to turn to loan-banking on a larger or smaller scale in order to make a living. The canonical **prohibition** against taking **interest** by Christians, which was stressed in successive Church councils (especially the Fourth Lateran Council of 1215), and the vast opportunities for capital investment in land and sea trade open to the wealthy Christian made <u>lending on interest for consumer and emergency needs virtually a **Jewish monopoly** in Western and Central Europe between the 12th and 15th centuries.</u> By the 13th century the notion that the **Wucherer ("usurer")** was a Jew was already current, for example, in the writings of Berthold of Regensburg, Walther von der Vogelweide, and Ulrich von Lichtenstein. The word **judaizare** became identical with **"taking interest."** Testimony from the 12th century shows that **moneylending** <u>was then becoming the main occupation of the Jews;</u> this was the case of those of Bacharach (1146) and of Muenzenberg (1188).

172

*However, there is little data to suggest that Jewish banking transactions were on a large scale even in the 13th century, but there is evidence that the bishop of Basle had **debts** with Basle Jews and that various **monasteries had Jewish creditors**.*

*The transition from a **natural economy to a money economy** in the course of the **"commercial revolution,"** and the stabilization of territorial principalities opened new possibilities for Jewish banking activity, especially in the Rhineland and in southern Germany. Jews from Siegburg, Trier, Mainz, Speyer, Strasbourg, and Basle as well as from Ulm and Nuremberg appear as sources of credit. The most important banking transaction in the first half of the 14th century went through the hands of Vivelin the Red, who transmitted 61,000 florins in gold which King Edward III of England paid to Baldwin of Trier for becoming allied with him against France. Margrave Rudolf III of Baden was indebted to David the Elder, called Watch, and to Jekelin of Strasbourg and his partners. Muskin and Jacob Daniels served the archbishop of Trier in the administration of his finances; during the first half of the 14th century, Daniels was probably the most important Jewish banker of the Rhineland. He was followed in the service of the archbishop by his son-in-law Michael. At the same time Abraham von Kreuznach at Bingen had a similar position with the archbishop of Mainz. Gottschalk von Recklinghausen and his company was another group on the lower Rhine. Such banking activity is recorded in other parts of Central Europe as far as Silesia.*

*<u>**Moneychanging** and **coinage** privileges were often combined with **moneylending**, and Jews were frequently the sole agents arranging loans.</u> From the first half of the 12th century **moneychanging** as a special form of banking is supported by documentary evidence. To spread the risk, partnerships of between two and ten persons were formed. As security, custom at first recognized mainly pledges, but from the middle of the*

173

13th century the letter of credit came into use, though princess till preferred to pledge jewels. Often, instead of a pawn, bail was given by several persons. In western Germany hypothecation of real estate was preferred, and in this way **Jews acquired** in pledge houses, vineyards, farms, **villages**, castles, **towns**, and even seigneuries. **Interest rates** do not seem to have exceeded **36%** but in the case of deferred payment they could rise to **100%** or beyond. From the 12th century popes and princes exploited the financial capacity of the Jews by **frequent remission of debts or forced loans.** The Black Death and consequent persecutions of Jews gave rulers an opportunity forcibly to **seize property** and to **restore pawns** and **letters of credit to debtors.** The liquidation of **Jewish debts** by King **Wenceslaus IV** of Bohemia around the end of the 14th century is a well-known example of such royal rapacity. With these and other measures and the rise of the merchant class, who gradually took over the function of loan-bankers to the princes and even to emperors during the 15th and early 16th centuries, the Jews were **deprived of imperial protection** and forced to leave the towns. They retired to the small seigneuries or migrated to Eastern Europe, where a less-developed economy offered them possibilities of making a livelihood. In Bohemia, Hungary, and in Poland and Lithuania both princes and nobility made use of their financial help. As the Eastern European kingdoms developed with the colonization of the forests, Jews played an increasing part in commerce and especially in the *arenda. In the larger towns some engaged in **moneylending** and banking activities.

In 12th-century France **moneylending** was an important Jewish business, but in the 13th century Jewish lenders came up against the superior competition of the Lombards, a rivalry even more intense in the Netherlands. In England, where *Aaron of Lincoln and *Aaron of York were powerful bankers, a special *Exchequer of the Jews was set up to centralize Jewish transactions. However in the 13th century the crown began to

174

rely on the greater resources of the Cahorsins and Italian bankers *and in **1290** the Jews were expelled*. In Italy Jewish bankers could expand their sphere of activity under the silent protection of the popes, despite resistance on the part of the Christian burghers (see *Popes and the Jews). From the second half of the 13th century they spread throughout central Italy and gradually expanded toward the north, migrating at first to the smaller and medium-sized towns. In Pisa and then in Florence the Da *Pisa family became important **loan-bankers**; in Florence in 1437 Cosimo de' Medici permitted a Jewish group to establish four loan-banks; in Venice in 1366 Jews, probably of German origin, obtained the right to lend on pledges. Here as in other places in northern Italy, Jewish loan-bankers from the south came into competition with Jews migrating from Germany or southern France. Finally only a few towns, such as Milan and Genoa, refused to admit Jewish loan-bankers. However, their activities were seriously challenged when the anti-Jewish preaching of the ***Franciscans*** resulted in the establishment of branches of the *Monti di Pietà toward the middle of the 15th century.

The Iberian Peninsula after the Christian reconquest offers many examples of large-scale credit activities and **tax farming** by Jews. It is known that they provided money for armaments against the **Moors**. El Cid borrowed from Raquel and Vidas, Jews of Burgos, for his expedition against Valencia. King Alfonso VI of Castile (1072–1109) also obtained loans from Jews for his military expeditions. His successors employed Jews in the financial administration, especially as **almoxarifes (revenue collectors)**, an activity combined with **moneylending**. Thus, Judah Ibn Ezra was in the service of Alfonso VII, Joseph Ibn Shoshan of Alfonso VIII, and Solomon Ibn Zadok (Don Çulema) and his son Çag de la Maleha were **almoxarifes** in the service of Alfonso X, while Meir ibn Shoshan served as his treasurer. When Sancho IV (1258–95) came to the throne, *Abraham el-

Barchilon was prominent in the financial administration, supervising the farming of the taxes. Generally, in Castile the Jews abstained from farming the direct taxes, which from 1288 the Cortes opposed. The Jews therefore tended to prefer the administration of the customs and other rights belonging to the office of almoxarife. The court of Aragon relied on Jewish financial administrators in a similar fashion. **King James I** employed Benveniste de Porta as a banker, probably giving him as security for his advances the office of bailiff of Barcelona and Gerona. Judah de la Cavalleria, the most powerful Jew in the Aragonese administration, had control over all the bailiffs of the kingdom. Under Pedro III the family of Ravaya were most influential. Though during the 14th century the Jews in Aragon and Navarre were subjected to increasing pressures, Judah Ha-Levi and Abraham Aben-Josef of Estella were general **farmers of the rents** under Charles II and Charles III of Navarre. In Castile – in spite of the Cortes' opposition – Jews such as the Abrabanel family in Seville continued to be active as almoxarifes. The young Alfonso XI appointed Joseph de Écija as his almoxarife mayor (c. 1322); Pedro the Cruel (1350–69) made Samuel b. Meir ha-Levi Abulafia of Toledo, known as the richest Jew of his time, his chief treasurer, and Henry of Trastamara had Joseph Picho as his financial officer (contador mayor) despite his promise to remove all Jews from royal office (1367).

THE CONVERSOS

The **persecutions of 1391** and the mass conversions which followed brought an important change. Some of the **Conversos were able to use the act of baptism** to climb to high positions in the financial administration: examples are Luis de la *Cavalleria, chief treasurer under John II of Aragon, Luis Sánchez, royal bailiff of the kingdom of Aragon (c. 1490), and his brother Gabriel Sánchez, who was treasurer-general. Under Henry IV of Castile

(1454–74) Diego Arias de Avila was the king's secretary and auditor of the royal accounts; in spite of Diego's unpopularity his son Pedro succeeded him. Even Isabella the Catholic depended on the financial advice of the Jew Abraham Senior, from 1476 chief tax gatherer in Castile, and Isaac Abrabanel, who after having been banker of Alfonso V of Portugal served as the queen's private financial agent and loaned her a considerable sum for the war against Granada. The **Converso** Luis de Santangel, chancellor and comptroller of the royal household and great-grandson of the Jew Noah Chinillo, loaned Isabella money to finance Columbus' expedition to America. Though some men like Isaac Abrabanel, who went to Naples, remained faithful to Judaism, a number of Jews of Spanish origin stayed in Portugal and, after accepting baptism, rose to financial influence there, especially in combination with the East Indian spice trade. Prominent among them were Francisco and Diogo *Mendes. The latter, who took up residence in **Antwerp**, became one of the most important merchant bankers there, lending money to the king of Portugal, the emperor, and Henry VIII of England. The firm "Herdeiros de Francisco e Diogo Mendes" was administered for some time after Diogo's death (1543) by Francisco's widow, Doña Beatrice de Luna (Gracia *Nasi) and her nephew João Miques (Joseph *Nasi). They subsequently **immigrated to Turkey**, where the latter combined commercial and banking activity with political influence. Another to rise to high position was Alvaro Mendes from Tavira, Portugal, who in Constantinople took the name Solomon *Abenaes. Jewish **money-changers and tax farmers** were to be found in many places of the Ottoman Empire. After the union between Spain and Portugal (1580), a number of influential Conversos took the opportunity to invest their capital in financing the various ventures of the crown, provisioning the army in Flanders and in the East Indies, and **supplying contracts for Africa**. Their activities **expanded** especially after the **financial crisis of 1626** and continued until the Portuguese revolt of **1640** which

restored independent sovereignty to the country. After this all members of the gente de nação (as Conversos were called) living in Spain became suspect. The last important financial venture by *New Christians in Portugal was the financing of the Brazil Company established in 1649. However, Jewish involvement in banking proper really begins with the activities of those Conversos who, fleeing the Inquisition in Portugal and Spain, settled in *Antwerp, *Hamburg, and *Amsterdam, some remaining nominally Christian and some openly returning to Judaism. In Antwerp the Ximenes and Rodrigues d'Evora families were outstanding among an important group of merchant bankers who had commercial relations extending as far as the East Indies and Brazil. While they remained Catholics (like the Mendes de Brito group in Portugal), those who emigrated to Hamburg and Amsterdam formed Sephardi communities. In Hamburg they participated in the founding of the bank in 1619; 30 (by 1623, 46) local Jews were among its first shareholders, and some of them were financial agents for various North European courts, especially those of Denmark and Schleswig-Holstein. Most famous in Antwerp were Diego Teixeira de Sampaio (Abraham *Senior), consul and paymaster general for the Spanish government, and his son Manuel (Isaac Ḥayyim Senior), who succeeded him as financial agent of Christina of Sweden. Manuel Teixeira was an outstanding member of the Hamburg exchange and participated actively in the transfer of Western European subsidies to the German or Scandinavian courts.

At Amsterdam at first only a few Jews were shareholders in the bank founded in 1609 and of the East India Company. One hundred and six Portuguese had accounts in 1620. Generally their resources were not sufficiently great to add any special weight to the formative stage of Amsterdam capitalism. Through Holland's developing overseas trade, especially with Brazil (until 1654) and then with the West Indies, as well as

178

*through the growth of the **Amsterdam capital market** and the*
*transfer of **subsidies and provisioning of armies** through*
Amsterdam, Jewish financiers rose to importance in the
exchange market**, and were especially active in **trading
***company shares**. Outstanding were the *Pinto family and*
Antonio (Isaac) Lopez *Suasso (Baron d'Avernas le Gras);
nevertheless the wealth of the Sephardi families remained far
below that of their Christian counterparts. In the second half of
the 18th century the Pinto family remained prominent, and
another influential financier of Sephardi origin was David Bueno
de *Mesquita.

Partly as a consequence of the marriage between Charles II of
England and Catherine of Braganza (1662), and especially after
William and Mary became joint sovereigns of England (1689),
*London, too, became a center of **Sephardi banking**, leading*
figures being Anthony (Moses) da Costa, Solomon de *Medina,
and Isaac Pereira. In the reign of Queen Anne (1702–
14), Manasseh *Lopes was a leading banker; during the
18th century Samson *Gideon, Francis and Joseph *Salvador, and
*the *Goldsmid brothers, leading members of the **Ashkenazi***
community, were outstanding. In the middle of the 18th century
Jacob Henriques claimed that his father had planned the
*establishment of the **Bank of England (1694).***

THE HOLY ROMAN EMPIRE

Only a few Jewish financiers, such as Joseph zum goldenen
Schwan at Frankfurt or Michel *Jud, were active in the German
principalities in the 16th century. In the early 17th century the
Hapsburgs employed the services of Jacob *Bassevi of
Treuenberg of Prague, Joseph Pincherle of Gorizia, and Moses
and Jacob Marburger of Gradisca. The rise of the absolute
monarchies in Central Europe brought numbers of Jews, mostly
*of **Ashkenazi origin**, into the position of negotiating loans for*

179

the various courts, giving rise to the phenomenon of ***Court Jews.** *The most famous and most active of them in financial affairs were, in the second half of the 17th and the beginning of the 18th century, Leffmann *Behrends in Hanover, Behrend *Lehmann in Halberstadt, Bendix Goldschmidt in Hamburg, Aaron Beer in Frankfurt, and Samuel* **Oppenheimer** *and Samson *Wertheimer in Vienna. Later Diego d' *Aguilar, and the *Arnstein and *Eskeles families became prominent. In the early 18th century Joseph* **Suess Oppenheimer** *was the outstanding figure in southern Germany; his financial influence was widespread, especially in Wuerttemberg, until his fall and execution in* **1738**. *Important court bankers around the end of the 18th century were Israel *Jacobson in Brunswick, the *Bleichroeder family in Berlin, Simon Baruch and Solomon Oppenheimer in Bonn, the* ***Rothschilds** *in Frankfurt, the Reutlinger, Seligmann, and *Haber families in Karlsruhe, the Kaulla family in Stuttgart, and Aron Elias Seligmann, later baron of Eichthal, in Munich.*

ITALY

In the 15th and beginning of the 16th century the Italian loan-bankers reached their greatest eminence, including the Pisa, *Volterra, Norsa, Del Banco, *Rieti, and Tivoli families. In their wealth and style of life these men belonged to the Renaissance milieu as much as the artists and men of letters. However, with the expansion of the institution of the Monte di Pietà and the restrictive policy of the popes of the Counterreformation, their influence declined. The Da Pisa disappeared from Florence in **1570**. *However there were still between 60 and 70 loan-bankers operating in Rome toward the end of the 16th century and a century later about 20 were still in existence. In the first half of the 16th century about* **500 loan-bankers** *were active throughout Italy; toward the end of the century about 280 remained in 131 places. Abraham del Banco* was involved in the establishment of the famous Venetian Banco Giro in **1619**.

19ᵗʰ and 20ᵗʰ centuries

Jewish banking in the 19ᵗʰ century begins with the rise of the house of *__Rothschild__ in Frankfurt, a city which became the new banking center of Europe as a result of the political upheaval caused by the French Revolution and the Napoleonic Wars. The founder of the house (which became the symbol of the 19ᵗʰ-century type of merchant banking), **Meyer Amschel Rothschild** started as a banker to the elector of Hesse-Kassel. His sons rose to prominence as the major European bankers Amschel Mayer in Frankfurt, Solomon Mayer in Vienna, Carl Mayer in Naples, James Mayer in Paris, and Nathan Mayer in London. After the death of Abraham Goldsmid and Francis Baring in 1810, Nathan Rothschild became the dominant figure in the London money market. The majority of the English financial dealings with the continent went through the Rothschilds' offices. After the Congress of Vienna (1815) the **Rothschilds** extended their business into most European states, specializing in the **liquidation of inflated paper currencies** and in the foundation of **floating public debts**. In 1818 they made loans to European governments, beginning with Prussia and following with issues to England, Austria, Naples, Russia, and other stales, partly in collaboration with Baring, Reid, Irving and Company. Between 1815 and 1828 the total capital of the Rothschilds rose from 3,332,000 to 118,400,000 francs.

THE MERCHANT BANKERS

Prominent merchant bankers in Germany besides the Rothschilds were Joseph *Mendelssohn and Samuel *Bleichroeder. **Mendelssohn** founded his firm in Berlin in 1795, and was joined by his brother Abraham *Mendelssohn in 1804;

they issued **state loans for industrial development** to several foreign countries, particularly Russia. Samuel Bleichroeder, **Berlin correspondent of the Rothschilds**, established his own business in 1803. His son Gerson Bleichroeder became a confidant of Bismarck and served as his agent for financing the war of **1866** and for the transfer of the French war indemnity in 1871. The Bleichroeder bank also made loans to foreign states. After the death of Gerson Bleichroeder in 1893 his partner Paul Schwabach continued the business. The brothers Moses, Marcus, and Gerson *Warburg founded a bank in Hamburg in 1798. Its main business was concerned with the Hamburg overseas trade, especially transactions with England and the United States. **Paul M. *Warburg**, a brother of Max M. *Warburg, head of the Hamburg bank before World War I, established a branch office in **New York**. Toward the end of the 18th century J.M. *Speyer, through his bank's **provisioning of armies** and exchange business, had a capital of 420,000 florins, the largest Jewish fortune in Frankfurt at that time. In 1809 G.J. Elissen opened a banking house which took the name of J.L. Speyer-Elissen in 1818 and Lazard Speyer-Elissen in 1838. **Philipp Speyer** and Co., the U.S. branch, **negotiated the American credit during the Civil War**, participated in the development of the railroads in America, and conducted transactions in Mexico and Cuba, partly in association with the **Deutsche Bank**. In 1928 Speyer amalgamated with C. Schlesinger, Trier, and Company to form Lazard Speyer-Elissen K.a.A., Frankfurt and Berlin. The bank established by Solomon *Oppenheim in Bonn in 1789 acquired a leading position; at the beginning of the 19th century Solomon moved to Cologne, where his son Abraham became one of the most influential bankers in the Rhineland, financing insurance associations, railroad construction, and industrial investment.

Jewish bankers played an important part in the development of **joint stock banks**. Ludwig *Bamberger and Hermann Markuse were among the founders of the **Deutsche Bank (1870),** which was active in financing German foreign trade. The Disconto-Gesellschaft, established by David Hansemann in 1851, which amalgamated with the Deutsche Bank in 1929, had several Jewish partners. Eugen *Gutmann was the main founder of the Dresdner Bank, and Abraham Oppenheim was one of the founders of the Bank fuer Handel und Industrie (Darmstaedter Bank; 1853). The leading personality in the Berliner Handelsgesellschaft (established in 1856) was Carl *Fuerstenberg. Richard Witting, brother of Maximilian Harden, was one of the directors of the National bank fuer Deutschland; when it merged with the Darmstaedter Bank in 1921, Jacob *Goldschmidt, then director of the latter, took control of the new enterprise. In 1932 the two other most important banks in Germany, the Deutsche Bank and the Dresdener Bank, were directed by Oskar *Wassermann and Herbert Gutman respectively.

In England, **banks** were established by Sir David *Salomons **(London and Westminster Bank, 1832)**, the Stern brothers (1833), Samuel *Montagu (1853), Emile Erlanger (1859), the Speyer brothers, *Seligman brothers, and S. Japhet and Co., many of them immigrants from Frankfurt; the Speyer bank negotiated loans on behalf of Greece, Bulgaria, and Hungary, as well as for Latin American states.
David *Sassoon and Company, established in Bombay in 1832, had branches throughout the Orient, handling extensive transactions. Sir Ernest *Cassel, partly in association with Sir Carl Meyer, established banks in Egypt and Turkey. Industrial banks were organized by Sir Moses *Montefiore and the Anglo-American Corporation, which was connected with the diamond and finance corporation of A. Dunkelsbueler, established by Sir Ernest *Oppenheimer. In South Africa the General Mining and Finance Corporation was set up by Hamilton Ehrlich and Turk, and one of the most important enterprises in South African

183

financing was the Barnato brothers' company.

In France Achille *Fould, a competitor of the Rothschilds, was a supporter of Napoleon III and later his finance minister. Together with his brother Benoit he inherited the Paris firm of Fould, Oppenheimer et Cie., which had been established by his father. Meanwhile the brothers Emile and Isaac *Péreire, who moved to Paris from Marseilles in 1822, financed railway construction in France and Spain. Through the Crédit Mobilier, organized in 1852, they mobilized credit for various investment projects, but ran into difficulties in 1867. Among the other important Jewish banks was the Banque de Paris et des Pays-Bas (1872), with Henri Bamberger as one of the directors. The leading position among the private banks was held by **Rothschild**; *from 1889 to 1901* **all loans to Russia** *from Paris were issued through the Rothschild bank. Baron Maurice de *Hirsch from Munich, son-in-law of the Brussels banker Raphael Jonathan *Bischoffsheim, invested successfully in railroad construction. Other Jewish banks were those of* **Louis Dreyfus** *and Lazard Frères. In Italy, where Luigi *Luzzatti's agricultural associations were largely philanthropic, Jewish bankers played a leading part in the foundation of the Banca Commerciale Italiana and the Credito Italiano. The* **Rothschilds**, Sterns, and Goldsmids also invested money in Spain and Portugal.*

RUSSIA AND EASTERN EUROPE

A number of Jewish banks were established in Vienna during the 19th century, the most influential of which was Arnstein and Eskeles. This bank however was declared bankrupt in **1859**. *Weikersheim and Company and from 1821 Salomon* **Rothschild** *also established banks in* **Vienna**. *Jews participated in the foundation of the Niederoesterreichische Eskomptgessellschaft (1853) and the Kreditanstalt (1855), which made an essential contribution to the development of the* **Vienna stock exchange** and extended international loan facilities, also investing in industry and railroads. Leading private banks in Hungary were of Jewish origin, such as the Ungarische Allgemeine Kreditbank (Hungarian General Credit Bank; established in 1867) with Siegmund Kornfeld as a general director, the Pester Ungarische Kommerzial-bank (Hungarian Commercial Bank at Pest), established in 1841 by Moritz Ullmann, and the Ungarische Hypotheken-bank (Hungarian Hypothecary Credit Bank; 1869) with Nándor (Ferdinand) Beck de Madarassy as its general director. In Prague the *Petschek family established a bank in 1920; in Galicia, under the Austrian regime, Brody (Nathanson, Kallir) and Lemberg had Jewish banks. Between the end of the 18th century and the beginning of the 19th Jewish banks of some importance rose in Russia. In St. Petersburg **Nicolai and Ludwig *Stieglitz**, immigrants from Germany, opened a bank in 1803, which under Ludwig (who with his brother was **converted to Christianity in 1812**) became one of the leading financial institutions in Russia. Otherwise Jewish banking activity was limited to southern Russia, especially to Berdichev and Odessa. In 1860 Yozel (Yerzel) *Guenzburg, originally a **tax farmer**, established the St. Petersburg bank J.Y. Guenzburg, and later the discount and credit bank there, managed by his son Horace; Guenzburg also established banks in Kiev and Odessa. Lazar (Eliezer) *Poliakoff opened a bank at Moscow in 1860 and participated in the foundation of the Moskowsky Zemelny Bank and other Moscow banks. Poliakoff and his two brothers also founded banks in southern Russia. Abram *Zak was director of the Petersburg Discount and Credit Bank (1871–93), and Soloveitchik established the Siberian Trade Bank. At the beginning of the 20th century private banks of some importance were those of H. *Wawelberg in St. Petersburg, and O. Chayes and R. Sonschein and Company in Odessa.

Toward the end of the 18th century several bankers such as Koenigsberger, Levy, and Simon Simoni emigrated from the

185

west to Poland. Jacob *Epstein, court purveyor to King Stanislas IIAugustus, founded an important **dynasty of bankers**. The Polish **revolt of 1863** caused the bankruptcy of many Jewish banks. The bank of Wilhelm Landauer in Warsaw, established in 1857, closed in that year. However, Landauer returned to Warsaw some years later and opened a joint stock company in 1913. Mieczyslaw Epstein founded the Warsaw Discount Bank in 1871.Leopold *Kronenberg took part in the foundation of the Warsaw Credit Union in 1869 and the following year established the first joint stock bank in Poland, Bank Handlowy at Warsaw. The Natanson family bank was in operation between 1866 and 1932. In Romania, Maurice *Blank (d. 1921) established the house Marmorosch, Blank and Company, which his son, Aristide, directed after him...

THE UNITED STATES

*Already in early colonial times individual Jews were active in America as money brokers, such as Asser *Levy, who functioned in New York City during the second half of the 17th century. Often such figures were helped by their extensive family or fellow-Jewish contacts overseas, as was the case with* **David** ***Franks**, who was instrumental in **raising money** for the British army during the **French and Indian War** with the aid of his brother Moses, a London financier. The best known Jewish financier of the times was the legendary patriot* ***Haym *Salomon**, an immigrant from Poland who succeeded under extremely trying conditions in raising large amounts of desperately needed cash for the American Revolution by negotiating bills of exchange with France and the Netherlands. Yet another figure who helped finance the war for American independence was Isaac *Moses, later among the founders of the Bank of New York. It was not until the middle of the 19th century, however, with the arrival in America of a large* **German-Jewish immigration,** *that Jewish banking houses on the*

European model came to exist in the United States. Some of the founders of these firms, like Philip and Gustav *Speyer of Speyer & Co., went to the United States as American representatives of already established European concerns; others, like August *Belmont*, crossed the Atlantic with a degree of previously acquired banking experience; still others, like the *Lehman brothers*, Meyer and Emanuel, were essentially self-made men. Among other Jewish banking houses started by immigrants from Germany that developed into financial powers during the years 1840–1880 were **Kuhn, Loeb Co.**, Lazard Frères, J.W. Seligman Co., **Goldman, Sachs & Co.**, and Ladenburg, Thalman & Co. All of these firms functioned essentially as *investment bankers* – the more established field of commercial banking offered relatively few opportunities to the German-Jewish immigrant – a capacity in which they helped to finance large numbers of American utilities and corporations whose rapid growth throughout the latter half of the 19th century created an insatiable demand for capital. To raise such funds these Jewish houses not only freely utilized their widespread European connections, particularly in France, England, and Germany, but created a chain of interlocking associations and directorates among themselves which enabled them quickly to mobilize sums many times larger than their individual holdings and to compete successfully with gentile firms several times their size. Not only was it common for the children and relatives of a given firm to marry each other, but marital alliances frequently occurred as well among different Jewish banking families, as was the case with the *Loebs, the *Kuhns, the *Schiffs, and the *Warburgs. Frequently too the children of such families married into families of large German-Jewish companies in a variety of other fields and the latter would then proceed to raise capital through the banking houses which they had joined. Socially, the result of such commercial and kinship ties was the creation of a German-Jewish banking and business *aristocracy* based in **New York City** whose descendants

187

continued for over a century to play a dominant role in the financial, cultural, and political life of the American Jewish community, and to a lesser extent, of the nation at large. The contribution of such Jewish banking houses to the process of capital formation in the United States in the late 19th and early 20th century was considerable by any standard. Several of them, such as Speyer & Co., August **Belmont** & Co., and J. & W. Seligman, raised large sums for the **federal government** both during and after the Civil War (the Jewish house of **Erlanger Co.**, on the other hand, obtained sizeable loans for **the Confederacy**); others, such as Kuhn, Loeb, were particularly active in the westward expansion of the railroads. In the late 19th century **Seligman Co.** alone was capitalized at an estimated $10,000,000, while during the Russo-Japanese War of **1905 Jacob *Schiff** of Kuhn, Loeb was able on short notice to float a bond issue of $200,000,000 on behalf of the **Japanese government**. Although the total assets of such Jewish firms were nevertheless small when compared to those of the American banking system as a whole, their **clannishness and ability to coordinate their actions** made them the focus of antisemitic agitation from the 1890s on, when caricatures of ruthless Jewish oligarchs at the head of an international Jewish money conspiracy began to abound in the ranks of the Populist movement. In reality, however, the fiscal policies of the German-Jewish firms tended to be highly conservative and their owners exercised their fortunes with an unusual degree of social as well as fiscal responsibility. Although a number of the great 19th-century Jewish banking houses such as Lazard Frères and Kuhn, Loeb have survived into the present, none has continued as a family or even exclusively Jewish concern and even the most prosperous of them have lost their former importance as a result of the steady trend in the American financial market toward the predominance of ever larger and more impersonal corporations. At the same time, the general field of commercial banking in the United States has remained relatively closed to Jewish

188

*participation despite **heavy Jewish involvement** in such related*
*fields as **stock brokerage, investment analysis, and corporate***
***management**. A study undertaken by B'nai B'rith in 1939*
revealed that out of 93,000 bankers in the United States only
0.6% were Jewish, and that even in New York City Jews formed
only 6% of banking executives as compared to 28% of the
general population. Similar statistics for a later period are
unavailable, but reports of discrimination against Jews in major
banks throughout the country persist and in 1968 the American
Jewish Committee publicly filed a complaint before the Human
Rights Commission of New York City charging the banking
*system with **job bias against Jews**.*

In the latter years of the 20th century and the early years of the
21st, the banking industry consolidated, and some old-line
"Jewish" firms were bought or incorporated into others as
buyouts and mergers changed the landscape. As Jews
assimilated into American life, many advanced in the workplace
less along ethnic lines and more along lines of achievement. To
be sure, there were many Jews in leadership positions in
prominent financial institutions: Felix *Rohatyn at Lazard
Frères, Bruce *Wasserstein at several large firms, Sanford
*Weill at Citibank, and others, but their financial success was
largely attributed to their business acumen rather than to their
religious or ethnic background.

George Soros, a Hungarian immigrant, became one of the most
successful investors and later spread his wealth to nonprofit
organizations and to political causes. Michael Steinhardt and
others made their mark in hedge funds or as independent
venture capitalists, accumulating great wealth but also making
large philanthropic contributions. Carl *Icahn and Irwin L.
Jacobs developed reputations as **corporate raiders. Abby*
***Joseph Cohen** was the leading investment strategist for*
***Goldman Sachs**, and Henry Kaufman, a well-known economist,*

*offered advice about the stock market that was followed by
many. In addition, on Wall Street, such firms as Schwab & Co.,
headed by Charles *Schwab, achieved great success as a low-
price stock-market firm.*

*Some investors – **Ivan *Boesky, Michael *Milken,** Marc *Rich –
became infamous for their questionable **financial activities,** but
whether their religion played a role is highly unlikely. They were
perceived as corrupt financial figures, not corrupt Jewish
financial figures.*

*In the last years of the 20th century, a number of Jews had
important positions in the nation's economic community. **Alan
*Greenspan,** a Republican, headed the Federal Reserve System
for almost 20 years and became a powerful force in
Washington. During the Clinton administration, Jewish
economists, including **Robert *Rubin, the Treasury** secre*tary,
and **Lawrence *Sommers**, his successor and later president of
Harvard University, held Cabinet-level positions, and James D.
*Wolfensohn headed the World Bank from 1995 to 2005. His
successor, chosen by President George W. Bush, was Paul D.
Wolfowitz, a veteran foreign policy and defense official in
Republican administrations. [Stewart Kampel (2nd ed.)]

Assessment of the Role of Jewish Bankers

As shown above, Jewish activity, in particular in the late Middle
Ages and in the 18th and 19th centuries, often played an
important, sometimes a central, constructive role in the
economy and social life of various countries, sometimes even
internationally. However, banking always remained a subsidiary
Jewish economic activity. Frequently, when Jews appeared to
command large assets, they gave this impression because they
mostly owned mobile property. The wealthy Jews always
formed a small group, particularly in comparison with the

wealthy nobles or Christian merchants. It was really only in the 19th century that Jewish financiers achieved **remarkable wealth**, largely resulting from the activities of some European courts in **consequence of the upheavals** brought about by the French Revolution and the Napoleonic **Wars**. With the growth of joint **stock banks and of central banks** in the middle of the 19th century the field of private banking became limited. Around the beginning of the 20th century, Jewish influence in finance and banking had reached its zenith; afterward **it declined** at an accelerating rate. **_(propaganda)_**

C. Earlier forms of Money

Tally Sticks

_by_ PJCWASHERE _on_ JANUARY 2, 2009

http://coburns.biz/tally-sticks/190

King Henry VIII, King of England, produced sticks of polished wood, with notches cut along one edge to signify the denominations. The stick was then split full length so each piece still had a record of the notches.

| Tally Stick | Seshat with tally stick |

The King kept one half for proof against counterfeiting, and then spent the other half into the market place where it would continue to circulate as money.

Because *only* Tally Sticks were **accepted** by Henry **for payment of taxes**, there was a built in demand for them, which gave people confidence to accept these as money.

He could have used anything really, so long as the people agreed it had value, and his willingness to accept these sticks as legal tender made it easy for the people to agree. Herein lies a key: **Money is only as valuable as people's faith in it.** Without that faith even today's money is just paper.

The tally stick system worked really well for 726 years. It was the most successful form of currency in recent history and the British Empire was actually built under the Tally Stick system, and yet most of us are not aware of its existence?

In 1694 the Bank of England at its formation attacked the Tally Stick System. They realized it was money outside the power of the money changers, (the very thing King Henry had intended).

What better way to eliminate the vital faith people had in this rival currency than to pretend it simply never existed and not discuss it. That seems to be what happened when the first shareholder's in the Bank of England bought their original shares with notched pieces of wood and *then* retired the system. You heard correctly, they bought shares. The Bank of England was set up as a *privately owned bank* through investors buying shares. Shareholders expect a return on investment. Their driver is the return and not what is best for the people the Bank says it serves.

These investors, whose names were kept secret, were meant to invest one and a quarter million pounds, but only three quarters of a million was received when it was chartered in 1694.

It then began to lend out many times more than it had in reserve, collecting interest on the lot.

This is not something you could just impose on people without preparation. The money changers needed to create the climate to make the formation of this private concern seem acceptable.

And here is how they did it. With King Henry VIII relaxing the Usury Laws in the 1500's, the money changers flooded the market with their gold and silver coins becoming richer by the minute.

The English Revolution of 1642 was financed by the money changers backing Oliver Cromwell's successful attempt to purge the parliament and kill King Charles. What followed was 50 years of costly wars. Costly to those fighting them and profitable to those financing them.

So profitable that it allowed the money changers to take over a square mile of property still known as the City of London, which remains one of the three main financial centers in the world today.

The 50 years of war left England in financial ruin. The government officials went begging for loans from guess who, and the deal proposed resulted in a government sanctioned, privately owned bank which could produce money from nothing, essentially legally counterfeiting a national currency for private gain.

Now the politicians had a source from which to borrow all the money they wanted to borrow, and the debt created was secured against public taxes.

You would think someone would have seen through this, and realized they could produce their own money and owe no interest, but instead the Bank of England has been used as a model and now nearly every nation has a Central Bank with fractional reserve banking at its core.

These central banks have the power to take over a nation's economy and become that nations real governing force. What we have here is a scam of mammoth proportions covering what is actually a hidden tax, being collected by private concerns.

The country sells bonds to the bank in return for money it cannot raise in taxes. The bonds are paid for by money produced from thin air. The government pays interest on the money it borrowed by borrowing more money in the same way. There is no way this debt can ever be paid, it has and will continue to increase.

If the government did find a way to pay off the debt, the result would be that there would be no bonds to back the currency, so to pay the debt would be to kill the currency.

With its formation the Bank of England soon flooded Britain with money. With no quality control and no insistence on value for money, prices doubled with money being thrown in every direction.

One company was even offering to drain the Red Sea to find Egyptian gold lost when the sea closed in on their pursuit of Moses.

By1698 the national debt expanded from £1,250,000 to £16,000,000 and up went the taxes the debt was secured on.

As hard as it might be to believe, in times of economic upheaval, wealth is rarely destroyed and instead is often only transferred. And who benefits the most when money is scarce? You may have guessed. It's those controlling what everyone else wants... it is the money changer's.

When the majority of people are suffering through economic depression, you can be sure that a minority of people are continuing to get rich.

Even today the Bank of England expresses its determination to prevent the ups and downs of booms and depressions, yet there have been nothing but ups and downs since its formation with the British pound rarely being stable.

Burning of Talley Sticks:
http://en.wikipedia.org/wiki/Burning_of_Parliament

Talley Stick burning

Burning of Parliament is the popular name for the fire which destroyed the Palace of Westminster, the home of the Parliament of the United Kingdom, on 16 October 1834. The blaze, which started from overheated chimney flues, spread rapidly throughout the medieval complex and developed into the biggest conflagration to occur in London since the Great Fire of 1666, attracting massive crowds. The fire lasted for many hours and gutted most of the Palace, including the converted St Stephen's Chapel (the meeting place of the House of Commons), the Lords Chamber, the Painted Chamber and the official residences of the Speaker and the Clerk of the House of Commons. Westminster Hall and a few other parts of the old Houses of Parliament survived the blaze and were incorporated into the New Palace of Westminster, which was built in the Gothic style over the following decades.

The fire was caused by the destruction of tally sticks. The mathematician Tobias Dantzig, in his book *Number: The Language of Science*, remarked on how a counting-device had brought about the destruction of both Houses of Parliament, and he quotes from a speech given by the English novelist and advocate of social reform, Charles Dickens, in 1855 (Charles Dickens, Speech to the Administrative Reform Association, June 27, 1855). Long before his time, the now-literate clerks of the Exchequer no longer had need of tally sticks; and in 1724, Treasury officials had ordered that their use be discontinued: but they remained valid, and were not completely abolished until 1826.

Dickens wrote:

...it took until 1826 to get these sticks abolished. In 1834 it was found that there was a considerable accumulation of them; and the question then arose, what was to be done with such worn-out, worm-eaten, rotten old bits of wood? The sticks were housed in Westminster, and it would naturally occur to any intelligent person that nothing could be easier than to allow them to be carried away for firewood by the miserable people who lived in that neighborhood. However, they never had been useful, and official routine required that they should never be, and so the order went out that they were to be privately and confidentially burned. It came to pass that they were burned in a stove in the House of Lords. The stove, over-gorged with these preposterous sticks, set fire to the paneling; the paneling set fire to the House of Commons; the two houses were reduced to ashes; architects were called in to build others; and we are now in the second million of the cost thereof.

The responsibility for disposing of the tally sticks fell to Richard Whibley, the Clerk of Works at the Palace. He decided against burning them on a bonfire out in the open, as he feared such an action would upset the neighbors. The decision was made to burn the sticks in the under floor coal furnaces that heated the House of Lords chamber. On the morning of October 16, Whibley assigned the task to two workmen, Joshua Cross and Patrick Furlong. The work went on all day; witnesses recalled seeing the men throw great handfuls of sticks onto the fires, despite the risk of the burning wood overheating the copper-lined brick flues.

The first indication that something was wrong came that afternoon when the housekeeper at the palace, Mrs. Wright, was showing round a party of visitors. She complained that the House of Lords' Chamber was full of smoke; whilst her visitors noted the exceptional amount of heat coming up through the floor. Nonetheless she did not pursue the matter any further. Cross and Furlong clocked off in the late afternoon, having completed their task. Mrs. Wright locked up the Lords chamber at 5pm. Within an hour it was discovered to be ablaze. It is believed the over-stoked furnaces heated the flues to such an extent that their copper linings collapsed, causing the exposed brickwork to heat up, and bursting through the stone floor of the chamber above. This allowed the fire to spread to the vast range of combustible wooden and fabric furnishings inside the Chamber itself.[1]

D. Banking

Source: *Encyclopaedia Judaica*. © 2008 The Gale Group. All Rights Reserved.http://www.jewishencyclopedia.com/articles/2444-banking

BANKING:

Banking means the taking of money on deposit (banks of deposit), and loaning it out on interest (banks of issue). In this sense Banking is comparatively recent; only a few banks of deposit existing in the Middle Ages, in Italy (Florence, Genoa, Lucca), while the earliest banks of issue of consequence were those of Amsterdam and Hamburg at the beginning of the seventeenth century. The financial activity of the Jews in the Middle Ages is generally called Banking; but this is erroneous, as they did not receive money of others on deposit, which is an essential element of Banking. Their operations were more of the **nature of finance banks**—that is, *loan corporations*—and were conducted under special economic conditions and relations to the state (for further particulars see also the article Usury).

Medieval Finance.

All the great Jewish financiers of the Middle Ages, such as Aaron of Lincoln and Aaron of York in England, Jahudan Cavalleria and Benveniste da Porta in Aragon, Esmel de Ablitas in Navarre, and Nathan Official in France, were associated with the royal treasuries of their respective countries, and in every instance their property fell into the hands of the crown; so that their banking operations were in the nature of indirect taxation. Details are not sufficiently clear to make a general statement. In several cases, however, the capital utilized by these financiers probably belonged in some measure to other Jews; so that their operations were really in the form of banking corporations, though the conditions were so dissimilar from those of modern Banking that it would be misleading to treat them as of the same order. In more modern times the financial operations of Jews have been more of the order of **finance loan corporations** than of banks of deposit and issue;

197

but as a large part of the business of modern Banking consists of similar loan operations, there is **less impropriety** in using the word for the modern form of Jewish financial transactions (see also Finance, Stock Exchange).

Source of Jewish Fortunes.

With the spread of the Maranos throughout the world-empire of Spain and Portugal (which countries were united 1580-1640), Jewish commerce entered a new phase, which is represented by the career of Don Joseph Nasi, who began his life as a banker in the firm of Mendes at Antwerp, the center of Spanish commerce. The Maranos became large factors or merchants, and, owing to **the unwise economic policy of the Spanish monarch**, were enabled to accumulate **large capital** from the profits of importation into Europe of the raw products of the **East and West Indies.** The firm of Gradis at Bordeaux, a branch of the Mendes family, established relations with Amsterdam as well as with the New World; so that ultimately they became the chief **exporters from France to Canada** (9,000,000 francs during the Seven Years' war), besides maintaining relations with the Maranos in Spain itself (Jacobs, "Sources," No. 13, p. 5; Grätz, in "Monatsschrift," new series, vii.-viii.). But among the chattels imported by such merchants **was bullion**; and thus their operations as **merchants led** to their activity as **bankers.** Ferdinand de Carvajal is thus reported to have brought into England no less than **£100,000 per annum** ("Trans. Jewish Soc. England," ii. 18). During the latter part of the seventeenth century and the early part of the eighteenth, a number of Marano merchants are found acting as **loan agents for European monarchs**. Thus Isaac Suasso, Baron Auvernes de Gras, is said to have advanced 2,000,000 florins to William of Orange for the **invasion** of England. With the great movements of Continental armies in connection with the wars of Louis XIV. **large fortunes** were gained by the Jews as **commissaries**; and these were then loaned out in banking operations. Thus, on the **one side**, Marlborough's troops were supplied by Sir Solomon Medina ("Dict. National Biography," x. 336) and Joseph Cortisos; while Jacob Worms performed a similar office for the

opposing army of Louis XIV. Worms afterward settled in Paris as a banker (Kahn, "Histoire des Juifs à Paris dans la XVIIIᵉSiècle," p. 39).

Hamburg and Amsterdam.

Meanwhile in Hamburg a bank had been opened in imitation of the Amsterdam bank; this still exists under the name of the "Hamburger Bank." Among the chief founders of the new venture was a Marano named Diego Teixera de Mattos; and of the forty original members of the bank twelve were Jews. (Grätz, "Gesch. der Juden," x. 17, note). Later on, in connection with the Hamburg bank were the two Abensurs, financial representatives of the king of Poland. They represent another source from which **Jewish capital was drawn**; the position of the Jews as **"factors"** to the Polish nobility in some degree resembling the standing and functions of the **Court Jews** who slowly collected around the smaller German courts and who managed their finance much in the way modern banks do in the case of court estates. Among these may be mentioned Michael of Berlin, court Jew to Joachim II. of Brandenburg (Grätz, *ib.* ix. 305, 314); Samson Wertheimer at Vienna, and Bassevi von Treuenberg at Prague (the last two connected with the imperial finances of the Hapsburgs). In the middle of the eighteenth century the Pintos, Delmontes, Bueno de Mesquita, and Francis Mels of Amsterdam were the leading financiers of northern Europe; while in London, which, owing to the relations of William III. with Holland, was financially dependent on Amsterdam, Mendes da Costa, Manasseh Lopez, and Baron d'Aguilar held prominent positions. The very first work on the operations of the **Amsterdam Exchange** was written by a Spanish Jew named Joseph de la Vega.

Rise of the **Rothschilds.**

When French influence became prominent in Holland in 1803, the financial operations of the powers opposing Napoleon were transferred to Frankfort-on-the-Main (Ehrenberg, "Das Zeitalter der Fugger," ii. 318), and the financial control of the anti-Napoleonic League fell into the hands of Mayer Amschel **Rothschild, court Jew** of William I., elector of Hesse-Cassel. His father, Frederick II., had died in 1785, leaving about £8,400,000, derived chiefly from the hire of soldiers to the British government to suppress the rebellion in America. As the fortune of the **Rothschilds** was ultimately dependent on the manipulation of this, it is curious to reflect that their **financial predominance** in the nineteenth century is in the last resort **due to America**. It is impossible in this place to pursue the financial career of the **Rothschilds**, which is the key to the history of Jewish Banking in the nineteenth century; but it may be remarked that the London house between 1818 and 1832 undertook loans amounting to £21,800,000, and that as early as 1824 the Paris house had risen to the position of financial magnates, undertaking in conjunction with Lafitte and Baring the French loan of 1824 (Nervo, "Les Finances Françaises sous la Restauration," ii. 294). (For the ramifications built up by Mayer Amschel Rothschild throughout western Europe.) The plan adopted by him **of establishing branches** in the more important European capitals, over which he placed **his sons**, was followed by other Jewish banking-houses.

With the reconstruction of Europe, after the fall of Napoleon in 1815, a new financial era began in which the capital hitherto diverted to warlike operations was transferred to industrial enterprise, owing to the introduction of steam. This was mainly operated from **London** with English capital; and the Jews did only a small portion of the business connected with the introduction of machinery and railroads into European commerce. But the international connections of great Jewish families, such as the Rothschilds, Sterns, Péreires, Hirschs, and Bischoffsheims caused them to be of considerable importance in the issuing of state loans between 1820 and 1860. Up to 1848 the practice **of apportioning loans** to large banking firms, who then distributed them to the public in **smaller lots,** was carried out; and in this way the **Rothschilds** especially had a **quasi-monopoly** of the loan market. In the fifties, however, their monopoly of international finance was broken down by the formation throughout western Europe of credit banks, many of them founded by **associations of Jewish bankers** of smaller caliber than the great financial families. Thus the Crédit Mobilier of

1852 was founded by the Péreires, Solomon Heine, and D'Eichthal (M. Aycard, "Histoire du Crédit Mobilier," 1867). The practice, after the year 1848, of opening the subscription to the loans to the public in general also tended to break down the monopoly of the great Jewish financial firms.

Capitalists Invest in Railroads.

It may be worthwhile to remark here that the idea promoted generally **by anti-Semitic** writers that the resources of all Jewish capitalists formed one fund is **ludicrously** at variance with the facts of the case. Heine, in a correspondence to the Augsburg "Allgemeine Zeitung," dated May 27, 1840, and reprinted in "Französische Zustände," refers to Rothschild and Fould as two "**rabbis of finance**," opposed just as strenuously to each other as were once "Rabbi Shammai and Rabbi Hillel in the old city **of Babylon**" (*sic*). Jewish firms competed with one another with as much eagerness as they did against non-Jewish firms. The Péreires, for example, obtained a concession for South Russian railways against the Rothschilds in 1856 (Reeves, "The Rothschilds," p. 334). With the introduction of railroads on the Continent many of the firms previously mentioned were closely connected, the Péreires with those of northern France, the Bishoffsheims with those of Belgium, and Baron de Hirsch with those of Turkey. Many Jewish firms and credit banks, especially the house of Bleichroeder, were concerned with the growth of railways in Germany and Austria. It was Baron Bleichroeder who operated the transfers of the milliards from France to Germany after the Franco-Prussian war. But with the nationalization of the German railroads the field of operation of the **Jewish banking-houses** in Germany was transferred from railroads to other industries which they have largely helped to create.

Throughout the latter half of the nineteenth century, however, others had been learning the **secret of international connections**, and by 1900 the monopoly of international finance had largely passed from Jewish hands. An organized attempt to precipitate this was made about 1885 by a number of Catholic financiers in France, who constituted the Union

201

Générale to overcome the financial predominance of the Jewish capitalists (Rothschilds, Pereires, etc.); but it proved a disastrous failure, and much of French anti-Semitism has been traced to this cause. Similarly, it is stated that the financial crisis of Germany and Austria in 1873, in which the inflation due to the introduction of the milliards came to an end, was also a source of anti-Semitism, because the shrewdness of the **Jewish bankers had foreseen the crash,** and they were enabled to evade it...

In the United States.

But in the two great wars Jewish financiers played a considerable role, owing doubtless to their European connections: Haym Solomon in the Revolutionary war (see "Transactions of the Jewish Historical Society of America,"*passim*), while Seligman Bros. and Speyer & Co. financed the North, and Messrs. Erlanger the South (J. C. Schwab, "Confederate States of America," p. 102, New York, 1901), in the great Civil war. More recently, in the great development of railway finance, the firm of **Kuhn, Loeb & Co.** has taken a prominent position.

Altogether, the influence of Jews on Banking has been only short-lived, and was due to the preliminary advantage given to them by their international position, which is nowadays shared by them with others. It is a significant fact that at the beginning of the twentieth century the typical Jewish banking house of Rothschilds gave up its original foundation at Frankfort.

E. Federal Reserve System

WHO STOLE AMERICA?

William E. Dannemeyer
U.S. Congressman, 1979-1992 (California)

If you want to take over a country, one of the first things you do is to seize control of the money supply. **Jacob Schiff** was the son of a Jewish rabbi, born in Frankfurt, Germany. He was sent to America in the late nineteenth century by the **European Rothschild** financial dynasty. One of his assigned tasks was to seize control of the money supply of the U.S. Government. At that time it was under the control of the U.S. Congress pursuant to Article 1, Section 8 of the U.S. Constitution which states:

"The Congress shall have Power to coin Money, regulate the Value thereof."

Baron MA Rothschild had stated this truism in the nineteenth century:

"Give me control over a nation's currency and I care not who makes the laws."

Jacob Schiff began his quest to take over the money supply of America by purchasing an interest in a banking concern in Indiana called Kuhn and Loeb. He married the daughter of Loeb, bought out the interest of Kuhn and as sole owner of Kuhn and Loeb, moved the business to New York in the late 19th century.

Jacob Schiff was not exactly welcomed with open arms by the financial potentates led by the House of Morgan then controlling the financial markets in New York. Schiff, as the Rothschild's agent in America, gradually was able to build a working relationship with the other banking houses in New York by sharing some Rothschild bonds and stock business with them.

Schiff was so successful in being accepted as a player in the N.Y. Banking scene that in 1908 he was among a handful of NY bankers who gathered at **Jekyll Island**, one of the House of Morgan's homes located in Georgia. These financial wizards plotted to take over the money supply of America. They had no small task before them.

They needed to get America to pass their hatched plan called the **Federal Reserve System which was nothing more than a private group of bankers**. It was not then nor has it ever been a part of the U.S. government. Some of the stockholders included: Rothchilds of London and Berlin; Lazard Brothers of Paris; Israel Moses Seif of Italy; Kuhn, Loeb and Warburg of Germany; and the Lehman Brothers, Goldman, Sachs and the Rockefeller families of New York.

The congressional stooge present at the meeting in 1908 at Jekyll Island was Senator **Nelson Aldrich** of New York. He was assigned the task of **shepherding** the outright **theft** of the U.S. money supply system called the Federal Reserve Act through Congress.

On December 23, 1913, he delivered in spades. Two days before Christmas is a good time to have Congress debate and vote on a major piece of legislation if your desire is to minimize the desire of members of Congress to really understand what they are voting on. The reason is not hard to find. Members of Congress have families and want to get home for Christmas like anyone else.

The Federal Reserve Act was passed by a vote of 298 to 60 in the House of Representatives and in the Senate by a majority and was sent to the White House for the signature of President Woodrow Wilson.

How President Wilson was elected in 1912 was all a part of the conspiracy organized by **Jacob Schiff** and his New York banking fraternity at the meeting at **Jekyll Island in Georgia in 1908.**

President Robert Taft, a well-respected Republican, was running for re-election in the Presidential election scheduled for 1912. He was on to the theft of our money supply organized by Jacob Schiff and his New York City banking friends. If President Taft was re-elected in 1912, it was clear that he would **veto any bill** passed by Congress to create the privately owned **Federal Reserve Act.**

The conspirators led by **Jacob Schiff** enlisted the help of former President Theodore Roosevelt, a Republican and convinced him to run on the third party Bull Moose ticket and split the Republican vote. The **scheme** worked and Woodrow Wilson was elected President in the 1912 election and when the Federal Reserve Act came to his desk in 1913, he rewarded his bankers and signed the act into law.

In 1913, the principle means of communicating to the people of America what Congress was doing were newspapers. The newspapers did not report this biggest theft in the 20th Century at all.

Almost a century later, 2007, we Americans are still experiencing the consequences of this theft of our money supply in 1913 by transferring control of it to private elitist banking families residing mostly in Europe and some in America.

It is not an exaggeration to say that these are the consequences of this historic event:

(1)   The American people lost control of how and to what extent Congress spends our money: Example, Congressional deficits are financed by irresponsibly expanding the money supply by the privately owned Federal Reserve System which results over time in an inflationary spiral which will lead to a total collapse of the dollar and the destruction of the middle class.

(2)   America disavowed the advice of George Washington to avoid entangling alliances with other countries and focus our energies on protecting the interests of the American people.

(3)   The creation of Imperial America which seeks to control the world and results in perpetual war to achieve perpetual peace. It goes by the name of the New World Order, led by the Council on Foreign Relations (CFR). The CFR has over 3,000 members, over 70% of whom are Zionist Jews.

===

http://en.wikipedia.org/wiki/Jekyll_Island

At the end of November 1910, Senator Nelson W. Aldrich and Assistant Secretary of the U.S. Treasury Department A. Piatt Andrew, and five of the country's leading financiers (Frank Vanderlip, Henry P. Davison, Charles D. Norton, Benjamin Strong, and Paul Warburg) arrived at the Jekyll Island Club to discuss monetary policy and the banking system, an event that led to the creation of the current Federal Reserve. According to the Federal Reserve Bank of Atlanta, the 1910 Jekyll Island meeting resulted in draft legislation for the creation of a U.S. central bank.

Parts of this draft (the Aldrich plan) were incorporated into the 1913 Federal Reserve Act, to unsure legal theft. On November 5–6, 2010, Ben Bernanke stayed on Jekyll Island to commemorate the 100-year anniversary of this original meeting. The Conference was the first official confirmation of the revelations made initially in 1949 by Ezra Pound to Eustace Mullins in his work *Secrets of The Federal Reserve* and later reported by G. Edward Griffin in his book *The Creature from Jekyll Island.*

Chapter 6

Persecution of the Jews

Using a "scapegoat" to hide the strangling of America

The international Jewish bankers made it through the hundredth anniversary of **their** Federal Reserve System, which had run the government debt up from $1 billion in 1913 to over $17 trillion in 2013, without receiving a scratch by using Blacks in America as scapegoats to fool their white non-Jewish brethren. It has been almost thirty years since the Honorable Minister Louis Farrakhan warned America about the Jewish stranglehold on the U.S. government. It has been four years since the release of *The Secret Relationship between Blacks and Jews Vol. 2,* which exposes how Jews make Blacks the scapegoats to keep non-Jews busy fighting one another while they make off with the loot. And now the real rulers of America, Ashkenazi Jews, have come out of the closet and now **openly** run America's money supply and her foreign policy. However, the question remains is "how can the American people be so content to suck on a dry bone, when all the meat is gone?"

When the Jewish dominated financial industry collapsed in 2008 sending America into an economic tailspin, the economic pundits tried to blame the financial fall of America on **black people** who were **baited** into taking out variable rate mortgages on homes that they could not afford. Biblically, the "scapegoat" was a sacrificial goat ritually laden with the sins of the people and then driven into the wilderness as part of the Jewish ceremony of Yom Kippur, the Day of Atonement. The rite is described in Leviticus 16:7-10, 20-22.

The book, *The Secret Relationship between Blacks and Jews,*

Vol. 2, allows us unprecedented access to the private confessions of Jewish scholars and rabbis about their strategy of using the Black man and woman as scapegoats for their own economic and political advancement. One of the most revered Jewish scholars, Dr. Henry L. Feingold, wrote of the American Jews that there was a "**concealed advantage** in living in a society which reserved most of its fear and rancor for its blacks." Jewish author Eli Evans wrote that Southern Jews attribute the lack of anti-Semitism in the region to "the presence of the Negro," who acted as "the lightning rod for prejudice" which allowed Jews the freedom to thrive. Dr. Louis Schmier uses the same language in his analysis: "the presence of blacks acts as a lightning rod to attract antagonistic attitudes which otherwise might be directed against the Jews." Jewish folklorist David Max Eichhorn wrote that the Southern Jew was spared acts of hatred in America "mainly because of the ubiquitous presence of a **convenient scapegoat**, the black." Author Leon Harris discussed the remarkable rise of Jewish-owned department stores in the South, like Neiman-Marcus and Rich's, and he reasons that "the exploitation and consequent hatred of the 'niggers' on the part of many Southern whites **diverted** much of the hostility that might otherwise have been directed at Jews."

Sen. Bernie Sanders has revealed the report of the Government Accountability Office, which stated that more than $4 trillion in near zero-interest Federal Reserve loans and other financial assistance went to the banks and businesses of at least 18 current and former Federal Reserve regional bank directors in the aftermath of the 2008 financial collapse. This $4 trillion dollars that went to bailout banks using money printed by the Federal Reserve was in addition to the $700 billion bailout money "stolen" from the Treasury Department at the end of the Bush administration.

These incredible bank robberies have also had a devastating economic impact on the average American. The Federal Reserve released figures on June 11, 2012 showing that the net worth of the typical American family fell by **40%** between 2007 and 2009. The Bush administration used 9/11 as the pretext for destroying Iraq, while people in his administration walked off with $2.3 trillion in 2001 from the Defense Department, $700 billion in 2008 from the Treasury Department and $4 trillion from 2008 to 2009 from the Federal Reserve. We are talking big money here.

The results of these financial raids on the American people are catalogued by Cliff DuRand in his May 13, 2013 article "The American Dream Is Dead; Long Live the New Dream":

"This upward mobility was a reality for most citizens of the United States for several generations, from 1820 to 1970. For 150 years, real wages rose. In the quarter century from 1947 to 1973, average real wages rose an astounding 75 percent. But that shared prosperity came to a halt in the mid '70s. In the next 25 years, from 1979 to 2005, wages and benefits rose less than 4 percent... From 1983 to 2008, total GDP grew from $6.1 trillion to $13.2 trillion in constant 2005 dollars... The wealthiest 5 percent of American households captured 81.7 percent of the gain. The bottom 60 percent of households not only failed to share in the overall increase, they suffered a **7.5 percent loss."**

Minister Farrakhan warned America in 1985 that the Nation of Islam was America's only hope to break the stranglehold of the Jewish lobby on the government. America has not listened and now the Jewish bankers have stepped from behind the scenes to run both America's foreign policy and money, outright. With the swearing in of another Ashkenazi Jew as Federal Reserve Chairman and the appointment of Stanley Fischer as Vice-Chairman, the blurring of citizenship and national loyalties will be complete. Stanley Fischer holds citizenship in two countries, the U.S. and Israel. He was once the head of the Israeli Central Bank and mentored the current Fed Chairman, Ben Bernanke and the next Chairman, Janet Yellen. How does one move from a high ranking position in one country to a high ranking position in another? Whose interest would he or she serve?

209

Let us give you a list of 12 high ranking **non-elected** American officials who are also citizens of Israel and the positions that they hold or held: 1. Henry Kissinger, **Secretary of State**, 2. Douglas Feith, Under Secretary of Defense, 3. Paul Wolfowitz, Deputy Defense Secretary, 4. Richard Perle, chairman of the Pentagon's Defense Policy Board, 5. Michael Chertoff, head of **Homeland Security**, 6. Michael Mukasey, **US Attorney General**, 7. Dov Zakheim, Pentagon Comptroller from May 4, 2001 to March 10, 2004 during which time $2.3 trillion went missing from the Pentagon's budget, 8. Lewis "Scooter" Libby, Vice President Dick Cheney's Chief of Staff, 9. Elliott Abrams, National Security Council Advisor, 10. Ari Fleischer, White House Spokesman for the Bush (Jr.) Administration, 11. David Frum, White House speechwriter for the Bush (Jr.) Administration, 12. John Bolton, Senior Advisor to President Bush (Jr.).

These people are key players who make and execute foreign policies which can and has led America into wars to defend Israel and her interests instead of America's. In fact all of the above 12 have been implicated in the biggest false flag hoax the world has ever suffered, **"9/11"**, according to many researchers and revealed in a well-researched video on the Israeli/Jewish involvement in 9/11 called MISSING LINKS: http://www.youtube.com/watch?v=IQqWM0nRRPU. If the positions that these 12 hold or held were occupied by citizens of some other country like China or Libya, would the American people be so complacent?

For 100 years Jewish bankers and Wall Street gamblers used black people as scapegoats and slid out of the slaughtering pen with their wealth in tact leaving black folk and middle income white Gentiles holding the bag and blaming each other. This is unlike what happened in Europe as we will demonstrate in this chapter when Jews were either killed or run out of countries once their money schemes were figured out.

Starting in 2013 (the 100th anniversary of the Fed) there was a dramatic increase in the incidence, or at least the reporting, of Whites murdering young black people and Blacks taking to the streets to protest these killings. Was all of this staged to keep both the Blacks (sheep) and Whites (sheepdogs) going at one another so

210

that no one would notice that all their money was gone and safely **diverted** off shore to Jewish bank accounts? Were white people given Blacks to chew on like a dog is given a dry bone while his Jewish master cooked and ate the meat? The ADL was also set up in 1913 and has since been calling everyone who would question the Federal Reserve an anti-Semite. When will the American people stop allowing Abe Foxman and his ADL to call Minister Farrakhan an anti-Semite just because he spotted the robbery and the robber a long time ago? Meanwhile, Blacks should support Muhammad's Economic Blueprint and stop being the dry bones that everybody in the valley chews on.

Why have the Jews been persecuted?

Are Jews persecuted for "who they are" or "what they do"? Are they persecuted and not forgiven for "what they did" or "what they continue to do"? Black people are persecuted in America because of "who they are," black descendants of slaves. Blacks cannot stop being Black.

Jews would have us to believe that Christians hate them because the Jews were instrumental in the killing of Jesus, 2000 years ago. They accuse the Christians of being unforgiving and therefore hypocrites to their principles taught by Jesus of forgiveness. Therefore whenever the Jews are attacked, they cry foul and sink the world into some type of guilt trip. They have done this quite successfully. The world is backing them as they take the Palestinians' lands, because of the Jews suffering during the Holocaust and their claim that God gave them Palestine as the "Promised Land."

However, in the previous chapters we think that we have removed the cloak hiding their identity. They were not in bondage in Egypt and not liberated by Moses and given Palestine as the "Promised Land" by God. We have also began to show how the Jews got so rich by loaning money with interest charges, loaning money to both sides of a war and being the personal bankers of kings. In this process of moneylending we found that they have one set of rules for lending between Jewish "brothers" and another set of rules when lending to non-Jews. Treating people differently could cause a problem, if found out. We know how showing

211

favoritism or practicing unjust behavior can cause big problems between people.

The father of Protestantism, Martin Luther wrote a book in 1543 called *The Jews and Their Lies* which presents many accusations against them and what they do including "usury" and avarice. Let us look at a few quotes from this book:

> "Princes and government sit by, snore and have their mugs (mouth) open, let the Jews take from their purse and chest, steal and rob whatever they will. That is, they permit themselves and their subjects to be abused and sucked dry and reduced to beggars with their own money, through the usury of the Jews." (Luther 1543: 30)
>
> "If a thief steals ten gulden he must hang; if he robs people on the highway, his head is gone. But a Jew, when he steals ten tons of gold through his usury, is dearer than God Himself." (Ibid: 30)
>
> "And into the temple they had placed money changers, merchants and all manner of avaricious trade, that our Lord Christ said they had made of God's house a den of thieves." (Ibid: 33)
>
> "For I see in writings how they curse us Goyim and wish us all evil in their schools and prayers. They rob us of our money through usury, and wherever they are able, they play us all manner of mean tricks: (what is worst of all) they mean to have right and well in this, that is, they think they have rendered God a service in this and teach that such should be done." (Ibid: 34)
>
> "...Why, they hold us Christians in captivity in our own country; they let us work in the sweat of our noses, while they appropriate money and goods, sitting behind the stove, are lazy, gluttlers and guzzlers, live well and easy on goods for which we have worked, keep us and our goods in captivity through their cursed usury, mock us and spit on us, because we must labor and permit them to be noblemen at our expense; thus they are our lords and masters, we their servants with our property, sweat and labor! And to thank us and reward us, they curse our Lord!" (Ibid: 37)

"I hear it said that Jews give large sums of money and thereby are helpful to the government. Yes, from what do they give it? Not of their own, but from the property of the rulers and their subjects whom they deprive of their possessions through usury! The rulers take from the subjects what the Jews have taken, that is: subjects must give money and suffer themselves to be fleeced for the Jews so they can remain in the land freely to lie, slander, curse and steal. Should not the despairing Jews have a good laugh over the way we suffer ourselves to be fooled and be led around by the nose to give our money in order that they may stay in the land to practice all manner of wickedness? On top of that they even become rich on our sweat and blood, but we become poor and are sucked dry by them?" (Ibid: 47)

The Jews know better

Go back over in your mind the power of compound interest and how the interest charges become astronomical after 50 years. Now imagine that in the Bible a system was set up to relieve society of this debt burden every seven years, so that the burden of debt would not destroy the people. Please take the time to read from the Jews' own hands about the system they were given to relieve debt called the "Sabbatical Year" and the "Jubilee." Again we bring this information directly from the "Jews' mouth":

http://www.jewishencyclopedia.com/articles/12967-sabbatical-year-and-jubilee

SABBATICAL YEAR AND JUBILEE:

Biblical Injunctions

The septennate or seventh year, during which the land is to lie fallow, and the celebration of the fiftieth year after seven Sabbatical cycles. As regards the latter, the Hebrew term "yobel"

213

refers to the blast of the shofar on the Day of Atonement announcing the jubilee year (comp. שׁופרות היובלים = "trumpets of rams' horns"; Josh. vi. 4), though Ibn Ezra thinks it signifies the transfer of properties (comp. יובל; Isa. xviii. 7). So important was the law regarding the jubilee that, like the Decalogue, it was ascribed to the legislation on Mount Sinai (Lev. xxv. 1). It was to come into force after the Israelites should be in possession of Palestine: "When ye come into the land which I give you" (*ib.*). The law provides that one may cultivate his field and vineyard six years, but "in the seventh year shall be . . . a Sabbath for the Lord," during which one shall neither sow nor reap as hitherto for his private gain, but all members of the community—the owner, his servants, and strangers—as well as domestic and wild animals, shall share in consuming the natural or spontaneous yield of the soil.

The fiftieth year, *i.e.*, that following the last year of seven Sabbatical cycles, is the jubilee; during it the land regulations of the Sabbatical year are to be observed, as is also the commandment "ye shall return every man unto his possession" (*ib.* verse 10), indicating the compulsory restoration of hereditary properties (except houses of laymen located in walled cities) to the original owners or their legal heirs, and the emancipation of all Hebrew servants whose term of six years is unexpired or who refuse to leave their masters when such term of service has expired (Gen. xviii. 6; 'Ar. 33b; see Josephus, "Ant." vi. 8, § 28).

The regulations of the Sabbatical year include also the annulment of all monetary obligations between Israelites, the creditor being legally barred from making any attempt to collect his debt (Deut. xv. 1 *et seq.*). The law for the jubilee year has not this provision.

Technically the Talmud distinguishes the Sabbatical year for the release or quitclaim of loans as "shemiṭṭah," more distinctly "shemiṭṭat kesafim" (money-release), in contradistinction to "shebi'it" (seventh) or "shemiṭṭat ḳarḳa'ot" (land-release). There is this difference, however, that loans are not annulled before the expiration (= "the end") of every seven years, as the Mosaic law (*ib.*) provides, whereas the land-release, the shemiṭṭat ḳarḳa'ot, begins with the seventh year. The general term for the

214

Sabbatical cycle is "shabua'" = "septennate" (Sanh. v. 1).

Reasons for Observance.

Several reasons are advanced for these laws:

(1) In the Cabala the number seven is a symbolic division of time, and is sacred to God. The week of Creation consisted of seven days, the last being the Sabbath. The Feast of Weeks is so called because it occurs seven weeks after Passover, the fiftieth day being Pentecost. These days are parallel to the years of shemiṭṭah and yobel. The duration of the world is 7,000 years, the seven thousandth year being the millennium, the Great Sabbath of the Lord (Sanh. 97a).

(2) The physico-economic and socialistic theories are that rest from labor is an absolute necessity both for animal and for vegetable life; that continuous cultivation will eventually ruin the land. The law of the Sabbatical year acts also as a statute of limitation or a bankruptcy law for the poor debtor, in discharging his liability for debts contracted, and in enabling him to start life anew on an equal footing with his neighbor, without the fear that his future earnings will be seized by his former creditors. The jubilee year was the year of liberation of servants whose poverty had forced them into employment by others. Similarly all property alienated for a money consideration to relieve poverty, was to be returned to the original owners without restoration of the amount which had been advanced.

(3) The rabbinical view, however, is that these laws were made to promote the idea of theocracy: that one year in seven might be devoted "to the Lord," as the weekly Sabbath is devoted to rest from manual labor and to the study of the Law. The jubilee was instituted primarily to keep intact the original allotment of the Holy Land among the tribes, and to discountenance the idea of servitude to men. "For unto me the children of Israel are servants; they are my servants" (Lev. xxv. 55); and they shall not be servants to servants, as God's bond has the priority (Sifra, Behar Sinai, vii. 1.). That the main object was to keep intact each tribe's inheritance is evident from the fact that shemiṭṭah and yobel were not inaugurated before the Holy Land had been conquered and apportioned among the tribes and their families. The first shemiṭṭah year is said to have occurred twenty-one years after the arrival of the Hebrews in Palestine, and the first yobel thirty-three years later (ib. i. 3.). The jubilee was proclaimed "throughout all the land unto all the inhabitants thereof"; only when all the tribes were in possession of Palestine was the jubilee observed, but not after the tribes of Reuben and

215

Gad and the half-tribe of Manasseh had been exiled (ib. ii. 3); nor was it observed during the existence of the Second Temple, when the tribes of Judah and Benjamin had been assimilated (Sheb. x. 2; 'Ar. 32b). After the conquest of Samaria by Shalmaneser the jubilee was observed nominally in the expectation of the return of the tribes—according to some authorities, Jeremiah brought them back (ib. 33a)—and till the final exile by Nebuchadnezzar.

Fifty- and Forty-nine-Year Cycles.

There is a difference of opinion in the Talmud as to whether the jubilee year was included in or excluded from the forty-nine years of the seven cycles. The majority of rabbis hold that the jubilee year was an intercalation, and followed the seventh Sabbatical year, making two fallow years in succession. After both had passed, the next cycle began. They adduce this theory from the plain words of the Law to "hallow the fiftieth year," and also from the assurance of God's promise of a yield in the sixth year sufficient for maintenance during the following three years, "until the ninth year, until her fruits come in" (Lev. xxv. 22), which, they say, refers to the jubilee year. Judah ha-Nasi, however, contends that the jubilee year was identical with the seventh Sabbatical year (R. H. 9a; Giṭ. 36a; comp. Rashi *ad loc.*). The opinion of the Geonim and of later authorities generally prevails, that the jubilee, when in force during the period of the First Temple, was intercalated, but that in the time of the Second Temple, when the jubilee was observed only "nominally," it coincided with the seventh Sabbatical year. In post-exilic times the jubilee was entirely ignored, though the strict observance of the shemiṭṭah was steadily insisted upon. This, however, is only according to a rabbinical enactment (Tos. to Giṭ. 36a, *s.v.* "Bizeman"), as by the Mosaic law, according to R. Judah, shemiṭṭah is dependent on the jubilee and ceases to exist when there is no jubilee (Giṭ. *l.c.* and Rashi *ad loc.*).

That the Sabbatical year was observed during the existence of the Second Temple is evident from the history of the Maccabees (I Macc. vi. 51, 55). The Mishnah includes in the examination of witnesses questions as to dates, in giving which there must be specified the Sabbatical year, the year, month, week, day, and hour (Sanh. v. 1).

216

Palestinian Area of Shemiṭṭah.

The area of the Holy Land over which the shemiṭṭah was in force included in the time of the First Temple all the possessions of the Egyptian emigrants ("'Ole Miẓrayim"), which territory extended south to Gaza, east to the Euphrates, and north to the Lebanon Mountains. Ammon and Moab in the southeast were excluded. In the period of the Second Temple the area of the Babylon emigrants ("'Ole Babel"), headed by Ezra, was restricted to the territory west of the Jordan and northward as far as Acre (Acco). The Rabbis extended the shemiṭṭah to Syria, in order not to tempt settlers of the Holy Land to emigrate thither (Yad. iv. 3). The area of Palestine was divided into three parts, Judea, Galilee, and the transjordan districts, where shemiṭṭah existed in more or less rigorous observance (see Sheb. ix. and Yer. *ad loc.*).

The duration of the shemiṭṭah year was from autumn to autumn, beginning with New-Year's Day; but as a precaution against any infringement of the Law, the Rabbis extended the time and prohibited sowing and planting thirty days before Rosh ha-Shanah. Still later they prohibited the sowing of grain from Passover, and the planting of trees from Pentecost preceding the shemiṭṭah year, in order not to derive any benefit from the fruits bearing in that year (Sheb. i. 1, ii. 1). The extension of the time is known as "'ereb shebi'it" (= "preceding the seventh"). The penalty for non-observance of the shemiṭṭah year is exile; for eating the fruits of the seventh year (*i.e.*, of the sixth year's growth), pestilence (Abot v. 11, 12).

Rabbinical Extensions; Bankruptcy.

The rabbinical enactment extended the shemiṭṭat kesafim or money-release to countries other than the Holy Land, but confined the shemiṭṭat ḳarḳa'ot or land-release to Palestine within Ezra's boundary lines of occupation during the period of the Second Temple. The money-release was obviously independent of the Holy Land and was intended to free from his debts the poor in every land, and at a certain period of time. On the other hand, this bankruptcy law checked all business enterprises which the Jews were engaged in after they had largely abandoned agricultural pursuits. Hillel the Elder then amended the law by his institution of the Prosbul. In addition to this subterfuge, there are various exceptions which exclude the following debts from the operation of shemiṭṭah: wages, merchandise on credit, loans on pledges, a note guaranteed by mortgage, one turned over to the bet din for collection (according to the theory of the prosbul), and one which stipulates that the debtor waives the shemiṭṭah defense as regards this particular note (but he cannot waive the law in general; Sheb. xi.; Yer. *ad loc.*; Giṭ. 36a, b, 37a).

The shemiṭṭat kesafim was undoubtedly intended for the poor debtor, though the rich man also might take advantage of the general law. The Mishnah, however, plainly expresses the Rabbis' satisfaction with the debtor who does not make use of the shemiṭṭah in order to be relieved of his obligations (Sheb. x. 4). The Rabbis nevertheless desired that "the law of the shemiṭṭah shall not be forgotten" (Giṭ. 36b).

Implications of practicing "Shemittat kesafim" or money-release

As stated above you have two major types of Sabbaticals (Shemittahs), one for the land (agricultural) and one for money. The agricultural or land shemittah was only to be practiced in Palestine, however the money shemittah was applicable wherever the Jews lived. Still, there were many gimmicks used by the Jewish creditors to not even release fellow Jews from their debt obligations.

According to their religious practices, the Jews were **never** obligated to relieve the debt owed to them by **non-Jews**. And here is the potential for conflict in countries where there is a lot of money-lending by Jews to non-Jews. At the end of the seven year cycle what if non-Jews find out that the Jews release each other from debt obligations but not them? How would they feel and what might they do?

Pogrom (http://en.wikipedia.org/wiki/Pogrom)

A **pogrom** is a violent riot aimed at massacre or persecution of an ethnic or religious group, particularly one aimed at Jews. The term originally entered the English language to describe 19th- and 20th-century attacks on Jews in the Russian Empire (mostly within the Pale of Settlement in present day Ukraine and Belarus). Similar attacks against Jews at other times and places also became retrospectively known as pogroms. --

If these pogroms against the Jews are based on "who they are" instead of "what they do," then one would expect the incidence of persecution to be a random walk through time. However, if the persecutions happen periodically every seven years or so, then that persecution may be caused by the reaction of non-Jews to being treated differently when it comes to debt obligations. Keeping up with the Sabbatical and Jubilee years was the responsibility of the Rabbis. Their ruling on what year the Sabbatical Year falls is what their Jewish community would have to go by.

When the Jews were run out of one country, they found another home and set up camp. Over time they regrouped their wealth and began their "trade" of money-lending. Once the burden of debt on the general populace or the ruling class became too great, everybody sought some type of debt relief. Everybody did not have the Hebrew Bible and until recently, starting in 1382 with the Wycliffe Bible and later the King James Bible (1611), the common people did not have access to the Old Testament of the Bible. Therefore, only the elite or priests had access to the knowledge of the Sabbatical Year and its debt release obligations. This is why in many of the pogroms it was a member of one of the Christian priesthoods who started the pogrom.

As I stated earlier the Jews like to use their history of persecution to blackmail the rest of the world into feeling sorry for them and being afraid of criticizing them. Therefore, the Jews take great pride in keeping records of their persecutions. We will present this raw data of their persecutions starting in 224 AD to the present. A number of websites carry this same list of persecutions

219

including: www.simpletoremember.com and
www.whatreallyhappened.com. Other similar lists can be found on
www.eretzyisroel.org and
http://en.wikipedia.org/wiki/Timeline_of_antisemitism#cite_note-
11.

    In this analysis we use the list provided on
www.simpletoremember.com. The other lists are almost identical
to this one. This list is quite extensive covering 217 recorded
incidents over 1700 years, covering 27 countries and over 80 cities.
Many of the countries and towns experienced multiple attacks as
the Jews were allowed to come back, but were subsequently run
out again. Why?

Jewish Persecution

http://www.simpletoremember.com/articles/a/HistoryJewishPersecution/

DATE	PLACE	EVENT
224 C.E.	Italy	Forced Conversion
250 C.E.	Carthage	Expulsion
325 C.E.	Jerusalem	Expulsion
351 C.E	Persia	Book Burning
357 C.E.	Italy	Property Confiscation
379 C.E.	Milan	Synagogue Burning
415 C.E.	Alexandria	Expulsion
418 C.E.	Minorca	Forced Conversion
469 C.E.	Ipahan	Holocaust
489 C.E.	Antioch	Synagogue Burning
506 C.E.	Daphne	Synagogue Burning
519 C.E.	Ravenna	Synagogue Burning
554 C.E.	Diocese of Clement (France)	Expulsion
561 C.E.	Diocese of Uzes (France)	Expulsion
582 C.E	Merovingia	Forced Conversion
612 C.E.	Visigoth Spain	Expulsion
628 C.E.	Byzantium	Forced Conversion
629 C.E.	Merovingia	Forced Conversion

633 C.E.	Toledo	Forced Conversion
638 C.E.	Toledo	Stake Burnings
642 C.E.	Visigothic Empire	Expulsion
653 C.E.	Toledo	Expulsion
681 C.E.	Spain	Forced Conversion
693 C.E.	Toledo	Jews Enslaved
722 C.E.	Byzantium	Judaism Outlawed
855 C.E.	Italy	Expulsion
876 C.E.	Sens	Expulsion
897 C.E.	Narbonne	Land Confiscation
945 C.E.	Venice	Ban on Sea Travel
1009 C.E.	Orleans	Massacre
1012 C.E.	Rouen, Limoges & Rome	Massacre
1012 C.E.	Mayence	Expulsion
1021 C.E.	Rome	Jews Burned Alive
1063 C.E.	Spain	Massacre
1095 C.E.	Lorraine	Massacre
1096 C.E.	Northern France & Germany	1/3 of Jewish Population Massacred
1096 C.E.	Hungary	Massacre
1096 C.E.	Ralisbon	Massacre
1099 C.E.	Jerusalem	Jews Burned Alive
1100 C.E.	Kiev	Pogrom
1140 C.E.	Germany	Massacres
1146 C.E.	Rhine Valley	Massacre
1147 C.E.	Wurzburg	Massacre
1147 C.E.	Belitz (Germany)	Jews Burned Alive
1147 C.E.	Carenton, Ramenu & Sully (France)	Massacres
1171 C.E.	Blois	Stake Burnings
1181 C.E.	France	Expulsion
1181 C.E.	England	Property Confiscation
1188 C.E.	London & York	Mob Attacks
1190 C.E.	Norfolk	Jews Burned Alive
1191 C.E.	Bray (France)	Jews Burned Alive
1195 C.E.	France	Property Confiscation
1209 C.E.	Beziers	Massacre

1212 C.E.	Spain	Rioting and blood bath against the Jews of Toledo.
1215 C.E.	Rome	Lateran Council of Rome decrees that Jews must wear the "badge of shame" in all Christian countries. Jews are denied all public sector employment, and are burdened with extra taxes.
1215 C.E.	Toulouse (France)	Mass Arrests
1218 C.E.	England	Jews Forced to Wear Badges
1231 C.E.	Rome	Inquisition Established
1236 C.E.	France	Forced Conversion/Massacre
1239 C.E.	London	Massacre & Property Confiscation
1240 C.E.	Austria	Property confiscation. Jews either imprisoned, converted, expelled, or burned.
1240 C.E.	France	Talmud Confiscated
1240 C.E.	England	Book Burning
1240 C.E.	Spain	Forced Conversion
1242 C.E.	Paris	Talmud Burned
1244 C.E.	Oxford	Mob Attacks
1255 C.E.	England	Blood libel in Lincoln results in the burning / torture of many Jews & public hangings.
1261 C.E.	Canterbury	Mob Attacks
1262 C.E.	London	Mob Attacks
1264 C.E.	London	Mob Attacks
1264 C.E.	Germany	Council of Vienna declares that all Jews must wear a "pointed dunce cap." Thousands murdered.

1267 C.E.	Vienna	Jews Forced to Wear Horned Hats
1270 C.E.	Weissenberg, Magdeburg, Arnstadt, Coblenz, Singzig, and Erfurt	Jews Burned Alive
1270 C.E.	England	The libel of the "counterfeit coins" - all Jewish men, women and children in England imprisoned. Hundreds are hung.
1276 C.E.	Bavaria	Expulsion
1278 C.E.	Genoa (Spain)	Mob Attacks
1279 C.E.	Hungary & Poland	The Council of Offon denies Jews the right to all civic positions. The Jews of Hungary & Poland are forced to wear the "red badge of shame."
1283 C.E.	Mayence & Bacharach	Mob Attacks
1285 C.E.	Munich	Jews Burned Alive
1290 C.E.	England	King Edward I issues an edict banishing all Jews from England. Many drowned.
1291 C.E.	France	The Jewish refugees from England are promptly expelled from France.
1292 C.E.	Italy	Forced conversions & expulsion of the Italian Jewish community.
1298 C.E.	Germany	The libel of the "Desecrated Host" is perpetrated against the Jews of Germany. Approximately 150 Jewish communities undergo forced conversion.

1298 C.E.	Franconia, Bavaria & Austria	Reindfel's Decree is propagated against the Jews of Franconia and Bavarai. Riots against these Jewish communities, as well as those in Austria, result in the massacre of 100,000 Jews over a six-month period.
1306 C.E.	France	Expulsion
1308 C.E.	Strasbourg	Jews Burned Alive
1320 C.E.	Toulouse & Perpigon	120 Communities Massacred & Talmud Burned
1321 C.E.	Teruel	Public Executions
1328 C.E.	Estella	5,000 Jews Slaughtered
1348 C.E.	France & Spain	Jews Burned Alive
1348 C.E.	Switzerland	Expulsion
1349 C.E.	Worms, Strasbourg, Oppenheim, Mayence, Erfurt, Bavaria & Swabia	Jews Burned Alive
1349 C.E.	Heilbronn (Germany)	Expulsion
1349 C.E.	Hungary	Expulsion
1354 C.E.	Castile (Spain)	12,000 Jews Slaughtered
1368 C.E.	Toledo	8,000 Jews Slaughtered
1370 C.E.	Majorca., Penignon & Barcelona	Mob Attack
1377 C.E.	Huesca (Spain)	Jews Burned Alive
1380 C.E.	Paris	Mob Attack
1384 C.E.	Nordlingen	Mass Murder
1388 C.E.	Strasbourg	Expulsion
1389 C.E.	Prague	Mass Slaughter & Book Burning
1391 C.E.	Castille, Toledo, Madrid, Seville, Cordova, Cuenca & Barcelona	Forced Conversions & Mass Murder
1394 C.E.	Germany	Expulsion
1394 C.E.	France	Expulsion
1399 C.E.	Posen (Poland)	Jews Burned Alive

1400 C.E.	Prague	Stake Burnings
1407 C.E.	Cracow	Mob Attack
1415 C.E.	Rome	Talmud Confiscated
1422 C.E.	Austria	Jews Burned Alive
1422 C.E.	Austria	Expulsion
1424 C.E.	Fribourg & Zurich	Expulsion
1426 C.E.	Cologne	Expulsion
1431 C.E.	Southern Germany	Jews Burned Alive
1432 C.E.	Savory	Expulsion
1438 C.E.	Mainz	Expulsion
1439 C.E.	Augsburg	Expulsion
1449 C.E.	Toledo	Public Torture &. Burnings
1456 C.E.	Bavaria	Expulsion
1453 C.E.	Franconia	Expulsion
1453 C.E.	Breslau	Expulsion
1454 C.E.	Wurzburg	Expulsion
1463 C.E.	Cracow	Mob Attack
1473 C.E.	Andalusia	Mob Attack
1480 C.E.	Venice	Jews Burned Alive
1481 C.E.	Seville	Stake Burnings
1484 C.E.	Cuidad Real, Guadalupe, Saragossa & Teruel	Jews Burned Alive
1485 C.E.	Vincenza (Italy)	Expulsion
1486 C.E.	Toledo	Jews Burned Alive
1488 C.E.	Toledo	Stake Burnings
1490 C.E.	Toledo	Public Executions
1491 C.E.	Astorga	Public Torture & Execution
1492 C.E.	Spain	Expulsion
1495 C.E.	Lithuania	Expulsion
1497 C.E.	Portugal	Expulsion
1499 C.E.	Germany	Expulsion
1506 C.E.	Lisbon	Mob Attack
1510 C.E.	Berlin	Public Torture & Execution
1514 C.E.	Strasbourg	Expulsion

1519 C.E.	Regensburg	Expulsion
1539 C.E.	Cracow & Portugal	Stake Burnings
1540 C.E.	Naples	Expulsion
1542 C.E.	Bohemia	Expulsion
1550 C.E.	Genoa	Expulsion
1551 C.E.	Bavaria	Expulsion
1555 C.E.	Pesaro	Expulsion
1556 C.E.	Sokhachev (Poland)	Public Torture & Execution
1559 C.E.	Austria	Expulsion
1561 C.E.	Prague	Expulsion
1567 C.E.	Wurzburg	Expulsion
1569 C.E.	Papal States	Expulsion
1571 C.E.	Brandenburg	Expulsion
1582 C.E.	Netherlands	Expulsion
1593 C.E.	Brunswick	Expulsion
1597 C.E.	Cremona, Pavia & Lodi	Expulsion
1614 C.E.	Frankfort	Expulsion
1615 C.E.	Worms	Expulsion
1619 C.E.	Kiev	Expulsion
1635 C.E.	Vilna	Mob Attack
1637 C.E.	Cracow	Public Torture & Execution
1647 C.E.	Lisbon	Jews Burned Alive
1648 C.E.	Poland	1/3 of Jewry Slaughtered
1649 C.E.	Ukraine	Expulsion
1649 C.E.	Hamburg	Expulsion
1652 C.E.	Lisbon	Stake Burnings
1654 C.E.	Little Russia	Expulsion
1656 C.E.	Lithuania	Expulsion
1660 C.E.	Seville	Jews Burned Alive
1663 C.E	Cracow	Public Torture &. Execution
1664 C.E.	Lemberg	Mob Attack
1669 C.E.	Oran (North Africa)	Expulsion
1670 C.E.	Vienna	Expulsion
1671 C.E.	Minsk	Mob Attacks

1681 C.E.	Vilna	Mob Attacks
1682 C.E.	Cracow	Mob Attacks
1687 C.E.	Posen	Mob Attacks
1712 C.E.	Sandomir	Expulsion
1727 C.E.	Russia	Expulsion
1738 C.E.	Wurtemburg	Expulsion
1740 C.E.	Liule Russia	Expulsion
1744 C.E	Bohemia	Expulsion
1744 C.E.	Livonia	Expulsion
1745 C.E.	Moravia	Expulsion
1753 C.E.	Kovad (Lithuania)	Expulsion
1757 C.E.	Kamenetz	Talmud Burning
1761 C.E.	Bordeaux	Expulsion
1768 C.E.	Kiev	3,000 Jews Slaughtered
1772 C.E.	Russia	Expulsion
1775 C.E.	Warsaw	Expulsion
1789 C.E.	Alsace	Expulsion
1801 C.E.	Bucharest	Mob Attack
1804 C.E.	Russian Villages	Expulsion
1808 C.E.	Russian Countryside	Expulsion
1815 C.E.	Lubeck & Bremen	Expulsion
1820 C.E.	Bremes	Expulsion
1843 C.E.	Austria & Prussia	Expulsion
1850 C.E.	New York City	500 People, Led by Police, Attacked & Wrecked Jewish Synagogue
1862 C.E.	Area under General Grant's Jurisdiction in the United States	Expulsion
1866 C.E	Galatz (Romania)	Expulsion
1871 C.E.	Odena	Mob Attack
1887 C.E.	Slovakia	Mob Attacks
1897 C.E.	Kantakuzenka (Russia)	Mob Attacks
1898 C.E.	Rennes (France)	Mob Attack
1899 C.E.	Nicholayev	Mob Attack
1900 C.E.	Konitz (Prussia)	Mob Attack
1902 C.E.	Poland	Widespread Pogroms

1904 C.E.	Manchuria, Kiev & Volhynia	Widespread Pogroms
1905 C.E.	Zhitomir (Yolhynia)	Mob Attacks
1919 C.E	Bavaria	Expulsion
1915 C.E.	Georgia (U.S.A.)	Leo Frank Lynched
1919 C.E.	Prague	Wide Spread Pogroms
1920 C.E.	Munich & Breslau	Mob Attacks
1922 C.E.	Boston, MA	Lawrence Lowell, President of Harvard, calls for Quota Restrictions on Jewish Admission
1926 C.E.	Uzbekistan	Pogrom
1928 C.E.	Hungary	Widespread Anti-Semitic Riots on University Campuses
1929 C.E.	Lemberg (Poland)	Mob Attacks
1930 C.E.	Berlin	Mob Attack
1933 C.E.	Bucharest	Mob Attacks
1938-45 C.E.	Europe	Holocaust

Known persecutions due to money-lending:

*414 **Persecution**, such as occurred in Alexandria in **414** or the oppressive measures promulgated in the Byzantine Empire beginning with Constantine and intensified under Justinian, may have contributed to the fact that from the fifth century Jewish merchants followed their Greek and Syrian counterparts to Gaul and not only traded in luxury goods but also loaned money.

1096 C.E. The Rhineland communities were relatively wealthy, both due to their isolation, and because they were not restricted as Catholics were against moneylending. Many crusaders had to go into debt in order to purchase weaponry and equipment for the expedition; as Western Catholicism strictly forbade usury(unlike Orthodox Catholicism, which merely regulated it), many crusaders inevitably found themselves indebted to Jewish moneylenders...The crusaders rationalized the killing of Jews as an extension of their Catholic mission.

1181

Philip Augustus annuls all loans made by Jews to Christians and takes a percentage for himself. A year later, he confiscates all Jewish property and expels the Jews from Paris.

1190 March 16

500 Jews of York were massacred after a six day siege by departing Crusaders, backed by a number of people indebted to Jewish money-lenders.[11]

1290 July 18

Edict of Expulsion: Edward I expels all Jews from England, allowing them to take only what they could carry, all the other property became the Crown's. Official reason: continued practice of usury.

1498

Prince Alexander of Lithuania forces most of the Jews to forfeit their property or convert. The main motivation is to cancel the debts the nobles owe to the Jews. Within a short time trade ground to a halt and the Prince invites the Jews back in.

1593 February 25

Pope Clement VIII confirms the Papal bull of Paul III that expels Jews from Papal states except ghettos in Rome and Ancona and issues Caeca et obdurata ("Blind Obstinacy"): "All the world suffers from the usury of the Jews, their monopolies and deceit. ... Then as now Jews have to be reminded intermittently anew that they were enjoying rights in any country since they left Palestine and the Arabian desert, and subsequently their ethical and moral doctrines as well as their deeds rightly deserve to be exposed to criticism in whatever country they happen to live."

1619

Shah Abbasi of the Persian Sufi Dynasty increases persecution against the Jews, forcing many to outwardly practice Islam. Many keep practicing Judaism in secret.

Persecution Hypothesis

Our hypothesis simply stated is that the *"Jews are persecuted because they practiced debt forgiveness or money-release every seven years between Jews but not between non-Jews, and this discrimination in money-release caused Jews to be persecuted periodically in Europe."*

As we look at the data we notice that many of the occurrences happen in consecutive years, such as in 1146, 1147 and 1261, 1262. In a few years we had multiple incidents over a wide area such as in 1096, 1147, 1181 and 1240. These can be attributed to the same stimulation or one area hearing about what was going on in other places and deciding to follow their lead.

After we clean the data of these redundancies, we can search the data for possible signs of patterns over time. We first took a section of the data stretching from 1463 to 1519 which had a string of these persecutions. We put them in a "scatter plot" (see Graph 1), which is just graphing the points on a graph with the y-axis (vertical) representing the year and the x-axis (horizontal) representing its place in a sequence. For instance, point 2 on the x-axis corresponds to the year 1473 on the y-axis.

In graph 2 we try to fit a sine curve or "snake", as I call it, to the data. One can see that our sine curve hits a few points, but not all. However, if we stretch the "snake" out (Graph 3), we can get a good match. So there seems to be some pattern between the intervals.

Now let's look at the total data file of persecutions from 224 AD to 1938 AD given in Table 1. Since we are trying to determine if there is some underlying pattern to the intervals between persecutions, we first calculate the time intervals between each occurrence. For instance there is an interval of 26 years between 224 AD and 250 AD. We have intervals as large as 133 years and as short as 2 years. We need to do a little statistical analysis using some very simple tools as the average, the mode and the median as defined below:

Average=Sum/count; A calculated "central" value of a set of numbers.

Mode=The **mode** is the value that appears most often in a set of data.

Median =The *median* is the numerical value separating the higher half of a data sample, a population.

For our data the average interval is 15.03 years. The median is 9.5 years, but the mode is 7 years.

This is giving us a hint at what may lie beneath. Let us go back to the data which produced graphs 1,2 and 3 and place it in tabular form (Table 1). The intervals between these incidents of persecution vary from a minimum of 4 years to a maximum of 10 years over this 56 year period. The average interval is 7 years. Notice that "7 years" is the interval of the Sabbatical.

Now we stretch all of the data over this grid produced by the 7 year intervals. We start in year 225, then add 7 years to it, we get the next predicted persecution at 232. We continue this process until we have a grid stretching from 225 AD to 1940 AD (Table 2). Now we place the actual persecution years next to the closest predicted dates. The next step is to see how close our predicted dates match with actual dates. We do this by subtracting the actual date from the predicted, such as predicted 1898 minus actual 1897 equals 1. As we look at our table the "Predicted minus Actual Persecutions" (Pred-Act) figures are sometimes positive and sometimes negative and sometimes zero. "Zero" means we hit it on the dot. In fact over the 115 data points we hit the nail on the head 27 times and our median and mode deviations for the entire data set are both zero.

Now we take the absolute value of these differences or deviations so that we can find our average deviation of our predictive model. As we see from the "Summary Statistics" for Table 2, the average deviation is 1.313043 years which transforms to 479.26 days. In other words our model predicts each of these persecutions for 1700 years to within a little over a year, which is pretty good.

Now if we compute the intervals between consecutive

persecutions and compute the average, we come up with an average interval of 6.96875. The mode and median intervals are both exactly 7.

Graph 1: Scatter Plot
Persecutions 1463-1519

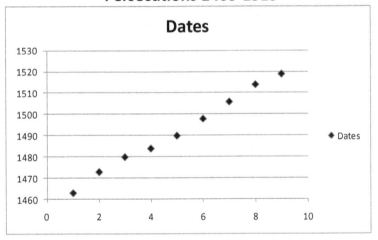

Graph 2: Fitting curve (snake)
Persecutions 1463-1519

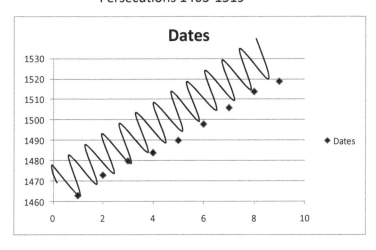

Graph 3: Stretching curve (snake) out
Persecutions 1463-1519

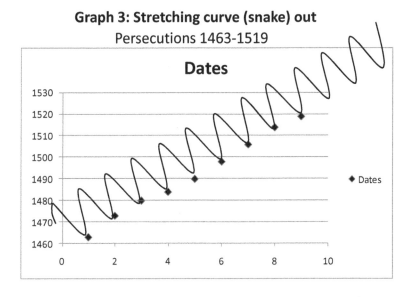

Table 1: Persecutions 1463-1519

Persecutions	Interval
1463	
1473	10
1480	7
1484	4
1490	6
1498	8
1506	8
1514	8
1519	5
Average	7

Table 2: Persecution of Jews

7 Years	Persecution	Pred-Act	ABS	Interval
225	224	1	1	
232				
239				
246				
253	250	3	3	
260				
267				
274				
281				
288				
295				
302				
309				
316				
323	325	-2	2	
330				
337				
344				
351	351	0	0	
358	357	1	1	6
365				
372				
379	379	0	0	
386				
393				
400				
407				
414	414	0	0	

7 Years	Persecution	Pred-Act	Abs	Interval
421				
428				
435				
442				
449				
456				
463				
470	469	1	1	
477				
484				
491	489	2	2	
498				
505	506	-1	1	
512				
519	519	0	0	
526				
533				
540				
547				
554	554	0	0	
561	561	0	0	7
568				
575				
582	582	0	0	
589				
596				
603				
610	612	-2	2	
617				
624				
631	629	2	2	
638	638	0	0	9

7 Years	Persecution	Pred-Act	Abs	Interval		7 Years	Persecution	Pred-Act	Abs	Interval
645						862				
652	653	-1	1			869				
659						876	876	0	0	
666						883				
673						890				
680	681	-1	1			897	897	0	0	
687						904				
694	693	1	1			911				
701						918				
708						925				
715						932				
722	722	0	0			939				
729						946	945	1	1	
736						953				
743						960				
750						967				
757						974				
764						981				
771						988				
778						995				
785						1002				
792						1009	1009	0	0	
799						1016				
806						1023	1021	2	2	
813						1030				
820						1037				
827						1044				
834						1051				
841										
848										
855	855	0	0							

Continued..

7 Years	Persecution	Pred-Act	Abs	Interval		7 Years	Persecution	Pred-Act	Abs	Interval
1058					Continued..	1268	1267	1	1	6
1065	1063	2	2			1275	1276	-1	1	9
1072						1282	1283	-1	1	7
1079						1289	1290	-1	1	7
1086						1296	1298	-2	2	8
1093	1096	-3	3			1303	1306	-3	3	8
1100	1099	1	1	3		1310	1308	2	2	2
1107						1317	1320	-3	3	12
1114						1324				
1121						1331	1328	3	3	
1128						1338				
1135						1345	1348	-3	3	
1142	1140	2	2			1352	1354	-2	2	6
1149	1147	2	2	7		1359				
1156						1366	1368	-2	2	
1163						1373	1377	-4	4	9
1170	1171	-1	1			1380	1380	0	0	3
1177						1387	1388	-1	1	8
1184	1181	3	3			1394				
1191	1190	1	1	9		1401	1399	2	2	
1198						1408	1407	1	1	8
1205	1209	-4	4			1415	1415	0	0	8
1212	1212	0	0	3		1422	1422	0	0	7
1219	1218	1	1	6		1429	1431	-2	2	9
1226						1436	1438	-2	2	7
1233	1231	2	2			1443				
1240	1239	1	1	8		1450	1449	1	1	
1247						1457				
1254	1255	-1	1			1464	1463	1	1	
1261	1261	0	0	6		1471	1473	-2	2	10

7 Years	Persecution	Pred-Act	Abs	Interval		7 Years	Persecution	Pred-Act	Abs	Interval
1478	1480	-2	2	7		1695				
1485	1484	1	1	4		1702				
1492	1490	2	2	6		1709	1712	-3	3	
1499	1498	1	1	8		1716				
1506	1506	0	0	8		1723				
1513	1514	-1	1	8		1730	1727	3	3	
1520	1519	1	1	5		1737	1738	-1	1	11
1527						1744	1744	0	0	6
1534						1751	1753	-2	2	9
1541	1539	2	2			1758	1757	1	1	4
1548	1550	-2	2	11		1765	1768	-3	3	11
1555	1555	0	0	5		1772	1772	0	0	4
1562	1561	1	1	6		1779				
1569	1567	2	2	6		1786	1789	-3	3	
1576						1793				
1583	1582	1	1			1800	1801	-1	1	
1590	1593	-3	3	11		1807	1808	-1	1	7
1597	1597	0	0	4		1814	1815	-1	1	7
1604						1821	1820	1	1	5
1611	1614	-3	3			1828				
1618	1619	-1	1	5		1835				
1625						1842	1843	-1	1	
1632	1635	-3	3			1849				
1639	1637	2	2	2		1856				
1646	1647	-1	1	10		1863	1862	1	1	
1653	1652	1	1	5		1870	1871	-1	1	9
1660	1660	0	0	8		1877				
1667	1669	-2	2	9		1884	1887	-3	3	
1674						1891				
1681	1681	0	0							
1688	1687	1	1	6						

Table 2 (continued) and Summary Statistics

7 Years	Persecution	Pred-Act	Abs	Interval
1898	1897	1	1	
1905	1904	1	1	7
1912	1915	-3	3	11
1919	1919	0	0	4
1926	1926	0	0	7
1933	1933	0	0	7
1940	1938	2	2	5
	sum dev	-21		
		avg dev	1.313043	
		days dev	479.2609	
	count	115	avg inter.	6.96875
	mode	0	mode	7
	median	0	median	7

We think we have found out why the "snake" has been persecuted over time. He carries his dirty **practice of money-lending** and **usury** with him **wherever** he goes. The mistake that he always makes is that he practices his "dirty religion" of financial discrimination in a manner that can be found out by the non-Jews. That is, the Jews practice debt forgiveness or money-release among themselves every 7 years, but do not forgive the debts of their non-Jewish neighbors and debtors. When they are found out, they are killed or run out of town. It is as simple as that.

So when Minister Farrakhan accuses the Jews of practicing a "dirty religion", the Jews and their defenders should check themselves and their sneaky ways before attacking The Minister. Now let's speculate a little over how some wise Jews might look at some of their brothers who try to practice their religion to the letter of the law, which when done in a careless manner can get every other Jew killed. Did the Jews who turned in other Jews to Hitler

239

do so to get rid of ignorant practitioners of their "dirty religion"? The wiser ones among them understood that they had to hide what they were doing from the general public and indeed found a stealthier way to use financial secrets which were originally taught to them or which they stole from other civilizations. The straight seven year Sabbatical was straightforward. However, it is complicated by the addition of the Jubilee year after 7 Sabbatical years. Oh, it gets fun from here on.(smile)

Chapter 7

Revealing the mathematical secret code of the Financial Raiders

The Decline of the dollar

Black people should look up and take notice that the financial crises that have gripped America since September 11, 2001, are indications that "the chickens have come home to roost" in the lofty heights of Wall Street. The Most Honorable Elijah Muhammad warned us of this day in an article originally published in the 1960s but reprinted in the *Final Call Newspaper* called "The Decline of the dollar":
http://www.finalcall.com/columns/hem/dollar_decline.htm

> "The stronghold of the American Government is falling to pieces. She has lost her prestige among the nations of the earth. One of the greatest powers of America was her dollar. The loss of such power will bring any nation to weakness, for this is the media of exchange between nations. The English pound and the American dollar have been the power and beckoning light of these two great powers. But when the world went off the gold and silver standard, the financial doom of England and America was sealed.

> The pound has lost 50 per cent of its value. America's dollar has lost everything now as power backing for her currency, which was once backed by gold for every $5.00

note and up. All of her currency was backed by silver from a $1.00 note and up.

Today, the currency of America is not backed by any sound value, silver or gold. The note today is something that the government declares it will give you the value in return but does not name that value. They definitely are not backing their currency with silver or gold.

This is the number one fall, and it is very clear that the loss of the power of the American dollar means the loss of the financial power of America. What will happen, since there is no sound backing for her notes, we do not know.

What should we expect even in the next 12 months under the fall of the power of America's dollar? This means that we have 100 per cent inflation. What could happen under 100 per cent inflation? Your guess is as good as mine. The power of gold and silver was once abundant in America. But the touch of the finger of God against the power of so mighty a nation has now caused the crumbling and fall of America.

We can easily and truthfully liken the fall of America to the prophetic symbolic picture given in the (Bible) Revelation of John (18:2). The name Babylon used there does not really say whether it is ancient Babylon or a picture of some future Babylon.

The description it gives is as follows: "And he [angel] cried mightily with a strong voice [with authority] saying, Babylon the great is fallen, is fallen and is become the habitation of devils [Allah has declared the people to be a race of devils], and the hole of every foul spirit and a cage of every unclean and hateful bird." The description here given to the Babylon by the Prophets compares with the present history and people of America and their fall."

Over the last few decades we have witnessed all the warnings of The Messenger to come true. What does it mean when a man of God predicts exactly what is to come before it happens? Black people in America have been warned to "Come out of her, my people." The Most Honorable Elijah Muhammad, like the Moses of the Bible, admonished our people to separate, but instead we chose to integrate with what now is turning out to be a "burning house."

The Honorable Minister Louis Farrakhan has given us our last chance to set up an "economic Ark" which will save us from "The Fall of America." Black people may not feel that we are smart enough to handle money, build an economy and feed ourselves. We may look up to white people and especially the Jews as the "gods" of business and economics. We may feel that we could never compete with them and should just continue to beg them for jobs and "keep hope alive."

However, what if the Jews' great wealth and economic achievement was the result of a trick, a hidden mathematical code, which told them when to invest and when to divest? We are going to show you these financial raiders' "code" in this book, Allah willing. But first let us show you what wise white scientists of economics are saying about the impending crash, panic and depression soon to hit America.

Predictions of next "Great Depression"

The Messenger warned us of America's fall when America was flying high in the 1960s, but now chickens are just about ready to come home to roost at the other end of another cycle. Financial pundits are making predictions of **when, not if** America will have another financial crisis that may lead to a "25 year depression".

An article published on www.sodahead.com quotes Jim Richards, the CIA's Financial Threat and Asymmetric Warfare Advisor on his predictions of a $100 trillion meltdown:

"Everybody knows we have a dangerous level of debt. Everybody knows the Fed has recklessly printed trillions of dollars. These are secrets to no one," he said. "But all signs are now flashing bright red that our chickens are about to come home to roost."

Richards is not the only "expert" who is predicting this crash. Andrew Henderson published an article on April 13, 2014 called "Top US dollar collapse predictions":

Top 5: US dollar collapse predictions

The US dollar is in bad shape. Having lost 97% of its purchasing power of one hundred years [ago], it's easy to argue that the dollar has suffered a slow but steady collapse.

And many financial experts claim this is the beginning. In an era when central banks are printing money to infinity and racking up debts like never before, something has to give. For those in the know, the question isn't if the dollar will collapse… but rather, when.
As the United States plays a less and less significant role in the world economy and countries like Russia and China threaten to replace the dollar as the global reserve currency, here are five of the most chilling predictions about the future of the dollar.

5. Harvard economist starts a "bank run" over dollar collapse fears
Classical economist and Harvard professor Terry Burnham

244

told the world that he was withdrawing $1 million from his Bank of America checking account because of the negative consequences Ben Bernanke and Janet Yellen have had on the US dollar, and trying to start a bank run by getting others to do the same.

He claimed a dollar collapse is also underway because the Fed's manipulations had two adverse effects on the currency: decreasing overall wealth by distorting markets, and redistributing wealth from unsophisticated investors to the political elite through the currency.

Burnham said he couldn't stand getting paid zero interest by Bank of America anymore, and didn't trust them to keep his money safe. At zero interest, he was losing tens of thousands of dollars in purchasing power every year due to inflation, while his well-connected bank benefitted.

4. The US dollar collapse will be worse than the situation in Spain or Greece

Billionaire Donald Trump says the dollar is on the edge of economic ruin, and an economic collapse is the only remedy. He painted an ugly picture of the US economy during an appearance on Fox News. In fact, he issued a warning to Americans to prepare for "financial ruin".

Trump claims the United States is no longer a rich country, because rich countries don't borrow money. In the interview, Trump claimed that the US is becoming a third world nation forced to borrow money and issue debt.

Trump also suggested an answer to the question "When will the us dollar collapse?", saying when US debt hits the $21 to $22 trillion mark, things will get much, much worse.

3. Even the US government will stop using the dollar

Jeff Berwick, editor of The Dollar Vigilante, predicts that things will get so bad that even the American government will view their own dollar as toxic waste. He says the average American is in "la la land" obsessing over TV shows or the next Presidential race. He says what just happened in Ukraine could easily happen in the United States.

245

And while Ukraine saw their currency crisis coming for some time, the US dollar collapse could happen overnight, he says. Berwick says the US is "turning a corner" and headed for total financial ruin as early as "this year", and quotes Jim Rogers who says "there is no paper money in 2014 and 2015 that's going to be worth much of anything." Berwick often predicts the "end of the monetary system as we know it" and claims that, once all of the capital controls have been implemented and the US government starts confiscating assets to pay creditors like China, it will not even accept the tainted US dollar.

2. Federal Reserve insolvency will cause a 90% drop in the dollar
Financial expert and author of _Currency Wars_ Jim Richards believes the "international monetary system is headed for a collapse." Richards sets the record straight on what an "economic collapse" is, saying it doesn't mean we all go live in caves. In fact, he says, we've seen three economic collapses in the last one hundred years.
In his new book, Richards suggests the dollar will see the worst of the next economic collapse as part of the "death of money," lamenting that "we are on a global dollar standard". He says a fiat currency standard can work but only if countries inject confidence into the system and welcome business with open arms. Of course, neither of those is true in the United States.
Among Richards' chief reasons for predicting a dollar collapse: quantitative easing, a "lousy business environment", high taxes, and low growth. He says that dollar-euro swaps from the Fed will make the next collapse much bigger than the last one.

1. Russia will ban the US dollar
Russian legislator Mikhail Degtyarev has likened the US dollar to a "worldwide Ponzi scheme" "… one he has claimed will end with the collapse of the dollar in 2017. He submitted a bill to protect Russians against the "collapsing

US debt pyramid", saying growing rates of US debt would cause a US dollar collapse if spending isn't remedied. Degtyarev's bill would ban US dollars from circulating in Russia and forbid private citizens from holding Russian bank accounts in US dollars. Those with dollar-denominated accounts would have to convert their accounts to other foreign currencies (his bill would not ban the euro, pound, yen, or renmibi). However, Degtyarev has proposed some wacky bills before, such as offering "menstruation leave" for women in the workplace.

While the bill acknowledges the weakness of the dollar, it's also rather authoritarian: anyone caught holding dollars would have them seized and reimbursed in rubles… thirty days later. However, the bill would not forbid Russians from holding offshore bank accounts denominated in dollars or buying goods priced in dollars online. And, like any good law, the government would be exempt.

These are not all the players in this prediction game. For instance, Jonathan Cahn predicts in his book, *The Harbinger,* that the next big crash will be on September 17, 2015. He uses the Shemittah cycle of exactly 7 years added to September 17, 2008 for his prediction code. He is close but not close enough as we will show later.

Trying to explain business cycles led to the development of the field of macroeconomics. Economic researchers have come up with a number of models to explain these apparent cycles.

Wikipedia gives a good overall explanation of what a "business cycle" is and how the concept has developed over time:

http://en.wikipedia.org/wiki/Business_cycle

Business Cycle (Boom-Bust Cycle)

The term **business cycle** (or **economic cycle** or **boom–bust cycle**) refers to fluctuations in aggregate production, trade and activity over several months or years in a market economy.

The business cycle is the upward and downward movements of levels of gross domestic product (GDP) and refers to the period of expansions and contractions in the level of economic activities (business fluctuations) around its long-term growth trend.

These fluctuations occur around a long-term growth trend, and typically involve shifts over time between periods of relatively rapid economic growth (an expansion or boom), and periods of relative stagnation or decline (a contraction or recession).

Business cycles are usually measured by considering the growth rate of real gross domestic product. Despite being termed cycles, these fluctuations in economic activity can prove unpredictable.

In 1860 French economist Clement Juglar first identified economic cycles 7 to 11 years long, although he cautiously did not claim any rigid regularity. Later, economist Joseph Schumpeter (1883–1950) argued that a Juglar Cycle has four stages:

1. expansion (increase in production and prices, low interest-rates)
2. crisis (stock exchanges crash and multiple bankruptcies of firms occur)
3. recession (drops in prices and in output, high interest-rates)
4. recovery (stocks recover because of the fall in prices and incomes)

Schumpeter's Juglar model associates recovery and prosperity with increases in productivity, consumer confidence, aggregate demand, and prices.

In the mid-20th century, Schumpeter and others proposed a typology of business cycles according to their periodicity, so that a number of particular cycles were named after their discoverers or proposers:[8]

- the Kitchin inventory cycle of 3 to 5 years (after Joseph Kitchin);
- the Juglar fixed-investment cycle of 7 to 11 years (often identified[as "the" business cycle)
- the Kuznets infrastructural investment cycle of 15 to 25 years (after Simon Kuznets – also called "building cycle")
- the Kondratiev wave or long technological cycle of 45 to 60 years (after the Soviet economist Nikolai Kondratiev).

Interest in the different typologies of cycles has waned since the development of modern macroeconomics, which gives little support to the idea of regular periodic cycles

In 1946, economists Arthur F. Burns and Wesley C. Mitchell provided the now standard definition of business cycles in their book *Measuring Business Cycles*:

Business cycles are a type of fluctuation found in the aggregate economic activity of nations that organize their work mainly in business enterprises: a cycle consists of expansions occurring at about the same time in many economic activities, followed by similarly general recessions, contractions, and revivals which merge into the expansion phase of the next cycle; in duration, business cycles vary from more than one year to ten or twelve years; they are not divisible into shorter cycles of similar characteristics with amplitudes approximating their own.

According to A. F. Burns:

Business cycles are not merely fluctuations in aggregate economic activity. The critical feature that distinguishes them from the commercial convulsions of earlier centuries or from the seasonal and other short term variations of our own age is that the fluctuations are **widely diffused over the economy** – its industry, its commercial dealings, and its tangles of finance. The economy of the western world is a system of closely interrelated parts. He who would understand business cycles must master the workings of an economic system organized largely in a network of free enterprises searching for profit. The problem of how business cycles come about is therefore inseparable from the problem of how a capitalist economy functions.

This article gives a good overview. However I do not agree with the statement: *"Interest in the different typologies of cycles has waned since the development of modern macroeconomics, which gives little support to the idea of regular periodic cycles."* Professional macroeconomists do not want the people to understand and learn how these "regular periodic cycles" work because they would be out of a job, plus they would not have a leg up on the investment outsiders as they used insider information to fleece the flock and raid the stock.

Everything that is living has some type of cycle. You breathe rhythmically. The earth has a cycle of spring, summer, fall and winter. Animals have a gestation period. Plants have a life cycle. The rhythms of a culture can turn into economic cycles. In countries that celebrate Christmas retail sales leading up to December 25 are predictable and needed to insure the profitability of the whole year.

The five day work week with the two day weekend produces a social and economic rhythm or cycle in a community and country. We take it for granted that a week has always been seven days, but this is not so. The Ancient Egyptian year consisted of a week of 10 days and 3 weeks in a 30 day month. The Egyptians had on their calendar "good and bad" days on which to carry out various tasks. There would definitely be a clash of civilizations when people who operate on a 10 day week have to do business with a society based on a 7 day week. Imagine a person who practiced a 10 day week trying to understand the activities of a person who worked 5 days and rested from work the next 2 days. Now imagine a people who did their investments and divestments using a secret code or interval. They would be the ultimate insider traders, raiding people's wealth with a code. This is one of the major ways that Jews got so rich, along with usury.

Instead of our economic teachers and leaders making economics and business easy to understand, they go out of their way to confuse the people. Take former Chairman of the Federal Reserve, Alan Greenspan. Let us take a few of his quotes published on http://www.brainyquote.com/quotes/authors/a/alan_greenspan.html# 6VMroqV7xcdSbV85.99

"I believe that the general growth in large [financial] institutions have occurred in the context of an underlying structure of markets in which many of the larger risks are dramatically -- I should say, fully -- hedged." -- 2000

"Indeed, recent research within the Federal Reserve suggests that many homeowners might have saved tens of thousands of dollars had they held adjustable-rate mortgages rather than fixed-rate mortgages during the past decade, though this would not have been the case, of course, had interest rates trended sharply upward." -- February 2004

"Improvements in lending practices driven by information technology have enabled lenders to reach out to households with previously unrecognized borrowing capacities." -- October 2004

Even though some down payments are borrowed, it would take a large, and historically most unusual, fall in home prices to wipe out a significant part of home equity. Many of those who purchased their residence more than a year ago have equity buffers in their homes adequate to withstand any price decline other than a very deep one." -- October 2004

"The use of a growing array of derivatives and the related

application of more-sophisticated approaches to measuring and managing risk are key factors underpinning the greater resilience of our largest financial institutions .... Derivatives have permitted the unbundling of financial risks." -- May 2005

And in case you didn't quite get it yet, here are my two favorites:

> *"I know you think you understand what you thought I said but I'm not sure you realize that what you heard is not what I meant."* (http://www.goodreads.com/quotes/204034-i-know-you-think-you-understand-what-you-thought)

> *"I guess I should warn you, if I turn out to be particularly clear, you've probably misunderstood what I've said."* (http://www.brainyquote.com/quotes/quotes/a/alangreens169 876.html)

Alan Greenspan has a B.S., M.A. and PhD in economics, was head of the Federal Reserve but inspired William A. Fleckenstein to write a book about his years at the Federal Reserve entitled: *Greenspan's Bubbles: The Age of Ignorance at the Federal Reserve (2008)*. Now this author would have us to believe that Greenspan did not know what he was doing when he engineered bubbles and busts during his tenure at the Federal Reserve from 1987 to 2006. He quit just before the housing bubble burst in 2007 which led to the financial crisis of 2008. Just to show you how sneaky he was, let me quote an article from http://en.wikipedia.org/wiki/Alan_Greenspan :

> "In 1977, Greenspan obtained a PhD degree in economics from New York University. His dissertation is not available from the university since it was removed at Greenspan's request in 1987, when he became Chairman of the Federal Reserve Board. However, in April 2008, *Barron's* obtained a copy, and notes that it includes "a discussion of soaring

252

housing prices and their effect on consumer spending; it even anticipates a bursting housing bubble".

Fleckenstein used the run up to the "Dot-Com Bubble" as a perfect example of how central bankers like Greenspan at the Federal Reserve feed bubbles by "printing money" or at the least **lowering interest rates** to allow speculators to borrow cheap money to buy stocks in anticipation of making a "killing" on the stock market. The increased money supply allows more speculators, small and large, to buy more stock on the open market which drives the prices of stocks even higher. This all comes to a screeching halt one day after the central bank **increases interest rates** which forces **stock liquidations** held by **speculators** who bought stock on **borrowed money**. Greenspan and others claim that nobody knows when that day of reckoning will occur, but this
is not true, insiders do.

What time is it?

Below is a letter which I wrote to the Honorable Minister Louis Farrakhan on September 9, 2012. In it I basically describe how I came up with the Jews' secret code. After this letter I did further analysis and went further back in time to check my theory. We are now approaching the climax and our people need to know who the Honorable Minister Louis Farrakhan is and then act accordingly:

In the name of Allah, The Beneficent, The Merciful, I bear witness that there is no God but Allah and that Muhammad is His Messenger

As Salaam-Alaikum

MEMORANDUM

TO: Minister Louis Farrakhan, National Representative of the
Honorable Elijah Muhammad

FROM: Bro. Dr. Ridgely A. Mu'min Muhammad

DATE: September 9, 2012

RE: What time is it?

May Allah continue to bless you with increased health and strength.

At the end of Saviours' Day 2012 I was blessed to attend the after dinner table talk discussion hosted by you at the Palace. In your discussion you asked your student ministers to comment on the issue of what time did they think that we were living in. At that time I had not attempted the analysis which I am presenting now.

I began this line of analysis when President Obama seemed to approve gay marriages in May of this year which was reported in the New York Times on May 9 and featured on the May 21 cover of Newsweek portraying Obama as "The First Gay President". At the same time I was working on an article defending your Sacramento statements on gay marriage which I called "Homosexual Behavior as Population Control." Of course if everyone became homosexuals that would cause the "desolation" of the human species. This led me to look at Daniel 12:11-13:

"11 And from the time that the daily sacrifice shall be taken away, and the abomination that maketh desolate set up, there shall be a thousand two hundred and ninety days.

12 Blessed is he that waiteth, and cometh to the thousand three hundred and five and thirty days.

13 But go thou thy way till the end be; for thou shalt rest, and stand in thy lot at the end of days."

In trying to research the meaning of the "end of days" and what the "abomination" meant, I found that there were many attempts at interpretation of the 1290 and 1335 days. Some scholars tried to turn the days into years. Some scholars wondered about the 45 day difference between the two counts of days. Other scholars tried to reconcile these numbers with the 1260 days or 42 months mentioned in Revelations 12:6. I noticed that the difference between 1290 and 1260 is 30 while the difference between 1335 and 1260 is 75. I noticed that from the time that Obama was elected on November 4, 2008 until the time that he was inaugurated on January 20, 2009 was almost 75 or to be exact 77 days later.

I thought; "Could these events be a clue as to the time that we are living in?" Could the ceasing of the "daily sacrifice" be his election? However, according to what I have been able to glean from my research, the "daily sacrifice" of *one lamb* in the morning and *one lamb* in the evening must take place in the Jewish temple in Jerusalem. This practice supposedly ended with the destruction of the Temple in Jerusalem in 70 AD. Now Biblical scholars argue that the site of Solomon's Temple is now the site of the Muslim's Mosque (Dome of the Rock) where Prophet Muhammad was carried in a night vision. Therefore, some argue that until the Jews take that spot, they cannot resume the "daily sacrifice."

I think that the "daily sacrifice" was instituted not to

remember the Exodus from Egypt, which never happened, but to await the Messiah and to remember their plans to sacrifice him when he shows up at the end of the 6,000 years. When he arrives then the waiting and symbolic sacrificing can stop. We know that it was powerful Jews that "selected" Obama to be president. Maybe they have planned to sacrifice him and use his death as an excuse to get at the real Messiah. His death would be blamed on the Muslims. However, you, Brother Minister have thus far foiled their plans, in my opinion. It seems that they looked at how you dealt with Malcolm when he betrayed The Messenger; how you said words that helped to produce an atmosphere that the enemy could use to get rid of "two birds with one stone" or sacrificing two lambs in one day. You made it very clear to us on a recent Tuesday night Believers' meeting that you will not fall for that "small time stuff." When they killed your brother Khadafy, they just knew that you would jump. To their dismay you did not take the bait. Now they have to go back to the drawing board. They have bet a lot on this Obama scheme, so I think they may be stuck with this hand to play in this divine game for the lives of our people and the future of the world.

I also believe that they somehow will raise the assassination of Malcolm back up again to remind Black people how "Muslims" killed their Black "Prince" or "messiah", making us appear as an enemy to our people. Now that Obama has been molded in the image of the "Messiah", they would love to sacrifice him and turn our people and the world against us. If President Obama is not re-elected, then my ideas may just be wild speculations. This is why I feel no need to make them public. But I did have a dream last week that forced me to get up and start writing this letter to you.

256

Even if I am not correct about the 2008 election of President Obama representing the ending of the "daily sacrifice", the underlying math that this analysis brings out is interesting. In Daniel 12:11 we are told "And from the time that the daily sacrifice shall be taken away, and the abomination that maketh desolate set up, there shall be a thousand two hundred and ninety days." So what is 1290 days from November 4, 2008? Thanks to the date function on my Excel spreadsheet, the answer is May 17, 2012.

Now on May 9th and again on May 21st of 2012 this issue of gay marriage pops up with our president. Obama becomes the first president to sanction "gay marriage" which by some may be seen as an "abomination". Marriage is different from "civil union" because now you bring the church and God into the picture to accept what God condemns.

So now when you add the other part of the "days" as described in Daniel 12:12, you have 1335 plus May 17, 2012, you come to Tuesday, January 12, 2016. I found this number 1290+1335 or 2625 a very interesting number when we look at the calendar and events over the last 200 or so years. This number 2625 represents 7.19 years based on our calendar. And 2625 is a multiple of 7 (7x375=2625). The number of 7 is very important within this 6,000 year dispensation of the white race. Moses told them to remember the Sabbath day and keep it holy, because on the 7th day God supposedly rested from the process of creation. The "Sabbath day" is not Friday, Saturday or Sunday, but the 7th day of the week which does not stay constant from month to month or year to year with our calendar. For instance, the first day of the first month of the year may fall on a Tuesday as in 2002 or a Wednesday as in 2003. The importance of these shifts and the Jews compensating for these shifts will be discussed below.

In Leviticus 25:2 God commands the children of Israel "When ye come into the land which I give you, then shall the land keep a Sabbath unto the lord." This meant that the land would be left fallow on the 7th year of a series. Seven of these seven year cycles would end in a "Jubilee" as described in Lev. 25:8-10;

"8 And thou shalt number seven Sabbaths of years unto thee, seven times seven years; and the space of the seven Sabbaths of years shall be unto thee forty and nine years.

9 Then shalt thou cause the trumpet of the jubilee to sound on the tenth day of the seventh month, in the day of atonement shall ye make the trumpet sound throughout all your land,

10 And ye shall hallow the fiftieth year, and proclaim liberty throughout all the land unto the all the inhabitants thereof; it shall be a jubilee unto you; and ye shall return every man unto his possession, and ye shall return every man unto his family."

Many Bible scholars argue on the seeming contradiction of the "jubilee" being in the 50th year instead of the 49th year which is 7 times 7. Suppose that the 7 years is not our 7 times 365.25 days which would give us 2556.75 days, but instead the 2625 days as described in Daniel. 7 times 2625 days equals 18,375 days or 50.31 years. And because these 2625 days is a multiple of 7, every time you add another cycle of 2625 days, you will always end up on the same day of the week. This may be why the "jubilee" is celebrated in the 50th year instead of the 49th year to put things back in line with the underlying hidden cycle of 7.19 years which is more than the more obvious cycle of an even 7 years.

This number (2625 days) is so special that it also ensures that you line up the calendar that we use, the Gregorian calendar that even adds another year [day] every 4 years. For instance if you subtract 2625 days from Tuesday, November 4, 2008 you get Tuesday, August 28, 2001. Now this was so close to September 11, 2001 that I decided to play with intervals of 2625 centered on 9/11/01.

The table below is the result of these calculations along with some important events associated with these dates, all on a Tuesday. I have specific dates for such events as "9/11" and "Black Tuesday". These dates fall exactly as multiples of 2625 days. The other events highlighted are mostly within the same year as our calculations. Therefore, I do not have a perfect fit for all these important economic dates. However, if I were a betting man and had the type of capital to play with, i.e. be a wealthy Jew, I would be tempted to position myself to capitalize on something happening around January 26, 2016. For it seems that the Jews interpret this "jubilee" not with giving back, but with taking back from their Gentile sheep whatever wealth they could accumulate before the shearing: minor shearing/fleecing every 7.19 years and major shearing/fleecing every 50.31 years.

I want to point out that this date, January 26, 2016, is the next end of my hypothesized 7.19 cycle or "end of days" and could signal when the Jews plan to fulfill their last big move against the Nation of Islam. Whether I am correct or not, I thank Allah for you, because you have proven to the world that you know what to do RIGHT ON TIME guided by Allah and His Christ.

The Holy Qur'an states in Surah 41:29:

"And those who disbelieve will say: Our Lord, show us those who led us astray from among the jinn and the men that we may trample them under our feet, so that they may be the lowest."

I wonder how the white Gentiles may respond; if it is proven that their white Jewish brothers have been fleecing them on a regular basis using this hidden time interval of 2625 days? At any rate, I thank Allah for you and your understanding of the TIME and what MUST be DONE.

Thank you for taking the time to read this letter.

Peace, Bro Ridgely (Doc)

Cycles of

2625 days

25	Tuesday, January 26, 2016	
24	Tuesday, November 18, 2008	Bank Bailout (11/12/08)
23	Tuesday, September 11, 2001	WTC 911 (9/11/01)
22	Tuesday, July 05, 1994	
21	Tuesday, April 28, 1987	"Black Monday (10/19/87)
20	Tuesday, February 19, 1980	
19	Tuesday, December 12, 1972	
18	Tuesday, October 05, 1965	

17	Tuesday, July 29, 1958	
16	Tuesday, May 22, 1951	
15	Tuesday, March 14, 1944	
14	Tuesday, January 05, 1937	
13	Tuesday, October 29, 1929	Black Tuesday" (10/29/29)
12	Tuesday, August 22, 1922	
11	Tuesday, June 15, 1915	
10	Tuesday, April 07, 1908	
9	Tuesday, January 29, 1901	Panic of 1901 (5/21/01)
8	Tuesday, November 21, 1893	Panic of 1893
7	Tuesday, September 14, 1886	
6	Tuesday, July 08, 1879	
5	Tuesday, April 30, 1872	Panic of 1873
4	Tuesday, February 21, 1865	
3	Tuesday, December 15, 1857	Panic of 1857
2	Tuesday, October 8, 1850	
1	Tuesday, August 1, 1843	
0	Tuesday, May 24, 1836	Panic of 1837

As you see from my table of cycles, the next rung on this

ladder is January 26, 2016. I find it interesting that Jonathan Cahn predicted the next big stock market crash for September of 2015, while Russian legislator Mikhail Degtyarev predicts that the U.S. dollar will "collapse" in 2017.

When I wrote the above letter in 2012, I was not aware that the Feds had started a process they call "quantitative easing" or simply flooding the market with money not backed by anything. Again from Wikipedia:

http://en.wikipedia.org/wiki/Quantitative_easing

> A third round of quantitative easing, "QE3", was announced on 13 September 2012. In an 11–1 vote, the Federal Reserve decided to launch a new $40 billion per month, open-ended bond purchasing program of agency mortgage-backed securities. Additionally, the Federal Open Market Committee (FOMC) announced that it would likely maintain the federal funds rate near zero "at least through 2015." According to NASDAQ.com, this is effectively a stimulus program that allows the Federal Reserve to relieve $40 billion per month of commercial housing market debt risk. Because of its open-ended nature, QE3 has earned the popular nickname of "QE-Infinity." On 12 December 2012, the FOMC announced an increase in the amount of open-ended purchases from $40 billion to $85 billion per month.

Notice that "QE-Infinity" started on September 13, 2012 and zero interest rates will persist until "at least through 2015". So the bubble begins to be inflated with cheap money in 2012, only to see the pin stuck in at the end of 2015; which makes January 26, 2016 a very interesting date indeed.

Trailing the "Great Snake"

On May 21, 2014 the 9/11 Memorial at "ground zero"

officially opened to the public. This "Memorial" will forever remind the public of those horrible moments that happened on September 11, 2001 and cement in future minds the official conspiracy theory that 19 Arab hijackers flew airplanes into the World Trade Center buildings 1 and 2 which caused the total collapse of those buildings killing 2,749 people. A few hours after the first skyscraper was hit TV cameras were focused on these buildings giving the world an opportunity to see them collapse in real time. The whole world saw this at once and according to scientific analysis, the shock of this horrendous event was felt by our planet itself. According to http://www.glcoherence.org/monitoring-system/about-system.html, "...two National Oceanic and Atmospheric Administration (NOAA) space weather satellites monitoring the earth's geomagnetic field also displayed a significant spike at the time of the September 11th attack ...indicating the stress wave possibly caused by mass human emotion created modulations in the geomagnetic field."

Thanks to "9/11" we all saw "...*fire come down out of heaven to the earth in the presence of men*" and we were all deceived by the official explanation for the collapse of those buildings as was prophesied in Revelations 13:13-14. The U.S. government claims that we were attacked by terrorists who were trying to take away our freedoms. Well our freedoms were indeed taken away due to the government's reaction to "9/11": 1. We are under constant surveillance, 2. We are strip-searched at the airports and 3. All Muslims are suspected terrorists and enemies of the state.

Black people and Muslims not under the Teachings of Nation of Islam do not understand white people and therefore could never understand how white people felt on October 16, 1995 when almost 2 million black men who were 95% Christians showed up on a Monday in front of the U.S. Capitol shouting "Allah-u-Akbar" lead by Minister Louis Farrakhan at the historic Million Man March. Black people and the world saw the most spectacular outpouring of

263

love and brotherhood, while Whites saw a threat and a potential army. In 1995 Black Muslims earned the title of peacemakers, but after the Satanic magic which was "9/11", all Muslims since 2001 are perceived as the enemies of God and the American way of life.

The American people and the world were manipulated by master deceivers such as Edward L. Bernays (The father of spin) who boasts: *"Those who manipulate the unseen mechanism of society constitute an invisible government which is the true ruling power of our country. We are governed, our minds molded, our tastes formed, our ideas suggested largely by men we have never heard of. In almost every act of our lives whether in the sphere of politics or business, in our social conduct or our ethical thinking, we are dominated by the relatively small number of persons who understand the mental processes and social patterns of the masses. It is they who pull the wires that control the public mind."* (Bernays 2004: 37)

Dr. Larry Burk in his 2006 article "**Mass Hypnosis on 9/11: Waking up from the Trance"** describes what he saw as a step by step method of hypnosis used to enslave the thinking of the masses: (http://nc911truth.blogspot.com/2006/07/mass-hypnosis-on-911-waking-up-from.html)

"**1)** Prior to 9/11 slightly less than half the country had willingly voted for Bush in 2000, and the rest of us had been programmed since childhood that Americans are the good guys through seemingly innocent games such as Cowboys and Indians.

2) When the first plane hit WTC 1, everyone turned on their TV's, and paid rapt attention; staring at the smoking hole just like watching a pendulum.

3) Rapid induction of mass trance occurred from the sudden shock of watching the 2nd plane hit WTC 2 live on

TV generating an immediate altered state of consciousness throughout the country.

4) Trance deepening is often done by having the subject walk down a flight of stairs in their mind, so on 9/11 there were repeated news reports of people running down the steps in the towers, followed by the actual towers coming down over and over again on TV.

5) Hypnotic suggestions were given on TV all afternoon designed to create the desired unconscious programming; in this case fear, by news reports of scary terrorists and stories of heroic passengers fighting hijackers.

6) Testing the depth of trance is usually done with a pin to check numbness of the skin, but on 9/11 it was done with the collapse of smoldering 47-story WTC 7, going largely unnoticed despite the fact that no steel-framed towering inferno skyscraper in history had ever collapsed.

7) Post-hypnotic suggestions were installed as anchors such that at the mere mention of 9/11, the masses would go back into trance, squawk with fear, rather like chickens, minus the silly arm flapping, but substituting flag waving instead.

8) The trance was reinforced later by movies like United 93 which trigger hypnotic anchors that prevent people from waking up and discovering the truth, and if necessary, another false flag terrorist attack can be used to rehypnotize the masses."

In other words the people were traumatized and given a hypnotic suggestion similar to an engram. An "engram" is a "stimulus impression" which could be reactivated by the recurrence of "the energetic conditions which ruled at the generation of the engram." Just the mentioning of "9/11" is a triggering mechanism which makes people around the world recoil from Muslims when they hear the words "call 911."

So now to make sure that the world never forgets the "magic" of that day a memorial has been opened. A part of that memorial includes the remains of 1,100 victims yet to be identified. Let's look at the cold facts. The victim identification statistics reported in a February 23, 2005 *AP* article are listed in the following table:

Of the	**2,800**	Victims
Fewer than	**300**	whole bodies found,
Fewer than	**1,600**	victims identified,
Over	**1,100**	victims remain unidentified,
Over	**800**	victims nearly identified by DNA alone,
Nearly	**20,000**	pieces of bodies found,
Over	**6,000**	pieces small enough to fit in test-tubes,
Over	**200**	pieces matched to single person,
Nearly	**10,000**	unidentified pieces frozen for future analysis.

In other words 2,800 people were "blown to smithereens." The aircraft impacts and fires could not have destroyed the DNA of so many victims. Nor have building collapses ever been known to destroy human remains beyond recognition. However, the buildings were destroyed in a manner that converted most of their non-metallic contents to homogeneous dust, including the bodies.

The official government investigation refused to test the debris for explosive materials even though a bomb was detonated in the basement of WTC 1 in 1993 in a failed attempt to bring it down. A real "9/11 Memorial" should also remind the public that many witnesses declared that they heard bombs go off as both buildings fell in 2001. A real "9/11 Memorial" should include scientific information that is available at locations like www.ae911truth.org such as:

266

1. Jet fuel can only reach 1,800°F, while steel which melts at 2,700°F was both melted and vaporized indicating high explosives. In fact there were smoldering fires and molten iron still being uncovered months after the buildings collapsed.
2. No steel-framed building BEFORE or SINCE 9/11 has ever collapsed due to fire.
3. Why was the U.S. military explosive THERMATE found in the dust of the collapsed World Trade Center buildings?
4. How did a 47-story skyscraper (WTO Building 7) collapse at 5:20 p.m. on 9/11 in the exact manner of a controlled demolition, though it was not struck by a plane?
5. Why was there no airplane debris where Flight 93 supposedly crashed in Pennsylvania—only a smoking hole in the ground?

And lastly, who were those Israeli men on top of a commercial van across the Hudson River filming the Towers **BEFORE THE FIRST** plane hit? How did they know to be there, and why were they celebrating after the plane hit the World Trade Center? The police arrested them and then let them go home to **ISRAEL**. Why?

The beasts that planned, orchestrated, covered up and deceived the whole world with "9/11" are free for now to continue their Satanic rituals geared to enslave humanity. Until now Satan's magic has worked, but he has left a trail leading back to his cave. By Satan executing this "Great Magic" on September 11, 2001, exactly in line with the Stock Market Crash on October 29, 1929, he allowed us to figure out his secret code of "2625 days" and track him back 400 years. Now we just need that "wooden spike" through the heart of this beast.

Blacks blamed for 2008 financial meltdown

Blaming the Community Reinvestment Act (CRA), Rep. Michele Bachmann, Republican Tea Party member from Minnesota said, "[President Bill Clinton] turned the two quasi-private, mortgage-funding firms into a semi-nationalized monopoly that dispensed cash to markets, made loans to large Democrat [sic] voting blocs and handed favors, jobs and money to political allies." This potential mix led inevitably to corruption and the Fannie-Freddie collapse. "Loans started being made on the basis of race, and often little else," she said.

For decades the banking industry openly "redlined" minority neighborhoods by refusing to generate mortgages while members of those neighborhoods were intentionally kept out of white neighborhoods. The CRA was passed to reverse those trends. Rep. Barney Frank, D-Mass., chairman of the Financial Services Committee on which Bachmann sits, penned a letter to the Star Tribune directly countering Bachmann's talking points: Bachmann … incorrectly points to the Community Reinvestment Act as a source of our current problems. CRA, originally passed in 1977, does not require banks or thrifts to make loans that are unsafe or unprofitable. In fact, federal law requires that CRA lending activities must be done consistent with safe and sound banking practices. In reality, most high-cost loans were originated by lenders that did not have a CRA obligation and lacked federal oversight.

The Congressional Black Caucus challenged Bachmann and other Tea Party members to substantiate their claim that the CRA and therefore, **black people** were the cause of the housing crisis and mass foreclosures that led to the collapse in the housing market, failures of financial institutions and eventually the stock market crash in the fall of 2008. The Honorable Minister Louis Farrakhan has taught us that The Most Honorable Elijah Muhammad warned us that we cannot fathom the depths of the wickedness of white people. We may never believe that so-called white people would destroy the wealth of their own country just to keep it away from black people, but let us shed more light on the present financial crisis and economic depression that we are in to analyze this hypothesis.

Lawsuits have been filed in Baltimore, MD and Memphis, TN against Wells Fargo Bank claiming that it targeted black people for these subprime loans which led to mass foreclosures, property devaluation and loss of tax revenue. And even more recently, Fannie Mae and Freddie Mac are suing Wells Fargo and other banks for selling them bundles of bad mortgage loans, subprime loans. Standard & Poor's gave a higher rating (AAA) to securities backed by subprime home loans, than it now assigns the US government (AA), which led Fannie, Freddie and other institutional bond holders to believe that their investments were safe.

Now, let us look at Baltimore's case against Wells Fargo. According to a June 6, 2009 article by Michael Powell entitled: *"Bank Accused of Pushing Mortgage Deals on Blacks"*, Beth Jacobson and her fellow loan officers at Wells Fargo Bank "rode the stagecoach from hell" for a decade, systematically singling out Blacks in Baltimore and suburban Maryland for high-interest subprime mortgages. Wells Fargo, Ms. Jacobson said in an interview, saw the black community as fertile ground for subprime mortgages, as working-class Blacks were hungry to be a part of the nation's home-owning mania. Loan officers, she said, pushed customers who could have qualified for prime loans into subprime mortgages. Another loan officer stated in an affidavit that employees had referred to Blacks as "mud people" and to subprime lending as "ghetto loans."

"We just went right after them," said Ms. Jacobson, who is white and said she was once the bank's top-producing subprime loan officer nationally. "Wells Fargo mortgage had an emerging-markets unit that specifically targeted **black churches**, because it figured

church leaders had a lot of influence and could convince congregants to take out subprime loans."

The New York Times, in an analysis of mortgage lending in New York City, found that black households making more than $68,000 a year were nearly five times as likely to hold high-interest subprime mortgages as Whites of similar or even lower incomes. (The disparity was greater for Wells Fargo borrowers, as 2 percent of Whites in that income group hold subprime loans and 16.1 percent of Blacks.)

A few points must be emphasized: 1. Blacks that qualified to get fixed low interest loans were steered like cattle (goyim) into subprime high interest loans, 2. The banks went after black community leaders such as preachers (**bell-wethers**) to convince Blacks (**sheep**) to fall for the "okie-doak" and 3. As a result of the housing crisis, the black community was **fleeced out of 50%** of its wealth. The question must be asked, why would Blacks be targeted for these subprime loans for "a decade" leading up to the financial crisis and then blamed (**scapegoated**) for the financial crisis of 2008?

In another statement by Michele Bachman she even tries to blame the Black Farmers lawsuit against the USDA for the shortage of money needed to help white farmers in the Midwest who suffered in 2011 from extreme flooding. Reps. Michele Bachmann (R-Minn.) and Steve King (R-Iowa) were interviewed by the press in Missouri and asked, if their calls for drastic cuts in federal spending would mean less money for emergency aid to help beleaguered farmers. King responded that there would be more money for the mostly white farmers if the government was not paying so much to settle cases involving racial discrimination against black farmers. Presidential candidate Bachmann joined King in saying that the mid-western farmers deserved the money and charged that a large percentage of the USDA settlement consisted of "fraudulent claims". King and Bachmann "scapegoated" black farmers to take the heat off of their Tea Party's call for drastic reductions in domestic spending, including emergency relief funds.

There is a pattern here that Blacks and Browns must see and understand. While the Tea Party is blaming the financial crisis and lack of money to aid white farmers on Blacks, they turn a blind eye on the hundreds of billions and even trillions of dollars printed and passed out by the **Federal Reserve** to banks in America and Europe. Only Minister Farrakhan and a few politicians like Rep. Dennis Kucinich dare to question the activities of the privately owned Federal Reserve (**Evil Shepherd**) which puts America further in debt every time it prints money in exchange for U.S. government bonds. On leaving office Bush and his banker buddies took $700 billion from the Treasury and another $4 trillion from the Federal Reserve, and then they put in a Black man as president to take the blame for the financial "Fall of America".

Now let us "connect the dots." According to the Census Bureau, by **2046** Whites will not be the majority ethnic population in America. Whites will be outnumbered by the Blacks, Native American, Hispanics and Asians. Curiously, the Congressional Budget Office estimates that at the rate we are going, by **2021** we will spend **$1.1 trillion on interest** annually, and by **2042**, the CBO says all tax revenue collected will be required just to pay the **interest** on the national debt, not the principal, leaving no money for education, transportation, agriculture, human services, national security or defense. Add to this that the nation most likely to hold most of that debt will be **China.** Many a fight on the streets starts off with "N---a, where is my money!!!" Welcome to the prelude to **World War III.** If this sounds a little too strong, read over this section again and you tell me why are Blacks continually "scapegoated"?

A little history from Herodotus may be helpful in understanding the mindset of these white people that we are dealing with. An ancient tribe of Whites from the Caucasus Mountains, the Scythians, reigned invincible for hundreds of years due to their ruthless war tactics. They would come out on one side of the mountains every seven years or so (their "business cycle"), raid the farmers in the valleys, then race back up into the caves and hillsides of Europe as they burned all the trees and fields while poisoning all the water holes behind them. Anyone pursuing them would have no resources to sustain an army. Now as the descendants of these Scythians hunker down in the modern caves and hillsides of Europe with the ill-gotten wealth of the world, what will we have to rebuild our broken communities?

Help Minister Farrakhan to help you or just keep your head in the sand until January 26, 2016. As Muslims we have been branded "Terrorists" and as Blacks we have been economically castrated, sacrificed to the sheepdogs and yet blamed for all of America's ills. The "Scythians" have poisoned the water, the land, air and even our minds. But we have the "Evil Shepherd's", the "Great Snake's" number and we will mathematically drive in our point in the next chapter.

Chapter 8

Tracking the "Great Snake" using Mathematics

Building the corral (Stock Market)

An old farmer once told me a story about how he made a lot of money retrieving another farmer's stray cattle. A farmer's cattle had gotten out of his fence and wandered into the nearby woods. So my friend, Arthur Pecan offered to get his cattle for him for a fee. Arthur Pecan built a corral near the edge of the woods. He put a hay wagon in the middle of the corral. He added a little molasses to sweeten the kitty. Each afternoon he would bring in more hay spiked with molasses and each day more cows would come from the woods to fill up on sweet hay. Mr. Pecan built two gates into his corral. One day he put a trailer at the end of one gate, closed the other gate. The cows just walked out of the opened gate, right up into his trailer. He collected his fee.

For the Jews to capture the Goyim's (sheep and sheepdog) discretionary money, they needed to build a "corral". The stock market and commodity markets have served this purpose for producing a place for the suckers to come and gamble with the hope of making a killing through speculation.

http://en.wikipedia.org/wiki/Corporation

> On 31 December 1600, the English monarchy granted the [British East India] company a 15-year monopoly on trade to and from the East Indies and Africa. By 1611, shareholders in the East India Company were earning an almost 150% return on their investment. Subsequent stock offerings demonstrated just how lucrative the Company had become. Its first **stock offering in 1613–1616** raised

£418,000, and its second offering in 1617–1622 raised £1.6 million.

So the first public stock offering was in 1613. This allowed common people from anywhere in the world to participate in the ownership of a corporation and to sell their stock to someone else at a profit, if the stock price went up. The stock market is born and the "trailer" was pulled up to the opened gate waiting on the greedy cattle or goyim who wanted to participate in the robbing of the planet. These corporations raped the non-white countries (sheep) bringing their wealth back to Europe and later the US. In the beginning of this rape of the planet only the kings, princes and aristocrats could feed. Now the common worker (sheepdogs) with a little extra money could participate.

Therefore I decided to see if my predictive model would work further back in time to the early 1600s. We found a great book which detailed the history of many financial panics and crashes going back to the 1600s: *Manias, Panics, and Crashes: A History of Financial Crises* by Charles P. Kindleberger (2000, fourth edition). In it he describes what is meant by "panics" and "crashes":

> "A crash is a collapse of the prices of assets, or perhaps the failure of an important firm or bank. A panic, 'a sudden fright without cause,' from the god Pan, may occur in asset markets or involve a rush from less to more liquid assets." (Kindleberger 2000: 105)

According to Kindleberger "speculative manias" precede crashes and panics. *Mania* connotes "a loss of touch with reality or rationality, even something close to mass hysteria or insanity. *Speculation* is no longer investment for use, when the goal becomes buying and selling stocks for profit. Objects of speculation over time are various and include metallic coins, tulips, government debt, selected companies, import commodities, banks, canals, export goods, foreign bonds, mines, mutual funds, real estate, agricultural land, railroad shares, joint-stock banks, copper, foreign exchange, gold, silver, new industries, derivatives and hedge funds.

Greed drives people to speculate. However, in many cases there are seasoned players and new comers. There are insiders, who know the deal, and outsiders who go on emotions and hunches.

"Speculation for profit leads away from normal, rational behavior to what has been described as 'manias' or 'bubbles.' The word *mania* emphasizes the irrationality; *bubble* foreshadows the bursting. In the technical language of some economists, a **bubble** is any deviation from 'fundamentals,' whether up or down…In this book, a **bubble** is an upward price movement over an extended range that then implodes. An extended negative bubble is a crash." (Ibid: 15, 16)

In the appendix of his book he lists a number of these crises/panics/crashes from **1621 thru 1997**. We have augmented his historical data and added some more recent dates along with brief histories of these events so the reader can see the pattern of the snake. On the farm, as long as a snake stays hidden in the bushes, he is relatively safe. However, if he ventures across the road at the wrong time, a pickup truck shows no mercy. Mathematics is my engine and history provides my wheels.

We have provided below dates for Panics and Crises followed by historical details on each of them. A careful analysis of the details reveals that each panic is preceded by an artificially manufactured **bubble** produced by "easy money" from the central banks and then the bankers stick a **pin** in the bubble by increasing **interest rates** thereby forcing the economy to slow down. And this pattern goes all the way back to 1621 which was the first great speculative **Bubble/Burst cycle**. As you read through the history of each of the panics/crashes keep an eye out for the role of the bankers in each bubble/burst cycle.

Panics and Crisis

Panics and Crises	Date Crisis	2625 Days or 7.18686	# Cycles
?????????		Tuesday, January 26, 2016	55
2008 Financial Crash	Sept. 16, 2008	Tuesday, November 18, 2008	54
"9/11"	Sept. 11, 2001	Tuesday, September 11, 2001	53
Economic Crisis in Mexico	Dec. 1994	Tuesday, July 05, 1994	52
Black Monday/Farm Crisis	Oct. 19, 1987	Tuesday, April 28, 1987	51
Silver Thursday	Mar. 17, 1980	Tuesday, February 19, 1980	50
1973-74 Stock Market Crash	Jan. 1973	Tuesday, December 12, 1972	49
		Tuesday, October 05, 1965	48
		Tuesday, July 29, 1958	47
		Tuesday, May 22, 1951	46
		Tuesday, March 14, 1944	45
Recession of 1937-38	Jul. 1937	Tuesday, January 05, 1937	44
Black Tuesday	Oct. 29, 1929	Tuesday, October 29, 1929	43
		Tuesday, August 22, 1922	42
J.P Morgan/Lusitania	May 5 1915	Tuesday, June 15, 1915	41
Panic of 1907	Oct. 1907	Tuesday, April 07, 1908	40
Panic of 1901	May 17 1901	Tuesday, January 29, 1901	39
Panic of 1893	May 1893	Tuesday, November 21, 1893	38
		Tuesday, September 14, 1886	37
Paris Bourse crash of 1882	Jan. 1882	Tuesday, July 08, 1879	36
Panic of 1873	Sept. 1873	Tuesday, April 30, 1872	35
Panic of 1866	May 1866	Tuesday, February 21, 1865	34
Panic of 1857	Oct. 1857	Tuesday, December 15, 1857	33
		Tuesday, October 8, 1850	32
		Tuesday, August 1, 1843	31
Panic of 1836-37	Dec. 1836	Tuesday, May 24, 1836	30
		Tuesday, March 17, 1829	29
Panic of 1819	June 1819	Tuesady, January 8, 1822	28
Rothschilds' corner British bonds	June 18, 1815	Tuesday, November 1, 1814	27
		Tuesday, August 25, 1807	26
Hamburg crisis of 1799	Nov. 1799	Tuesday, Jun 17, 1800	25

Panic of 1792	Mar. 1792	Tuesday, April 9, 1793	24
		Tuesday, January 31, 1786	23
		Tuesday, November 24, 1778	22
Credit Crisis of 1772	Jun. 1772	Tuesday, September 17, 1771	21
Banking Crisis of 1763	Sept. 1763	Tuesday, July 10, 1764	20
		Tuesday, May 3, 1757	19
		Tuesday, February 13, 1750	18
		Tuesday, December 7, 1742	17
		Tuesday, September 30, 1735	16
		Tuesday, July 23, 1728	15
Mississippi and South Sea Bubbles	Sept. 1720	Tuesday, May 16, 1721	14
		Tuesday, March 9, 1714	13
		Tuesday, December 31, 1706	12
		Tuesday, October 24, 1699	11
		Tuesday, August 16, 1692	10
		Tuesday, June 9, 1685	9
		Tuesday, April 2, 1678	8
		Tuesday, January 24, 1671	7
		Tuesaday, November 17, 1663	6
		Tuesday, September 9, 1656	5
		Tuesday, July 3, 1649	4
		Tuesday, April 26, 1642	3
Dutch Tulips, 1634-1638	Feb. 1637	Tuesday, February 17, 1635	2
		Tuesday, December 11, 1627	1
Tipper and See-saw	1621	Tuesday, October 3, 1620	0

History of each Panic Cycle:

Cycle

0 **1621 Tipper and See-saw**
(http://en.wikipedia.org/wiki/Kipper_und_Wipper0

Kipper und Wipper (German: *Kipper- und Wipperzeit*, literally "Tipper and See-saw") is the name given to a financial crisis during the start of the Thirty Years' War (1618–48). Starting around 1621, city-states in the Holy Roman Empire began to heavily debase currency in order to raise revenue for the Thirty Years' War, as effective taxation did not exist.

The name refers to the use of tipping scales to identify not-yet-debased coins, which were then taken out of circulation, melted, mixed with baser metals such as lead, copper or tin, and re-

277

issued. Often the states did not debase their own currency, but instead manufactured low-value imitations of coins from other territories and then spent them in yet other territories as far as possible from their own lands, hoping that the resulting damage would then occur to the economy of those other regions rather than their own. This worked for a while; but after a time, the general public caught on to the manipulation, resulting in pamphlets denouncing the practice, local riots and the refusal of soldiers and mercenaries to fight unless paid in "real", non-debased money. Also the states began to get back their own debased coins in taxes and customs fees. Due to these problems the practice largely stopped around 1623; however, the damage done was so large that it created financial disarray in almost all the city-states in the area. The same thing re-occurred on a smaller scale near the end of the century and again during the middle of the 18th century; however, the debasement spread from Germany to Austria, Hungary, Bohemia, and Poland.

2   Dutch Tulips, 1634-1638
(http://en.wikipedia.org/wiki/Tulip_mania)

Tulip mania or tulipomania (Dutch names include: *tulpenmanie, tulpomanie, tulpenwoede, tulpengekte* and *bollengekte*) was a period in the Dutch Golden Age during which contract prices for bulbs of the recently introduced tulip reached extraordinarily high levels and then suddenly collapsed.

"Jonathan Israel writes that the tulipmania should be viewed against the background of the general boom and as a mania of 'small-town dealers, tavern-keepers and horticulturalists'…Shares in the Amsterdam Chamber of the Dutch East India Company doubled between 1630 and 1639, mostly after early 1636…" (Kindleberger 2000: 110)

14   The Mississippi Bubble 1719-1720
(http://www.pbs.org/wgbh/pages/frontline/shows/dotcon/histori cal/bubbles.html)

The Mississippi Bubble -- which derives its name from the French Mississippi Company -- grew out of France's dire economic situation in the early 18th century. By the time of Louis XIV's death in 1715, the treasury was in shambles, with the value of metallic currency fluctuating wildly. The following year, the French regent turned to a Scotsman named John Law for help. Law, a gambler who had been forced into exile in France as the result of a duel, suggested the Banque Royale take deposits and issue banknotes payable in the value of the metallic currency at the time the banknotes were issued. Law's strategy helped the French convert from metallic to paper currency, and resulted in a period of financial stability, as well as his own increased fame and power.

In August 1717, Law incorporated the Companie des Indes (commonly known as the Mississippi Company), to which the French regent gave a monopoly on trading rights with French colonies, including what was then known as "French Louisiana." In August 1719, Law devised a scheme in which the Mississippi Company subsumed the **entire French national debt**, and launched a plan whereby portions of the debt would be exchanged for shares in the company. Based upon the expected riches from the trading monopoly, Law promised 120 percent profit for shareholders, and there were at least 300,000 applicants for the 50,000 shares offered. As the demand for shares continued to rise, the Banque Royale -- which was owned by the French government but effectively controlled by Law -- continued to **print paper banknotes**, causing inflation to soar.

"Amsterdam stood between Paris and London. It apparently did well. The Dutch were said to have sold their

Mississippi Compagnie des Indes at the **right psychological moment** and lost little in the crash. In April 1720, a bit prematurely perhaps, David Leeuw liquidated his South Sea stock and bought **Bank of England** and East India Company." (Kindleberger 2000: 122)

14 The South Sea Bubble 1720
(http://www.pbs.org/wgbh/pages/frontline/shows/dotcon/historical/bubbles.html)

During the same period that French speculators were driving up the price of shares in the Mississippi Company, English speculators were purchasing stock in the South Sea Company. Formed in 1711 by Robert Harley, the South Sea Company was created to convert £10 million of government war debt (incurred during the War of Spanish Succession) into its own shares. In exchange, the company would receive annual interest payments from the government and a monopoly on trade with the South Seas and South America. The exchange was successful and although the expected trade riches never materialized, the company continued with several other debt conversions.

"If a man is quick enough to get in and out ahead of the others, he may do well, as insiders do, even though the totality does badly…When the late buyers suspected they might not get their money back, the system collapsed. There is never enough money for all because the swindlers—the organizers of the South Sea Company, Ponzi, and the smart ones who **get out early**—have taken it, and the inflow of new money must eventually dry up." (Kindleberger 2000: 31, 32)

20 Amsterdam Banking Crisis of 1763
(http://en.wikipedia.org/wiki/Amsterdam_Banking_Crisis_of_1763)

On February 10, 1763, the Treaty of Hubertusburg was signed in Germany. This Treaty marked the end of the **Seven** Years' War, a war from 1756 to 1763 that involved all of the major European powers of the period. This treaty ended the war with no significant changes in borders. In the years during the War, Amsterdam banking firms reaped large profits with money trades and loans to other European banks, which lent the money to their governments that needed the money to finance their war efforts. To cover the loans, large quantities of goods were sent to Amsterdam. But in 1763, because of the end of the war, the abnormal high war prices plummeted and commodity and goods lost their value rapidly. More than 30 banking and trade firms went bankrupt, with an estimated debt of 20 million Dutch guilders. During the **economic boom and credit expansion** that followed the Seven Years' War, Berlin, for example, was the equivalent of an emerging market, and Amsterdam's merchant bankers were the primary **sources of credit**, with the Hamburg banking houses served as intermediaries between the two.

But some Amsterdam merchant bankers were leveraged far beyond their capacity... The post-Neufville **credit freeze**-up ultimately forced 38 Amsterdam firms into bankruptcy during August and September 1763.

21 Credit Crisis of
1772 (http://en.wikipedia.org/wiki/Credit_crisis_of_1772)

The peacetime **Credit Crisis of 1772** originated in London and then spread to other parts of Europe, such as Scotland and Netherlands...

From the mid-1760s to the early 1770s, **the credit boom**, supported by merchants and bankers, facilitated the expansion of manufacturing, mining and internal improvements in both Britain and the thirteen colonies.

Until the outbreak of the credit crisis, the period from 1770 to 1772 was considered prosperous and politically calm in both Britain and the American colonies. As the result of the Townshend Act and the breakdown of the Non-importation Act, the period was marked with a tremendous growth in exports from Britain to the American colonies. These massive exports were supported **by credit** that British merchants granted to American planters…

On June 8, 1772, Alexander Fordyce, a partner in the banking house Neal, James, Fordyce and Down in London, fled to France to **avoid debt repayment**, and the resulting collapse of the firm stirred up panic in London.

24 **Panic of 1792** (http://en.wikipedia.org/wiki/Panic_of_1792)

The Panic of 1792 was a financial credit crisis that occurred during the months of March and April of 1792, precipitated by the **expansion of credit** by the newly formed Bank of the United States as well as by rampant speculation on the part of William Duer, Alexander Macomb and other prominent bankers. Duer, Macomb and their colleagues attempted to drive up prices of US debt securities and bank stocks, but when they defaulted on loans, prices fell causing a bank run. Simultaneous **tightening of credit** by the Bank of the United States served to heighten the initial panic. Secretary of the Treasury Alexander Hamilton was able to deftly manage the crisis by providing banks across the Northeast with hundreds of thousands of dollars to make open-market purchases of securities, which allowed the market to stabilize by May of 1792.

25 **Hamburg crisis of 1799**
(http://www.econlib.org/library/YPDBooks/Lalor/llCy249.html)

The Hamburg crisis of 1799 was caused by the French occupation of Holland in 1795, which threw into the lap of the former the continental trade which had previously belonged to the latter, causing such a tremendous speculation and rise of prices and **extension of credit** in Hamburg during the succeeding **four** years that presently a crash came, in which 82 houses failed, with liabilities amounting to 29,000,000 marks. Thus the very event which seemed likely to contribute to the prosperity of Hamburg, serving to inflame the greed of her capitalists and obscure their vision, ended in her impoverishment.

27 **Rothschilds corner British government bonds** June 18, 1815

(http://en.wikipedia.org/wiki/Rothschild_family#The_Napoleonic_ Wars)

The Rothschilds already possessed a significant fortune before the start of the Napoleonic Wars (1803–1815), and the family had gained preeminence in the bullion trade by this time. From London in 1813 to 1815, Nathan Mayer Rothschild was instrumental in almost single-handedly financing the British war effort, organizing the shipment of bullion to the Duke of Wellington's armies across Europe, as well as arranging the payment of British financial subsidies to their continental allies. In 1815 alone, the Rothschilds provided £9.8 million (in 1815 currency, about £566 million or US$869 million today, when using the retail price index, and £6.58 billion or US$10.1 billion when using average earnings) in subsidy loans to Britain's continental allies

The brothers helped coordinate Rothschild activities across the continent, and the family developed a network of agents, shippers, and couriers to transport gold across war-torn Europe. The family network was also to provide Nathan Rothschild time and again with political and **financial information** ahead of his peers, giving him an advantage in the markets and rendering the house of Rothschild still more invaluable to the British government.

In one instance, the family network enabled Nathan to receive in London the news of Wellington's victory at the Battle of Waterloo a **full day** ahead of the government's official messengers. Rothschild's first concern on this occasion was to the potential financial advantage on the market which the knowledge would have given him; he and his courier **did not** immediately take the news to the government. It was then repeated in later popular accounts, such as that of Morton. The basis for the Rothschild's most famously profitable move was made after the news of British victory had been made public. Nathan Rothschild calculated that the future reduction in government borrowing brought about by the peace would create a bounce in British government bonds after a two-year stabilization, which would finalize the post-war restructuring of the domestic economy. In what has been described as one of the most audacious moves in financial history, Nathan immediately **bought up** the government bond market, for what at the time seemed an excessively high price, before waiting two years, then selling the bonds on the crest of a short bounce in the market in 1817 for a 40% profit. Given the sheer power of leverage the Rothschild family had at their disposal, this profit was an enormous sum.

28 Panic of 1819

(http://history1800s.about.com/od/thegildedage/a/financialp anics.htm)

- The first major American depression, the Panic of 1819 was rooted to some extent in economic problems reaching back to the war of 1812.
- It was triggered by a collapse in cotton prices. A **contraction in credit** coincided with the problems in the cotton market, and the young American economy was severely affected.

- Banks were forced to call in loans, and foreclosures of farms and bank failures resulted.
- The Panic of 1819 lasted until 1821.
- The effects were felt most in the west and south. Bitterness about the economic hardships resonated for years and led to the resentment that helped Andrew Jackson solidify his political base throughout the 1820s.
- Besides exacerbating sectional animosity, the Panic of 1819 also made many Americans realize the importance of politics and government policy in their lives.

30   **Panic of 1836-37** (Kindleberger 2000: 126, 226)

"The crisis was by no means a purely Ango-U.S. affair, although often discussed in these terms with emphasis on its impact on the evolution of Bank of England discount policy. Hawtrey states that it broke out in England in 1836 and 1837, spread to the United States, and then in May 1838…erupted in Belgium, France, and Germany to spread back again to England and the United States in 1839."

33   **Panic of 1857**
(http://history1800s.about.com/od/thegildedage/a/financial panics.htm)

The Panic of 1857 was triggered by the failure of the Ohio Life Insurance and Trust Company, which actually did much of its business as a bank headquartered in New York City. Reckless speculation in railroads led the company into trouble, and the company's collapse led to a literal panic in the financial district, as crowds of frantic investors clogged the streets around Wall Street.

Stock prices plummeted, and more than 900 mercantile firms in New York had to cease operation. By the end of the year the American economy was in shambles.

One victim of the Panic of 1857 was a future Civil War hero and US president, Ulysses S. Grant, who was bankrupted and had to pawn his gold watch to buy Christmas presents.

Recovery from the depression began in early 1859.

34 Panic of 1866

(http://en.wikipedia.org/wiki/Panic_of_1866#cite_note-Malcolm-1)

The Panic of 1866 was an international financial downturn that accompanied the failure of Overend, Gurney and Company in London, and the *corso forzoso* abandonment of the silver standard in Italy.

In Britain the economic impacts are held partially responsible for public agitation for political reform in the months leading up to the 1867 Reform Act. The crisis led to a sharp rise in unemployment to 8% and a subsequent fall in wages across the country. Similar to the "knife and fork" motives of Chartism in the late 1830s and 1840s, the financial pressure on the British working class led to rising support for greater representation of the people. Groups such as the Reform League saw rapid increases in membership and the organization spearheaded multiple demonstrations against the political establishment such as the Hyde Park riot 1866. Ultimately the popular pressure that arose from the banking crisis and the recession that followed can be held partly responsible for the enfranchisement of 1.1 million people as a result of Disraeli's reform bill.

"The conversion of Overend, Gurney & Co. to a public company in July 1865, at the peak of the boom and 'dividend race,' led to a 100 percent premium on the stock in October, causing the Bank of England to **raise its discount rate from 3 to 7 percent**; the crash did not occur until May 1866." (Kindleberger 2000: 99)

35 Panic of 1873

(http://history1800s.about.com/od/thegildedage/a/financial
panics.htm)

- The investment firm of Jay Cooke and Company went bankrupt in September 1873 as a result of rampant speculation in railroads. The stock market dropped sharply and caused numerous businesses to fail.
- The depression caused approximately three million Americans to lose their jobs.
- The collapse in food prices impacted America's farm economy, causing great poverty in rural America.
- The depression lasted for five years, until 1878.

The Panic of 1873 led to a populist movement that saw the creation of the Greenback Party.

"In the 1873 case, **'excessive tightness'** of money from September 1872 to May 1873, which caused the railroads to turn from issuing bonds to borrowing on short term, could have been seen as a sign of distress against which seasonal tightness precipitated the crash. Thus, the surprise of the business community is double curious." (Kindleberger 2000: 99)

36 Paris Bourse crash of 1882 Paris

(http://en.wikipedia.org/wiki/Paris_Bourse_crash_of_1882)

The Paris Bourse crash of 1882 was a stock market crash in France, and was the worst crisis in the French economy in the nineteenth century. The crash was triggered by the collapse of l'Union Générale in January. Around a quarter of the brokers on the bourse were on the brink of collapse. The closure of the exchange was prevented by a loan from the Banque de France which enabled sufficient liquidity to support settlement.

The crash led to a recession which lasted until the end of the decade immediately after the crash, the bank's founder accused that its downfall was caused by **Jewish-German banks** and Freemasons vying to destroy growing financial institutions that backed conservative Catholic political agendas. It is now generally accepted that there was no conspiracy to destroy the bank, however, it remains unclear why the collapse of the bank was so devastating.

During the 1882 crash, 14 of 60 stock brokers appeared to be in imminent danger of failure and 7 were completely bankrupt.

37 **Panic of 1893**

(http://history1800s.about.com/od/thegildedage/a/financial panics.htm)

Panic of 1893
- The depression set off by the Panic of 1893 was the greatest depression America had known, and was only surpassed by the Great Depression of the 1930s.
- In early May 1893 the New York stock market dropped sharply, and in late June panic selling caused the stock market to crash.
- A severe credit crisis resulted, and more than 16,000 businesses had failed by the end of 1893. Included in the failed businesses were 156 railroads and nearly 500 banks.
- Unemployment spread until one in six American men lost their jobs.
- The depression inspired "Coxey's Army," a march on Washington of unemployed men. The protesters demanded that the government provide public works jobs. Their leader, Jacob Coxey, was imprisoned for 20 days.
- The depression caused by the Panic of 1893 lasted for about four years, ending in 1897.

(http://en.wikipedia.org/wiki/Panic_of_1893)
One of the causes for the Panic of 1893 can be traced back

to Argentina. Investment was encouraged by the Argentinean agent bank, Baring Brothers. However, a failure in the wheat crop and a coup in Buenos Aires ended further investments. This shock started a run on gold in the U.S. Treasury, as investors were cashing in their investments. This occurred during "The Gilded Age", when the United States was experiencing economic growth and expansion. This expansion eventually became driven by railroad speculation. Railroads were over-built, incurring expenses that outstripped revenues...

In addition, farmers—particularly in wheat and cotton regions—struggled under a decline in prices for agricultural commodities.

One of the first clear signs of trouble came on February 23, 1893, ten days before the inauguration of U.S. president Grover Cleveland, with the bankruptcy of the Philadelphia and Reading Railroad, which had greatly overextended itself...

The Populists, a party that appealed to poor cotton and wheat farmers in the South and West, saw the Panic as confirmation that evil global conspiracies were to blame. In the words of historian Hasia Diner:

> Some Populists believed that Jews made up a class of international financiers whose policies had ruined small family farms. Jews, they asserted, owned the banks and promoted the gold standard, the chief sources of their impoverishment. Agrarian radicalism posited the city as antithetical to American values, asserting that Jews were the essence of urban corruption.

39 **Panic of 1901** (http://en.wikipedia.org/wiki/Panic_of_1901)

The Panic of 1901 was the first stock market crash on the New York Stock Exchange, caused in part by struggles between E. H. Harriman, **Jacob Schiff**, and J. P. Morgan/James J. Hill for the financial control of the Northern Pacific Railway. The **stock cornering** was orchestrated by James Stillman and William Rockefeller's **First National City Bank** financed with Standard Oil money. After reaching a compromise, the moguls formed the Northern Securities Company. As a result of the panic, thousands of small investors were ruined.

One of the causes of this stock market crash was Harriman's effort to gain control of Northern Pacific by buying up its stock. The panic began when the market crashed during that afternoon in May. Investors did not see it coming, but by 1:00pm, the decline in the market was beginning to show. First came the gradual decline in Burlington stock. It had been high all morning but suddenly a sharp weakness came about. Prices of stocks such as St. Paul, Missouri Pacific, and Union Pacific began to fall. Soon enough the whole market was drowning. Investors that had once held on tightly to their stocks were selling out of pure panic. Others caught on and an overwhelming cry of "Sell! Sell! Sell!" was heard throughout the floor of the New York Stock Exchange. During the selling, a rumor spread among traders that Arthur Housman, broker for J.P. Morgan, had died. Housman, the head of A.A. Housman & Company, was brought to the floor of the New York Stock Exchange to assure traders that J.P. Morgan was still doing business.

40 **Panic of 1907** (http://en.wikipedia.org/wiki/Panic_of_1907)

The Panic of 1907 – also known as the **1907 Bankers'
Panic** or **Knickerbocker Crisis** – was a United
States financial crisis that took place over a three week
period starting in mid-October, when the New York Stock
Exchange fell almost 50% from its peak the previous year.
Panic occurred, as this was during a time of
economic recession, and there were numerous runs on
banks and trust companies. The 1907 panic eventually
spread throughout the nation when many state and local
banks and businesses entered bankruptcy. Primary causes
of the run included a **retraction of market liquidity** by a
number of New York City banks and a loss of confidence
among depositors, exacerbated by unregulated side
bets at bucket shops. The panic was triggered by the failed
attempt in **October 1907** to corner the market on stock of
the United Copper Company. When this bid failed, **banks
that had lent money to the cornering scheme** suffered
runs that later spread to affiliated banks and trusts, leading
a week later to the downfall of the Knickerbocker Trust
Company—New York City's third-largest trust. The
collapse of the Knickerbocker spread fear throughout the
city's trusts as regional banks withdrew reserves from New
York City banks. Panic extended across the nation as vast
numbers of people withdrew deposits from their regional
banks.

The panic might have deepened if not for the intervention
of financier J. P. Morgan, who pledged large sums of his
own money, and convinced other New York bankers to do
the same, to shore up the banking system. At the time, the
United States did not have a central bank to inject liquidity
back into the market. By November, the financial
contagion had largely ended, only to be replaced by a
further crisis. This was due to the heavy borrowing of a
large brokerage firm that used the stock of Tennessee Coal,

Iron and Railroad Company (TC&I) as collateral. Collapse of TC&I's stock price was averted by an emergency takeover by Morgan's U.S. Steel Corporation—a move approved by anti-monopolist president Theodore Roosevelt. The following year **[1908]**, Senator Nelson W. Aldrich, father-in-law of John D. Rockefeller, Jr., established and chaired a commission to investigate the crisis and propose future solutions, leading to the creation of the **Federal Reserve System.**

A significant difference between the European and U.S. banking systems was the absence of a central bank in the United States. European states were able to extend the supply of money during periods of low cash reserves. The belief that the U.S. economy was vulnerable without a central bank was not new. **Early in 1907**, banker **Jacob Schiff** of **Kuhn, Loeb & Co**. warned in a speech to the New York Chamber of Commerce that "unless we have a central bank with adequate control of credit resources, this country is going to undergo the most severe and far reaching money panic in its history".

Aldrich convened a secret conference with a number of the nation's leading financiers at the Jekyll Island Club, off the coast of Georgia, to discuss monetary policy and the banking system in November 1910. Aldrich and A. P. Andrew (Assistant Secretary of the Treasury Department), Paul Warburg (representing **Kuhn, Loeb & Co.**), Frank A. Vanderlip (James Stillman's successor as president of the National City Bank of New York), Henry P. Davison (senior partner of J. P. Morgan Company), Charles D. Norton (president of the Morgan-dominated First National Bank of New York), and Benjamin Strong (representing J. P. Morgan), produced a design for a "National Reserve Bank".

41   Sinking of Lusitania May 7, 1915

(http://en.wikipedia.org/wiki/RMS_Lusitania)

RMS *Lusitania* was a British ocean liner, holder of the Blue Riband and briefly the world's biggest ship. She was launched by the Cunard Line in 1906, at a time of fierce competition for the North Atlantic trade. In 1915 she was torpedoed and sunk by a German U-boat, causing the deaths of 1,198 passengers and crew.

When she left New York for Liverpool on what would be her final voyage on 1 May 1915, submarine warfare was intensifying in the Atlantic. Germany had declared the seas around the United Kingdom to be a war-zone, and the German embassy in the United States had placed a newspaper advertisement warning people not to sail on *Lusitania*. On the afternoon of 7 May, *Lusitania* was torpedoed by a German U-Boat, 11 mi (18 km) off the southern coast of Ireland and inside the declared "zone of war". A second internal explosion sent her to the bottom in 18 minutes.

"Sinking of the Lusitania"

(http://www.threeworldwars.com/world-war-1/ww1.htm)

The next step in the maneuvering of the United States into the war came when the Cunard Lines, owner of the ocean liner, the *Lusitania*, turned the ship over to the First Lord of the Admiralty, Winston Churchill. It now became a ship of the English Navy and was under the control of the English government.

The ship was sent to New York City where it was loaded with **six million** rounds of ammunition, owned by **J.P.**

Morgan & Co., to be sold to England and France to aid in their war against Germany.

It was known that the very wealthy were interested in involving the American government in that war, and Secretary of State William Jennings Bryan was one who made note of this. "As Secretary [Bryan] had anticipated, the **large banking interests** were deeply interested in the World War because of wide opportunities for **large profits**. On August 3, 1914, even before the actual clash of arms, the French firm of **Rothschild Freres** cabled to **Morgan and Company** in New York suggesting the flotation of a **loan** of **$100,000,000,** a substantial part of which was to be left in the United States, to pay for **French purchases of American goods**."

England broke the German war code on December 14, 1914, so that "By the end of January, 1915, [British Intelligence was] able to advise the Admiralty of the departure of each U-boat as it left for patrol...."

This meant that the First Lord of the Admiralty, Winston Churchill, knew where every U-boat was in the vicinity of the English Channel that separated England and France.

The ocean liner was set to sail to England already at war with Germany. The German government had placed advertisements in the New York newspapers warning the American people considering whether or not to sail with the ship to England that they would be sailing into a war zone, and that the liner could be sunk.

Secretary Bryan promised that "he would endeavor to persuade the President (Woodrow Wilson) publicly to warn the Americans not to travel [aboard the *Lusitania*]. No such warning was issued by the President, but there can be no doubt that President Wilson was told of the character of the cargo destined for the *Lusitania*. He did nothing... "

Even though Wilson proclaimed America's neutrality in the European War, in accordance with the prior admonitions of George Washington, his government was secretly plotting to involve the American people by having the *Lusitania* sunk. This was made public in the book *The Intimate Papers of Colonel House*, written by a supporter of the Colonel, who recorded a conversation between Colonel House and Sir Edward Grey of England, the Foreign Secretary of England:

Grey: What will America do if the **Germans sink an ocean liner** with American passengers on board?

House: I believe that a **flame of indignation** would sweep the United States and that by itself would be **sufficient to carry us into the war**.

On May 7, 1915, the *Lusitania* was sunk off the coast of County Cork, Ireland by a U-boat after it had **slowed** to await the arrival of the English escort vessel, **the *Juno*,** which was intended to escort it into the English port. The First Lord of the Admiralty, Winston Churchill, issued orders that the **Juno was to return to port**, and the *Lusitania* sat alone in the channel. Because Churchill knew of the presence of three U-boats in the vicinity, it is reasonable to presume that he had planned for the *Lusitania* to be sunk, and it was. 1201 people lost their lives in the sinking.

43   **Black Tuesday Oct. 29, 1929**
(http://www.pbs.org/wgbh/pages/frontline/shows/dotcon/historical/bubbles.html)

The Bull Market of the Roaring Twenties (1924-1929)

The raging U.S. stock market of the late 1920s was hailed by many as evidence of a "new era" of economic fundamentals. Proponents of this theory pointed to evidence such as the establishment of the Federal Reserve in 1913; Coolidge administration policies including the extension of free trade, anti-inflation measures, and the relaxation of anti-trust laws; and corporate improvements such as increased worker productivity and expanded research and development.

In reality, the driving factor behind both the inflation and the bursting of the speculative bubble was the **expanding use of leverage** (i.e., debt) by individuals as well as corporations. The decade was marked by an enormous **expansion of consumer credit**, which Americans used to finance purchases of new products such as automobiles and radios, which were created using new techniques of mass production that additionally helped to drive down prices. Consumers also **used credit to purchase stocks**, and as the stock market escalated, investors began to take advantage of **margin loans** provided by their brokers. Their primary targets were industries involving new technologies, such as the automobile, motion picture, and aircraft industries. Radio stocks boomed, rising by 400 percent in 1928 alone, and the stock market attracted an immense public following.

On Sept. 3, 1929, the Dow Jones reached its high for the year before the bubble began to deflate. Oct. 24, which became known as "Black Thursday," marked the beginning of the stock market's downturn, remembered as the "Crash of 1929." Almost 13 million shares were traded on that day as an **unexpected panic** affected the markets. Although the following Friday was quieter, the Dow fell by a record 38 points on Monday, Oct. 28, and another 30 points on the infamous "Black Tuesday," Oct. 29, when a record 16.5 million shares changed hands. Following the chaos of October, the market briefly rallied through spring 1930 before plummeting again during the early 1930s.

44   Recession of 1937–

1938 (http://en.wikipedia.org/wiki/Recession_of_1937%E2%80%9338)

The **Recession of 1937–1938** was an economic downturn that occurred during the Great Depression in the United States.

By the spring of 1937, production, profits, and wages had regained their 1929 levels. Unemployment remained high, but it was slightly lower than the 25% rate seen in 1933. The American economy took a sharp downturn in mid-1937, lasting for 13 months through most of 1938. Industrial production declined almost 30 percent and production of durable goods fell even faster.

Unemployment jumped from 14.3% in 1937 to 19.0% in 1938. Manufacturing output fell by 37% from the 1937 peak and was back to 1934 levels. Producers reduced their expenditures on durable goods, and inventories declined, but personal income was only 15% lower than it had been at the peak in 1937. In most sectors, hourly earnings continued to rise throughout the recession, which partly compensated for the reduction in the number of hours worked. As unemployment rose, consumers' expenditures declined, thereby leading to further cutbacks in production.

Economists disagree about the causes of this downturn. It has been widely noted that the Undistributed profits tax enacted in 1936 caused a panic in Corporate America. Faced with the specter of taxation on retained earnings the business world immediately ceased most planned expansion and capital equipment purchases. Keynesian economists assign blame to cuts in federal spending and increases in taxes at the insistence of the US Treasury. Historian Robert C. Goldston also noted that two vital New Deal job programs, the Public Works

Administration and Works Progress Administration, experienced drastic cuts in the budget which Roosevelt signed into law for the 1937-1938 fiscal year. Monetarists, such as Milton Friedman, assign blame to the Federal Reserve's **tightening of the money supply** in 1936 and 1937. Austrian School economist Johnathan Catalan assigns blame to the relatively large **expansion of the money supply** from 1933 to 1937.

49   1973-74 Stock Market Crashes

(http://en.wikipedia.org/wiki/1973%E2%80%9374_stock_market_ crash)

The **1973–1974 bear market** was a bear market that lasted between January 1973 and December 1974. Affecting all the major stock markets in the world, particularly the United Kingdom, it was one of the worst stock market downturns in modern history. The crash came after the **collapse of the Bretton Woods system** over the previous two years, with the associated 'Nixon Shock' and United States **dollar devaluation** under the Smithsonian Agreement. It was compounded by the outbreak of the **1973 oil crisis** in October of that year. It was a major event of the 1970s recession.

In the 699 days between 11 January 1973 and 6 December 1974, the New York Stock Exchange's Dow Jones Industrial Average benchmark lost over 45% of its value, making it the seventh-worst bear market in the history of the index. 1972 had been a good year for the DJIA, with gains of 15% in the twelve months. 1973 had been expected to be even better, with Time magazine reporting, just 3 days before the crash began, that it was 'shaping up as a gilt-edged year'. In the two years from 1972 to 1974, the American economy slowed from 7.2% real GDP growth to −2.1% contraction, while inflation (by CPI) jumped from 3.4% in 1972 to 12.3% in 1974.

Worse was the effect in the United Kingdom, and particularly on the London Stock Exchange's FT 30, which lost 73% of its value during the crash. From a position of 5.1% real GDP growth in 1972, the UK went into recession in 1974, with GDP falling by 1.1%. At the time, the **UK's property market** was going through a major crisis, and a secondary banking crisis forced the Bank of England to bail out a number of lenders. In the United Kingdom, the crash ended after the **rent freeze** was lifted on 19 December 1974, allowing a readjustment of property prices; over the following year, stock prices rose by 150%. The definitive market low for the FT30 Index (a forerunner of the FTSE100 today), came on 6 January 1975 when the index closed at 146 (having reached a nadir of 145.8 intra-day). The market then practically doubled in just over 3 months. However, unlike in the United States, inflation continued to rise, to 25% in 1975, giving way to the era of stagflation. The Hong Kong Hang Seng Index also fell from 1,800 in early 1973 to close to 300.

50   Silver Thursday March 17, 1980

(http://en.wikipedia.org/wiki/Silver_Thursday#cite_note-3)

Silver Thursday was an event that occurred in the United States in the silver commodity markets on Thursday, **March 27, 1980**. A steep fall in silver prices led to panic on commodity and futures exchanges.

Nelson Bunker Hunt and William Herbert Hunt, the sons of Texas oil billionaire Haroldson Lafayette Hunt, Jr., had for some time been attempting to corner the market in silver. In 1979, the price for silver jumped from $6 per troy ounce ($0.193/g) to a record high of $48.70 per troy ounce ($1.566/g), which represents an increase of 712%. The brothers were estimated to hold one third of the entire world supply of silver (other than that held by governments). The situation for other prospective purchasers of silver was so dire that the jeweler Tiffany's took out a full page ad in *The New York Times*, condemning the Hunt Brothers and stating "We think it is unconscionable for anyone to hoard several billion, yes billion, dollars' worth of silver and thus drive the price up so high that others must pay artificially high prices for articles made of silver."

But on **January 7, 1980**, in response to the Hunts' accumulation, the **exchange rules regarding leverage** were changed, when **COMEX adopted "Silver Rule 7"** placing heavy restrictions on the purchase of commodities **on margin**. The Hunt brothers had **borrowed heavily to finance their purchases,** and as the price began to fall again, dropping over 50% in just four days, they were unable to meet their obligations, causing panic in the markets.

The Hunt brothers had invested heavily in futures contracts through several brokers, including the brokerage firm Bache Halsey Stuart Shields, later Prudential-Bache Securities and Prudential Securities. When the price of silver dropped below their

minimum margin requirement, they were issued a **margin call** for $100 million. The Hunts were unable to meet the margin call, and, with the brothers facing a potential $1.7 billion loss, the ensuing panic was felt in the financial markets in general, as well as commodities and futures. Many government officials feared that if the Hunts were unable to meet their debts, some large Wall Street brokerage firms and banks might collapse.

To save the situation, a consortium of US banks provided a $1.1 billion line of credit to the brothers which allowed them to pay Bache which, in turn, survived the ordeal. The U.S. Securities and Exchange Commission (SEC) later launched an investigation into the **Hunt brothers**, who had failed to disclose that they in fact held a **6.5% stake in Bache**.

51 "Black Monday" October 19, 1987
(http://www.thebubblebubble.com/1987-crash/)

The **Stock Market Crash of 1987** or "**Black Monday**" was the largest one-day market crash in history. The Dow lost 22.6% of its value or $500 billion dollars on October 19th 1987. **1986 and 1987 were banner** years for the stock market. These years were an extension of an extremely powerful **bull market** that had **started** in the **summer of 1982**. This bull market had been fueled by **low interest rates**, hostile takeovers, **leveraged buyouts** and merger mania. Many companies were scrambling to raise capital to buy each other out. The business philosophy of the time was that companies could grow exponentially simply by constantly acquiring other companies. In a leveraged buyout, a company would raise a massive amount of capital by selling junk bonds to the public. Junk bonds are bonds that pay high interest rates due to their high risk of default. The capital raised through selling junk bonds would go toward the purchase of the desired company. IPOs were also becoming a commonplace driver of market excitement. An IPO or Initial

301

Public Offering is when a company issues stock to the public for the first time…

The investing public eventually became caught up in a contagious euphoria that was similar to that of any other **historic bubble and market crash**. This euphoria made investors, as usual, believe that the stock market would "always go up."

During this growth boom, the SEC found it increasingly difficult to prevent shady IPOs and conglomerates from proliferating. In early 1987, the SEC conducted numerous investigations of illegal insider trading, which created a wary stance among many investors. At the same time, inflation and overheating became a concern due to the high rate of economic and credit growth. The **Federal Reserve rapidly raised short term interest rates** to temper inflation, which **dampened** some of stock investors' enthusiasm. Many institutional trading firms began to utilize portfolio insurance to protect against further stock dips. Portfolio insurance is a hedging strategy that uses stock index futures to cushion equity portfolios against broad stock market declines. As **interest rates rose**, many institutional money managers scrambled to hedge their portfolios at the same time. On October 19th 1987, the stock index futures market was flooded with billions of dollars' worth of sell orders within minutes, causing both the futures and stock markets to crash. In addition, many common stock investors attempted to sell simultaneously, which completely overwhelmed the stock market…

On October 19th 1987, $500 billion in market capitalization was evaporated from the Dow Jones stock index. Markets in nearly every country around the world plunged in a similar fashion. When individual investors heard that a massive stock market crash was occurring, they rushed to call their brokers to sell their stocks. This was unsuccessful because each broker had many clients. Many people lost millions of dollars instantly.

52   1994: Mexican peso crisis :
(http://en.wikipedia.org/wiki/Mexican_peso_crisis)

The **Mexican peso crisis** (also known as the **Tequila crisis**) was a currency crisis sparked by the Mexican government's sudden devaluation of the peso against the U.S. dollar in December 1994, which became one of the first international financial crises ignited by capital flight.

(https://economics.rabobank.com/publications/2013/september/the-tequila-crisis-in-1994/)

"The Tequila crisis in 1994" (September 19, 2013, by Maarten van der Molen)

Furthermore, in anticipation of joining the North American Free Trade Agreement **(NAFTA) in 1994**, Mexico started to further open up its economy. Mexico had to do so, as the free transfer of funds was a core principal of US treaties, including NAFTA. Next to a further trade liberalization for both goods and services, Mexico eliminated most capital and exchange controls. This paved the way for foreign investment in; securities, loans, direct investment, bonds (sovereign and private) and derivatives (Nordgaard, 2013)…

Part of the reform agenda was the introduction of a crawling peg to the US dollar in November 1991. Since then, the peso was allowed to float within a constant lower band and a slowly increasing upper band, therefore, a gradual depreciation was allowed. The pact served at least three purposes. First, it gave foreign investors additional assurance, as the risks of currency fluctuations were limited. Second, it allowed Mexican companies to borrow money in international markets to finance their expansion. Third, a managed exchange rate would help Mexico to fight domestic inflation (Musacchio, 2012).

After the nationalization of almost all private banks in 1982, Mexico privatized them again in 1991-92...

After the privatization of the banks, Mexico experienced an enormous credit boom, as all banks competed strongly to gain more market share to earn back their investments. This credit expansion later turned out fatal, as the performance of the existing portfolio was worse than expected. In addition, new loans were of poor quality due to this rapid expansion. Finally, banks borrowed in dollars to finance their expansion (Musacchio, 2012)...

Below we will discuss the triggers, which in our view, played an important role:

1) The liberalization of the financial account allowed money to flow freely in and out of Mexico.

2) The **low policy rate set by FED at the beginning of the '90s,** led to a search by investors for higher yields. Mexico, which was fighting inflation, had a relatively high policy rate, making it attractive for foreign investment. This resulted in a strong **increase** of portfolio investment. **In 1994, the FED raised its policy rate**, causing a lower

spread, as Mexico's central bank did not follow. The result was a **strong decline** in portfolio investment.

3) Until 1994, Mexico was running a current account deficit, which was compensated by the financial account. However, a sudden stop of the inflow of portfolio investment in March/ April, led to a considerable depletion of the foreign exchange reserves.

4) To stop the outflow of foreign currency in March 1994, Mexico's government started to issue short term dollar denominated debt, called *tesobonos*. By November 1994, 70% of foreign holdings was dollar denominated. The deterioration of the ratio of foreign exchange reserves to foreign denominated debt (with a short maturity) started to concern investors.

5) In the year prior to the crisis, Mexico's government was confronted by social unrest. Two political leaders were assassinated, while the province of Chiapas was confronted with violence. In addition, there were doubts about the fairness of the presidential elections of 1994.

53 "9/11" and Insider Trading
(http://911research.wtc7.net/sept11/stockputs.html)

Pre-9/11 Put Options on Companies Hurt by Attack Indicates Foreknowledge

Financial transactions in the days before the attack suggest that certain individuals used foreknowledge of the attack to reap huge profits.   The evidence of insider trading includes:

- Huge surges in purchases of put options (see below) on stocks of the two airlines used in the attack -- United Airlines and American Airlines
- Surges in purchases of put options on stocks of reinsurance companies expected to pay out billions to cover losses from the attack -- Munich Re and the AXA Group
- Surges in purchases of put options on stocks of financial services companies hurt by the attack -- Merrill Lynch & Co., and Morgan Stanley and Bank of America
- Huge surge in purchases of call options of stock of a weapons manufacturer expected to gain from the attack -- Raytheon
- Huge surges in purchases of 5-Year US Treasury Notes

In each case, the anomalous purchases translated into large profits as soon as the stock market opened a week after the attack: put options were used on stocks that would be hurt by the attack, and call options were used on stocks that would benefit.

Put and call options are contracts that allow their holders to sell and buy assets, respectively, at specified prices by a certain date. Put options allow their holders to profit from declines in stock values because they allow stocks to be bought at market price and sold for the higher option price. The ratio of the volume of put option contracts to call option contracts is called the put/call ratio. The ratio is usually less than one, with a value of around 0.8 considered normal.

Losers

American Airlines and United Airlines, and several insurance companies and banks posted huge loses in stock values when the markets opened on September 17. Put options -- financial instruments which allow investors to profit from the decline in value of stocks -- were purchased on the stocks of these companies in great volume in the week before the attack.

United Airlines and American Airlines

Two of the corporations most damaged by the attack were American Airlines (AMR), the operator of Flight 11 and Flight 77, and United Airlines (UAL), the operator of Flight 175 and Flight 93. According to *CBS News*, in the week before the attack, the put/call ratio for American Airlines was four.   The put/call ratio for United Airlines was 25 times above normal on September 6.

The spikes in put options occurred on days that were uneventful for the airlines and their stock prices.

On Sept. 6-7, when there was no significant news or stock price movement involving United, the Chicago exchange handled 4,744 put options for UAL stock, compared with just 396 call options -- essentially bets that the price will rise. On Sept. 10, an uneventful day for American, the volume was 748 calls and 4,516 puts, based on a check of option trading records.

The *Bloomberg News* reported that put options on the airlines surged to the phenomenal high of 285 times their average.

Over three days before terrorists flattened the World Trade

Center and damaged the Pentagon, there was more than 25 times the previous daily average trading in a Morgan Stanley "put" option that makes money when shares fall below $45. Trading in similar AMR and UAL put options, which make money when their stocks fall below $30 apiece, surged to as much as 285 times the average trading up to that time.

When the market reopened after the attack, United Airlines stock fell 42 percent from $30.82 to $17.50 per share, and American Airlines stock fell 39 percent, from $29.70 to $18.00 per share...

Winners

While most companies would see their stock valuations decline in the wake of the attack, those in the business of supplying the military would see dramatic increases, reflecting the new business they were poised to receive.

Raytheon

Raytheon, maker of Patriot and Tomahawk missiles, saw its stock soar immediately after the attack. Purchases of call options on Raytheon stock increased six fold on the day before the attack.

A Raytheon option that makes money if shares are more than $25 each had 232 options contracts traded on the day before the attacks, almost six times the total number of trades that had occurred before that day. A contract represents options on 100 shares. Raytheon shares soared almost 37 percent to $34.04 during the first week of post-attack U.S. trading.

Raytheon has been fined millions of dollars for inflating the costs of equipment it sells the US military. Raytheon has a secretive subsidiary, E-Systems, whose clients have included the CIA and NSA.

US Treasury Notes

Five-year US Treasury notes were purchased in abnormally high volumes before the attack, and their buyers were rewarded with sharp increases in their value following the attack.

The Wall Street Journal reported on October 2 that the ongoing investigation by the SEC into suspicious stock trades had been joined by a Secret Service probe into an unusually high volume of **five-year US Treasury** note purchases prior to the attacks. The Treasury note transactions included a single $5 billion trade. As the Journal explained: "Five-year Treasury notes are among the best investments in the event of a world crisis, especially one that hits the US. The notes are prized for their safety and their backing by the US government, and usually rally when investors flee riskier investments, such as stocks." The value of these notes, the Journal pointed out, has risen sharply since the events of September 11.

An analysis of the press reports on the subject of apparent insider trading related to the attack shows a trend, with early reports highlighting the anomalies, and later reports excusing them. In his book *Crossing the Rubicon* Michael C. Ruppert illustrates this point by first excerpting a number of reports published shortly after the attack:

- A jump in UAL (United Airlines) put options 90 times (not 90 percent) above normal between September 6 and September 10, and 285 times higher than average on the Thursday before the attack.
  -- CBS News, September 26
- A jump in American Airlines put options 60 times (not 60 percent) above normal on the day before the attacks.
  -- CBS News, September 26
- No similar trading occurred on any other airlines
  -- Bloomberg Business Report, the Institute for Counterterrorism (ICT), Herzliyya, Israel [citing data from the CBOE]
- Morgan Stanley saw, between September 7 and September 10, an increase of 27 times (not 27 percent) in the purchase of put options on its shares.
- Merrill-Lynch saw a jump of more than 12 times the normal level of put options in the four trading days before the attacks.

54 Financial Crisis of 2007-2008

We mentioned earlier how Blacks were brought in to be scapegoated for the fall of the financial system in 2008. Like many of you, I was watching this whole thing unfold in real time. One of the most striking things that I remember was the image of Treasury Secretary Henry Paulson giving testimony to the Senate Banking Committee. This man had a crooked pinky finger on his left hand. A man with his type of money could surely have gotten some plastic surgeon to fix that finger. Or was his finger left in that condition to remind him that when it was time to play his part in this "rip off game", he had better not forget his role?

Below I have lifted an article on the "Financial Crisis" from Wikipedia, then I added a series of clips from articles in a CNN

310

series called "The Crisis: A Timeline." As you read through these events notice the role of the "insiders": Paulson, Bernanke and Goldman Sachs as they "sac" the treasury and fleece the people all very "legally", after they had changed the laws. Then take the time to read the article in the appendix to this chapter entitled "The Secret Goldman Sachs Tapes" to witness this in-the-bed relationship between the Federal Reserve and Goldman Sachs:

(http://en.wikipedia.org/wiki/Financial_crisis_of_2007%E2%80%9308)

The **financial crisis of 2007–2008**, also known as the **Global Financial Crisis** and **2008 financial crisis**, is considered by many economists to have been the worst financial crisis since the Great Depression of the 1930s. It resulted in the threat of total collapse of large financial institutions, the bailout of banks by national governments, and downturns in stock markets around the world. In many areas, the housing market also suffered, resulting in evictions, foreclosures and prolonged unemployment. The crisis played a significant role in the failure of key businesses, declines in consumer wealth estimated in trillions of U.S. dollars, and a downturn in economic activity leading to the 2008–2012 global recession and contributing to the European sovereign-debt crisis.

The **bursting of the U.S. (United States) housing bubble**, which peaked in 2006, caused the values of securities tied to U.S. real estate pricing to plummet, damaging financial institutions globally. The financial crisis was triggered by a complex interplay of policies that encouraged **home ownership**, providing **easier access to loans** for (lending) borrowers, overvaluation of bundled subprime mortgages based on the theory that housing prices would continue to escalate, questionable trading practices on behalf of both buyers and sellers, compensation structures that prioritize short-term deal flow over long-term value creation, and a lack of adequate capital holdings from banks and insurance companies to back the financial commitments they were making. Questions regarding bank solvency, declines in credit availability and damaged investor confidence had an impact on global stock markets, where securities suffered large losses during 2008 and early 2009. Economies worldwide slowed during this period, as credit tightened and international trade declined.

Many causes for the financial crisis have been suggested, with varying weight assigned by experts. The U.S. Senate's Levin–Coburn Report concluded that the crisis was the result of "high risk, complex financial products; undisclosed **conflicts of interest**; the failure of regulators, **the credit rating agencies**, and the market itself to rein in the excesses of Wall Street." The Financial Crisis Inquiry Commission concluded that the financial crisis was avoidable and was caused by "widespread failures in financial regulation and supervision," "dramatic failures of corporate governance and risk management at many systemically important financial institutions," "a combination of **excessive borrowing**, risky investments, **and lack of transparency**" by financial institutions, ill preparation and inconsistent action by government that "added to the uncertainty and panic," a "systemic breakdown in accountability **and ethics**," "collapsing mortgage-lending standards and the mortgage securitization pipeline," **deregulation** of over-the-counter derivatives, especially credit default swaps, and "the failures of **credit rating agencies**" to correctly price risk. The **1999 repeal of the Glass-Steagall Act** effectively removed the separation between investment banks and depository banks in the

United States. Research into the causes of the financial crisis has also focused on the role of **interest rate spreads**.

Lower interest rates encouraged borrowing. From 2000 to 2003, the **Federal Reserve lowered the federal funds rate** target from **6.5% to 1.0%.** This was done to soften the effects of the collapse of the **dot-com bubble** and the **September 2001** terrorist attacks, as well as to combat a perceived risk of deflation. As early as 2002 it was apparent **that credit was fueling** housing instead of business investment as some economists went so far as to advocate that the **Fed "needs to create a housing bubble** to replace the Nasdaq bubble." Moreover, empirical studies using data from advanced countries show that **excessive credit growth** contributed greatly to the severity of the crisis...

Paulson proposal

U.S. Treasury Secretary Henry Paulson proposed a plan under which the U.S. Treasury would acquire up to $700 billion worth of mortgage-backed securities. The plan was immediately backed by President George W. Bush and negotiations began with leaders in the U.S. Congress to draft appropriate legislation.

Consultations among Treasury Secretary Henry Paulson, Chairman of the Federal Reserve Ben Bernanke, U.S. Securities and Exchange Commission chairman Christopher Cox, congressional leaders, and President Bush, moved forward efforts to draft a proposal for a comprehensive solution to the problems created by illiquid assets. News of the coming plan resulted in some stock, bond, and currency markets stability on September 19, 2008...

On September 21, Paulson announced that the original proposal, which would have excluded foreign banks, had been revised **to include foreign financial institutions** with a presence in the United States. The U.S. administration pressured other countries to set up similar bailout plans.

On September 23, the plan was presented by **Paulson and Bernanke** to the Senate Banking Committee, who rejected it as unacceptable.

- On September 24, President Bush addressed the nation on prime time television, describing how serious the financial crisis could become if action was not taken promptly by Congress.
- Also on September 24, 2008, Republican Party nominee for President, John McCain, and Democratic Party nominee for President, Barack Obama, issued a joint statement describing their shared view that "The effort to protect the American economy must not fail."

The plan was introduced on September 20, by Paulson. Named the Troubled Asset Relief Program, but also known as the Paulson Proposal or Paulson Plan... The proposal was only **three pages long**, intentionally short on details to facilitate quick passage by Congress.

There was concern that the current plan created a **conflict of interest** for Paulson. Paulson was a former **CEO of Goldman Sachs**, which stood to benefit from the bailout. Paulson had hired **Goldman executives** as advisors and Paulson's former advisors had joined banks that were also to benefit from the bailout. Furthermore, the original proposal **exempted Paulson** from judicial oversight. Thus there was concern that former **illegal activity** by a financial institution or its executives might be **hidden**.

The treasury staff member responsible for administering the bailout funds was Neel Kashkari, a former vice-president at **Goldman Sachs.**

The original proposal was submitted to the United States House

314

of Representatives, with the purpose of purchasing bad assets, reducing uncertainty regarding the worth of the remaining assets, and restoring confidence in the credit markets. The bill was then expanded and put forth as an amendment to H.R. 3997. The amendment was **rejected** via a vote of the House of Representatives on September 29, 2008, voting 205–228.

On October 1, 2008, the Senate debated and voted on an amendment to H.R. 1424, which substituted a newly revised version of the Emergency Economic Stabilization Act of 2008 for the language of H.R. 1424. The Senate accepted the amendment and **passed** the entire amended bill, voting 74–25. **Additional unrelated** provisions added an estimated $150 billion to the cost of the package and increased the length of the bill to 451 pages. (*See* Public Law 110-343for details on the added provisions.) The amended version of H.R. 1424 was sent to the House for consideration, and on October 3, the House voted 263–171 to enact the bill into law. President George W. Bush signed the bill into law within hours of its congressional enactment, creating the $700 billion Troubled Asset Relief Program (TARP) to purchase failing bank assets. TARP was dwarfed by other guarantees and lending limits; analysis by Bloomberg found the **Federal Reserve** had, by March 2009, committed **$7.77 trillion** to rescuing the financial system, **more than half the value** of **everything** produced in the U.S. that year.

The crisis: A timeline

http://money.cnn.com/galleries/2008/news/0809/gallery.week_that_broke_wall_street/10.html

Monday, Sept. 22 - Second thoughts

Meanwhile, news of the massive federal bailout that was

315

greeted with relief on Friday, sending the Dow up 369 points, began to sink in, and questions emerged. Taxpayers were enraged that Wall Street fat cats would get a **handout** while ordinary citizens were left to flounder. Members of Congress on both sides of the aisle began gearing up for Tuesday's hearing, expressing concern at the notion of handing Treasury a **blank check**, and at the plan's **lack of oversight**.

The markets expressed their own dismay, with the Dow **closing down 373** points as investors fretted about the bailout. The dollar was crushed, posting its biggest single-day drop in four years as traders absorbed just how **diluted** the bailout would leave the U.S. **currency**. Meanwhile, **oil surged more than $25**, its biggest dollar gain ever, to $130 a barrel before settling at $120 as big investors scrambled to fill obligations as the October contract expired.

Tuesday Sept. 23 - A spirited debate
Treasury **Secretary Henry Paulson** and **Federal Reserve** chairman Ben Bernanke went before the Senate Banking Committee to defend the Bush administration's bailout plan in a spirited debate. The two faced strong criticism from both Democrats and Republicans who argued that the program **needed more restrictions**.

Thursday, Sept. 25 - Deal, or no deal
Early in the afternoon, key lawmakers announced that they had reached an agreement on a set of principles for legislation in order to enact the Bush administration's proposal. Markets soared as investors believed the bill would soon be signed.
Late-night talks between lawmakers and Treasury Secretary Henry **Paulson failed** to end in agreement, shattering any hopes of a clean, bipartisan legislative effort, and putting in jeopardy chances of passing a bill by the end of the week.

Then, in another stunning event, Washington Mutual collapsed late Thursday night, marking the **biggest bank failure** in history. But after the troubled thrift was seized by the FDIC, federal regulators helped orchestrate a deal in which JPMorgan Chase paid $1.9 billion for WaMu's assets.

Friday, Sept. 26 - Back to the bargaining table

Wall Street was a grim scene Friday morning. Stocks were looking at a tough session after news of Washington Mutual's collapse the night before and **fears** that partisan bickering would further delay the Bush administration's $700 billion financial rescue plan.

Capitol Hill negotiators returned to the bargaining table Friday to work on details of the plan, while President Bush and leading lawmakers offered assurances that Congress and the administration would hammer out a deal.

Stocks stumbled through much of the day, but they rallied toward the end of the session on news that bailout talks has resumed, with Republicans and Democrats working towards a compromise. Investors positioned themselves for a Monday rally, on the hopes that a deal would be made by Sunday.

Sunday, Sept. 28 - Hard-won agreement

After days of intense negotiations on Capitol Hill, lawmakers unveiled the bailout's final legislation late Sunday afternoon. The bill calls for Treasury to buy as much as $700 billion in troubled mortgages and other assets from financial institutions, which was what Treasury Secretary Henry Paulson proposed when he first announced the plan on Sept. 18.

Monday, Sept. 29 - Crushing defeat

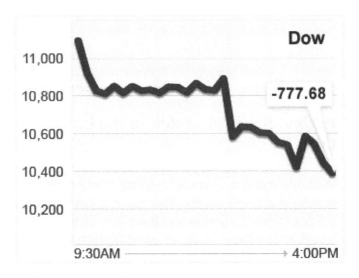

In a stunning development, the House of Representatives **voted down** the $700 billion financial bailout plan by a 228-205 margin after working days to hash out an agreement. Two-thirds of Republicans and one-third of Democrats voted against the measure.

The **defeat shocked the world**, following pledges by leaders of both parties to work together to avert economic disaster. Markets in the U.S. and abroad reacted with alarm. The Dow **plunged 778 points**, its largest one-day point drop ever, while Japan's Nikkei lost 4%, Australia's markets fell 4.3% and Taiwan's stocks retreated 3.6%.

It was unclear how Congress would proceed with the legislation.

After getting smacked down by the sudden defeat of the bailout plan in the House, stocks made a comeback as **investors bet** that lawmakers would eventually agree on a plan to rescue the economy.
The Dow Jones industrial average **rose** a whopping 485 points, making up much of the historic 777 point loss in the previous session.
But the credit markets remained frozen. And several closely watched measures of bank lending fear hit all-time highs, as

firms continued to hoard funds.
Most of the gains came late in the session after the Federal Deposit Insurance Corporation said it wants to temporarily increase the amount of money it can insure.

The agency's request to raise its $100,000 insurance limit was aimed at making anxious businesses and consumers less likely to withdraw funds from struggling banks. It was also seen by many as an attempt to **sway critics** of the $700 billion bailout plan.

House lawmakers **adjourned** for the day in observance of the **Jewish New Year**. President Bush, meanwhile, took to the airwaves to express his disappointment in the bailout's failure. "Our economy is depending on decisive action from the government," Bush said. "The sooner we address the problem, the sooner we can get back on the path of growth and job creation."

The bill was set to head to the Senate Wednesday.

Wednesday, Oct. 1 - The first hurdle

With credit market gauges showing historically tight lending, investors again were fearful that the government's financial rescue plan would not make it through a widely anticipated Senate vote.

But lawmakers came through Wednesday night, as the Senate passed a modified version of the bill that the House of Representatives rejected on Monday.

The revised measure was **passed** by a vote of 74 to 25 after more than three hours of floor debate in the Senate.

Presidential nominees Sens. Barack Obama, D-Ill., and John McCain, R-Ariz., voted in favor.

Friday, Oct. 3 - Bailout becomes law

Just hours after the Labor Department reported the biggest drop in jobs in more than five years, the House finally passed

319

a far-reaching plan to bail out the nation's financial system.

The 263-to-171 vote was the result of strong lobbying on the part of the White House and other supporters of the bill all week. After being amended by the Senate to include key sweeteners, including several tax breaks and an increase in the FDIC insurance cap to $250,000 from $100,000, members on both sides of the aisle agreed to switch their votes from "No" to "Yes." President Bush signed the bill into law later in the day.

Earlier Friday, Wachovia and Wells Fargo announced plans to merge, just four days after Citigroup said it would pay $2.2 billion for Wachovia's banking assets. Citigroup demanded that Wachovia and Wells Fargo terminate the proposed deal, valued at approximately $15.1 billion.

Monday, Oct. 6 - A bigger lifeline

As a stopgap until the Treasury's $700 billion financial rescue went into effect, the **Federal Reserve** announced Monday that it would **double** the amount of money it makes available to the nation's banks through auctions.

The **Fed** said it would make $600 billion available to banks through its Term Auction lending facility, and it signaled that number could increase to $900 billion later in the year.

But as investors realized that the government's bailout bill was not a cure-all, stocks went into a tailspin. The Dow **sank a record 800 points** before recovering somewhat, but it closed below 10,000 points for the first time since 2004.

Later Monday afternoon, Bank of America reported a 68% drop in profits and cut its dividend. The bank, which rescued both Countrywide Financial and Merrill Lynch in 2008, said it will raise $10 billion through a stock sale.

Tuesday, Oct. 7 - New kind of bailout

In a speech that day before the National Association of Business Economics in Washington, **Fed chief Ben Bernanke** said the economic **outlook has worsened**, and the financial crisis **will hurt** the economy well into next year. He also **implied** that more interest-rate cuts were on the way.

Later, the **Fed reported** that borrowing by consumers fell in August for the first time in more than 10 years, as budgets tightened and credit became scarcer.

Investors didn't like what they heard, and stocks fell to five-year lows. The Dow **tanked another 500 points.**

Friday, October 10 - Vertigo
President Bush addressed the nation and encouraged the American people to have **confidence** in the economy during a "deeply unsettling period" - but with the Dow losing nearly **700 points in the first five minutes** of trading, that was an understatement.

It was a volatile day on Wall Street as further signs of economic distress emerged. At one point the Dow dipped below the 8,000 mark, but ultimately closed down 128 to 8,451.19.

Market bellweather GE reported a 22% drop in net income to $4.3 billion for the third quarter, in line with expectations. Earnings from continuing operations fell 10% to 45 cents per share while revenues grew 11% to $47.2 billion.

Oil prices plunged more than $9 to a 13-month low Friday on **fears** that the weakening global economy would drive down demand for oil.

And General Motors had to issue a statement denying that it was considering bankruptcy after its shares lost 31% on

Thursday, when it closed at just $4.76, the stock's lowest price since 1950. GM shares ended Friday's session at $4.86.

Meanwhile, news emerged that House Democratic leaders are assembling a second economic stimulus package, which could cost as much as $150 billion, and will be geared toward helping struggling state and local governments.

Cycling up to January 26, 2016

I am writing this book in the fall of 2014. As I stated in Chapter 7 "QE-Infinity" started on September 13, 2012 and zero interest rates will persist "at least through 2015". So the Fed started feeding a new "stock market bubble" with cheap money in 2012, the Stock Market prices are shooting through the roof; the Dow Jones average moving from 12,101 in June of 2012 to highest in history with levels of 17,123 on September 12, 2014, an increase of 41% over a two year period. But the pin is already being forecasted to be stuck in this bubble at the end of 2015; which makes January 26, 2016 a very interesting date indeed. I seriously doubt that the "Dodd-Frank" regulatory reforms can do anything about what is about to happen (see Appendix to this chapter).

Brazil, Russia, India, China and South Africa (BRICS) now even Germany are setting up an alternative monetary fund outside of the IMF. They plan to remove the U.S. dollar as the global reserve currency. America is going to crash and she is preparing a scapegoat to take the blame. White police are shooting Black men down in the streets like dogs in plain daylight. Surplus military equipment has been given free of charge to municipalities, states and now even school districts in preparations for a race war between Black and White, the "sheep" and the "sheepdog" so that the "evil shepherd" can get away clean and blame the fall of the dollar and the fall of America on a new Civil War. America has plunged other countries like Iraq and Syria into civil war. Now Israel and her friends in America's ruling class are pumping up the race hatred between people while blaming the truth teller, Minister Farrakhan, for being "divisive." Aren't we tired of being "played"? Do we need a "Daniel" to read this "writing on the wall"?

Appendix to Chapter 8

The Secret Goldman Sachs Tapes

Michael Lewis
September 26, 2014
Bloomberg View

> *The Fed encourages its employees to keep their heads down, to obey their managers and to appease the banks. That is, bank regulators failed to do their jobs properly not because they lacked the tools but because they were discouraged from using them.*

Probably most people would agree that the people paid by the U.S. government to regulate Wall Street have had their difficulties. Most people would probably also agree on two reasons those difficulties seem only to be growing: an ever-more complex financial system that regulators must have explained to them by the financiers who create it, and the ever-more common practice among regulators of leaving their government jobs for much higher paying jobs at the very banks they were once meant to regulate. Wall Street's regulators are people who are paid by Wall Street to accept Wall Street's explanations of itself, and who have little ability to defend themselves from those explanations.

Our financial regulatory system is obviously dysfunctional. But because the subject is so tedious, and the details so complicated, the public doesn't pay it much attention.

That may very well change today, for today -- Friday, Sept. 26 --- the radio program "This American Life" will air a jaw-dropping story about Wall Street regulation, and the public will have no trouble at all understanding it.

The reporter, Jake Bernstein, has obtained 46 hours of tape recordings, made secretly by a Federal Reserve employee, of conversations within the Fed, and between the Fed and Goldman Sachs. The Ray Rice video for the financial sector has arrived.

First, a bit of background -- which you might get equally well from today's broadcast as well as from this article by ProPublica. After the 2008 financial crisis, the New York Fed, now the chief U.S. bank regulator, commissioned a study of itself. This study, which the Fed also intended to keep to itself, set out to understand why the Fed hadn't spotted the insane and destructive behavior inside the big banks, and stopped it before it got out of control. The "discussion draft" of the Fed's internal study, led by a Columbia Business School professor and former banker named David Beim, was sent to the Fed on Aug. 18, 2009.

It's an extraordinary document. There is not space here to do it justice, but the gist is this: The Fed failed to regulate the banks because it did not encourage its employees to ask questions, to speak their minds or to point out problems.

Just the opposite: The Fed encourages its employees to keep their heads down, to obey their managers and to appease the banks. That is, bank regulators failed to do their jobs properly not because they lacked the tools but because they were discouraged from using them.

The report quotes Fed employees saying things like, "until I know what my boss thinks I don't want to tell you," and "no one feels individually accountable for financial crisis mistakes because management is through consensus." Beim was himself surprised that what he thought was going to be an investigation of financial failure was actually a story of cultural failure.

Any Fed manager who read the Beim report, and who wanted to fix his institution, or merely cover his ass, would instantly have set out to hire strong-willed, independent-minded people who were willing to speak their minds, and set them loose on our financial sector. The Fed does not appear to have done this, at least not intentionally. But in late 2011, as those managers staffed up to take on the greater bank regulatory role given to them by the Dodd-Frank legislation, they hired a bunch of new people and one of them was a strong-willed, independent-minded woman named Carmen Segarra.

I've never met Segarra, but she comes across on the broadcast as a likable combination of good-humored and principled. "This American Life" also interviewed people who had worked with her, before she arrived at the Fed, who describe her as smart and occasionally blunt,

324

but never unprofessional. She is obviously bright and inquisitive: speaks four languages, holds degrees from Harvard, Cornell and Columbia. She is also obviously knowledgeable: Before going to work at the Fed, she worked directly, and successfully, for the legal and compliance departments of big banks. She went to work for the Fed after the financial crisis, she says, only because she thought she had the ability to help the Fed to fix the system.

In **early 2012**, Segarra was assigned to regulate Goldman Sachs, and so was installed inside Goldman. (The people who regulate banks for the Fed are physically stationed inside the banks.)

The job right from the start seems to have been different from what she had imagined: In meetings, Fed employees would defer to the Goldman people; if one of the Goldman people said something revealing or even alarming, the other Fed employees in the meeting would either ignore or downplay it. For instance, in one meeting a Goldman employee expressed the view that "once clients are wealthy enough certain consumer **laws don't apply to them.**" After that meeting, Segarra turned to a fellow Fed regulator and said how surprised she was by that statement -- to which the regulator replied, "You didn't hear that."

This sort of thing occurred often enough -- Fed regulators denying what had been said in meetings, Fed managers asking her to alter minutes of meetings after the fact -- that Segarra decided she needed to record what actually had been said. So she went to the Spy Store and bought a tiny tape recorder, then began to record her meetings at Goldman Sachs, until she was fired.

(How Segarra got herself fired by the Fed is interesting. In **2012**, Goldman was rebuked by a Delaware judge for its behavior during a corporate acquisition. Goldman had advised one energy company, El Paso Corp., as it sold itself to another energy company, Kinder Morgan, in which Goldman actually owned a $4 billion stake, and a Goldman banker had a big personal investment. The incident forced the Fed to ask Goldman to see its conflict of interest policy. It turned out that **Goldman had no conflict of interest policy** -- but when Segarra insisted on saying as much in her report, her bosses tried to get her to change her report. Under pressure, she finally agreed to change the language in her report, but she couldn't resist telling her boss that she wouldn't be changing her mind. Shortly after that encounter, she was fired.)

I don't want to spoil the revelations of "This American Life": It's far better to hear the actual sounds on the radio, as so much of the meaning of the piece is in the tones of the voices -- and, especially, in the breathtaking wussiness of the people at the Fed charged with regulating Goldman Sachs. But once you have listened to it -- as when you were faced with the newly unignorable truth of what actually happened to that NFL running back's fiancee in that elevator -- consider the following:

1. You sort of knew that the regulators were more or less controlled by the banks. Now you know.

2. The only reason you know is that one woman, Carmen Segarra, has been brave enough to fight the system. She has paid a great price to inform us all of the obvious. She has lost her job, undermined her career, and will no doubt also endure a lifetime of lawsuits and slander.

So what are you going to do about it? At this moment the Fed is probably telling itself that, like the financial crisis, this, too, will blow over. It shouldn't.

To contact the writer of this article: Michael Lewis at mlewis1@bloomberg.net

Chapter 9

How close is close enough?

As a scientist I must accept the fact that I could be in error. Therefore I must check myself. But in doing so, I will also give confidence to my readers that we are on to something. One thing that gives me confidence is that no matter how right or wrong I am with my "theories," The Teachings of The Most Honorable Elijah Muhammad as taught to us now by his best student, the Honorable Minister Louis Farrakhan is "right and exact." All I am doing is trying to put "meat on the bones" of a firm skeletal foundation. We have to fill in the blanks so that we can make our Teachings manifest themselves in action and institutions. We have the right teachings; we just lack "confidence."

Checking for alternative cycles

As stated in Chapter 7 we came up with the number 2625 days from observing similar economic and social patterns in comparison to the Bible book of Daniel's "end time prophecy" at the end of Chapter 12 in Daniel. "2625 days" has a special quality in terms of the 7 day week and Jewish attempts at keeping the "Sabbath" or seventh day holy.

Now we are going to take the raw data of the panics and analyze it to see if we can mathematically draw out hidden patterns just by using basic statistical tools. We then will compare alternative interval spacing to see which one best fits the data.

We will analyze the data in a series of steps; the first 4 of which are presented in Table 3: Panic Intervals. Since we are interested at checking if there are predictable intervals between the

Table 3: Panic Intervals

Panics	Step 1 Intervals	Step 2 short list	Step 3 Interval/7.142	Step 4 Stretch
1621				
1637.0876	16.0876		2.252534304	
1720.6708	83.5832		11.70305237	
1763.668	42.9972		6.02033044	
1772.41889	8.75089		1.225271633	
1792.167	19.74811		2.765067208	
1799.83504	7.66804		1.073654439	
1815.4627	15.62766		2.188134976	
1819.41615	3.95345		0.553549426	
1836.91992	17.50377		2.450821899	
1857.7502	20.83028		2.916589191	
1866.33128	8.58108		1.201495379	
1873.668	7.33672		1.027264072	
1882	8.332		1.166619994	
1893.33128	11.33128		1.586569588	
1901.3751	8.04382		1.126269952	
1907.7507	6.3756		0.892691123	
1915.3425	7.5918		1.062979558	
1929.8268	14.4843		2.028045365	1929.827
1937.5	7.6732		1.074376925	1937.5
1973	35.5		4.970596472	
1980.21096	7.21096	7.21096	1.009655559	
1987.8	7.58904	7.58904	1.062593111	
1994.91718	7.11718	7.11718	0.996524783	
2001.69589	6.77871	6.77871	0.949133296	1973
2008.71233	7.01644	7.01644	0.98241949	1980.211
Average	15.50849	7.142466		1987.8
Avg. days	5664.477	2608.786		1994.917
Median	8.332	7.11718		2001.696
Mode	#N/A	#N/A		2008.712

panics, we subtracted, for instance, the year 1621 from the year 1637.0876 which gives an interval of 16.0876 years. The fractions represents a part of a year, so "1637.0876" represents February of 1637.

The results of the interval calculations are presented under "Step 1: Intervals" column. As we see the intervals range from a low of 4 years to over 83 years (see Graph 4). The average interval between panics is 15.50849 years. The median is 8.332 years.

Graph 4: Raw Intervals

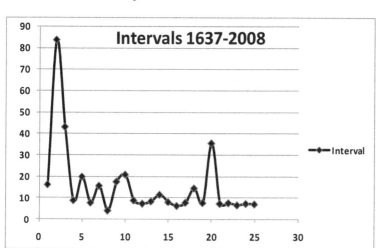

There are no two intervals exactly the same so we cannot measure the mode.

Although there are wide fluctuations in the length of intervals, we see that they are bunching up near 7 years and have more or less similar intervals from 1973 through 2008.71233. In "Step 2: short list" we have separated out those years and recalculated to obtain an average of 7.142 years and a median of 7.117 years.

Now let's look at the years from 1929.8268 to 2008.71233. First we put them on a scatter plot graph (Graph 5) and we notice that there could be some pattern here except for a kink between points 2 and 3 which represents on the y-axis, between 1937 and 1973. Before 1937 and after 1973 there seems to be some continuity.

Our next step (Step 3) is to divide the average interval (7.142) calculated between 1973 and 2008 into all of the intervals starting back with 16.0876 between 1637 and 1621. Now we have figures like 2.25, 11.70, 6.02 and 4.97. "2.25" means that there are a little over 2 intervals of 7.142 between 1621 and 1637.0786. "11.70" means that between 1637.0876 and 1720.767 (83.58) there are almost 12 intervals of 7.142 years. When we get down to the interval between 1937.5 and 1973 we have almost 5 (4.97) intervals of 7.142 years. This is very helpful. Now we can fill in the gap with 5 "dummy" intervals as demonstrated in "Step 4" and in Graph 6. Adding the "dummy" intervals as place holders "stretches" the data out over more intervals and lines up the dots to where they make almost a straight line (Graph 6).

Graph 5: Raw data

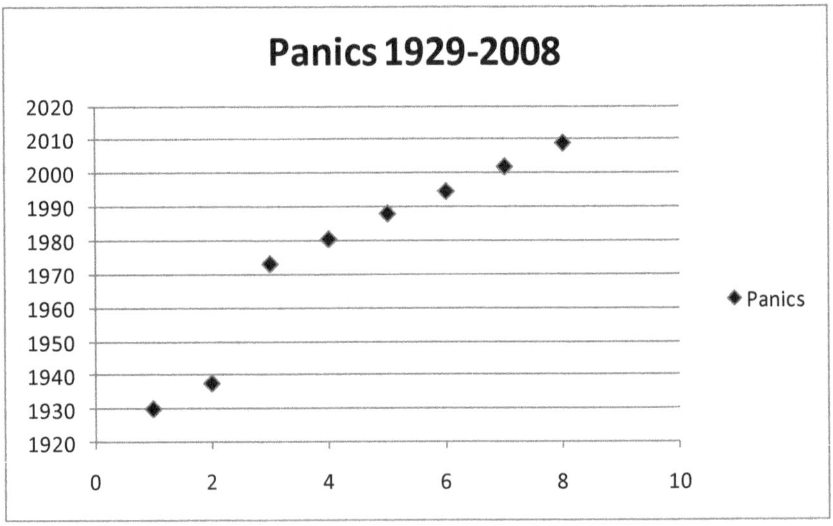

Graph 6: Adding "dummy" intervals

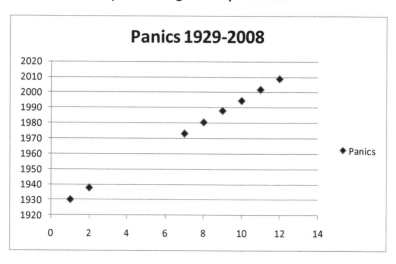

Panics 1929-2008

Graph 7: Fitting "Snake" to Plot

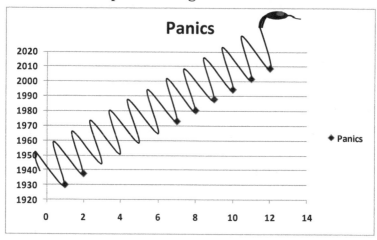

Panics

Now we can fit our "Snake" to the plot of points (Graph 7). We use this "Snake" or sine curve not just to connect the dots, but to show the underlying cycle of bubble development. First, within

331

each cycle between panics you first have a rise or bubble development starting 3 to 4 years into the cycle, then you have a fall when the bubble bursts at the end of a cycle. What about those 5 periods on our graph where there were no observed or recorded "panics"? This would be a problem if I were basing the reasons for these panics on **business cycles** such as the "Kitchin inventory cycle", or the "Juglar fixed-investment cycle" or the "Kuznets infrastructural investment cycle" which should produce some sign of activity as long as the economy is active.

What I believe we have instead is a small group of insiders who manipulate the markets and can **decide if** they are or are not going to pull the strings each time. Since they pull the strings based on an underlying pattern, they must lie dormant or hibernate like a snake **every now and then**, so that the general public would not catch on to who and how the financial markets are being manipulated. I am not saying that there are not some "naturally" occurring business cycles which are produced by the flow of goods and services over time. What I am saying is that superimposed over the "natural" economic system is a secret group of insider manipulators who play the outsiders for fools. When a snake hibernates, it is still breathing and its heart is pumping blood, but the intensity has slowed down so much that the snake would appear dead. As he hibernates the snake stays in its den to avoid detection until the next season.

On a historical note, remember we described in Chapter 6 how the big Jewish bankers schemed to get the Federal Reserve System in place and Jacob Schiff even warned the Chamber of Commerce in the spring of 1907 that if they did not set up a central bank, large financial crashes would occur. A large financial crash did occur in the fall of 1907 allowing Schiff to convince President Wilson to sign the Federal Reserve System bill in 1913, but many parts of it were not put in place because of opposition from members of congress who understood the dangers of the Federal Reserve. However, after another shock, "Black Tuesday" on October 29,

1929, the country almost went into bankruptcy by 1933. In exchange for the Federal Reserve and foreign bankers loaning America the money to recover, F.D. Roosevelt authorized the full powers of the Federal Reserve to be enacted.

So after a slight economic stumble in 1937, there were no more panics or crashes between 1937 and 1973. These were years of unprecedented economic growth and stability which the Federal Reserve System chairmen took credit for. However, this was the "snake" playing possum; staying out of sight to make a series of big strikes starting with the stock market crashes in 1973 through 1974.

The snake may not have just being playing possum on its own but laying low after the terrible experience of the Holocaust from 1938-1945 as we depicted in our chapter on "Persecution of the Jews." Not only were the Jews put in concentration camps during World War II, their banking institutions were nationalized in France in 1936 and 1945. However, under Georges Pompidou's French presidency the law was changed in 1973 that eliminated interest-free borrowing of the French government from the government owned Banque de France and gave the Rothschild Banque the chance to get back in the government lending business. Georges Pompidou was a former director of the Banque Rothschild from 1956-1962. The law that eliminated interest-free borrowing by the French treasury also opened the door for speculation in the foreign exchange markets in 1973. This coupled with President Nixon's decision in 1971 to remove dollar-gold convertibility, opened the door for the moneychangers to manipulate currencies and fleece whole nations again. So the cycles of boom-bust started again in 1973.

The "snake" struck in 1980 and 1987, then moved down to Mexico and struck in 1994. But the "Great Snake's" best day ever was September 11, 2001 when he fooled the whole world with making "fire come down from heaven" while running off with the loot. Before the economy and people could barely recover from

"9/11", the Fed produced the housing bubble and burst it causing the big financial market's collapse of 2008, which I liken to the fall of that great statue in the book of Daniel with the head of gold, breast and arms of silver, its belly and its thighs of bronze, its legs of iron, but feet partly iron and partly of clay. America's economy has collapsed but she is moving enough to convince some that she will be back and the great rise in stock prices between 2012 and 2014 is taken by some to represent her comeback. But it is all smoke and mirrors. The evil shepherd, "Great Snake", waits.

I like using the analogy of the "snake" for another reason. The Hyksos kings when they sat on the throne of Egypt took on the name, Apap or Apophis, the "Great Snake" of darkness and confusion. They also worshiped "Set" or "Seth" where our word "Satan" comes from, who was the enemy of Osiris; they were even called the "Scythians" or the "Sethians". They were proud in worshiping the devil or Satan then, but have fooled the people now into accepting them as "angels of light" (i.e. "Illuminati"), when in fact they are the angels of death and darkness (see 2 Thessalonians 2:3, 4).

Back to the data; Table 4 uses our average interval of 7.142466 which we derived from our "short list" to step us through time from 1623.14519 to 2008.8386 which represents our predicted dates on which panics should occur. Since we know the exact date of September 11, 2001 (2001.69589 converted to a general number), we subtract 7.142466 from 2001.69589 to get 1994.55342. We continue to subtract 7.142466 from each proceeding year until we reach 1623.14518. We add 7.142466 to 2001.69589 to get our last predicted crash that we have data for of 2008.83836. The last number in this series represents the next predicted panic, in this case 2015.98082.

Then we take the actual panics and place them on our time grid next to its closest match, such as for our predicted date or value of 1723.13972 we place next to it 1720.671, a date of an actual panic. We do this for each of our 26 observations.

Table 4

Step 5	Prediction	Dev.	Abs Dev.
Weeks	372.683672		
Days	2608.78571		
Panics	7.142466		
1621	1623.14519	2.145192	2.145192
	1630.28766		
1637.088	1637.43012	0.342524	0.342524
	1644.57259		
	1651.71506		
	1658.85752		
	1665.99999		
	1673.14245		
	1680.28492		
	1687.42739		
	1694.56985		
	1701.71232		
	1708.85478		
	1715.99725		
1720.671	1723.13972	2.468916	2.468916
	1730.28218		
	1737.42465		
	1744.56711		
	1751.70958		
	1758.85205		
1763.668	1765.99451	2.326512	2.326512
1772.419	1773.13698	0.718088	0.718088
	1780.27944		
	1787.42191		
1792.167	1794.56438	2.397376	2.397376
1799.835	1801.70684	1.871802	1.871802
	1808.84931		
1815.463	1815.99177	0.529074	0.529074

Panics	Prediction	Dev.	Abs Dev.
1819.416	1823.13424		
	1830.27671		
1836.92	1837.41917	0.499252	0.499252
	1844.56164		
	1851.7041		
1857.75	1858.84657	1.09637	1.09637
1866.331	1865.98904	-0.34224	0.342244
1873.668	1873.1315	-0.5365	0.536498
1882	1880.27397	-1.72603	1.726032
	1887.41643		
1893.331	1894.5589	1.22762	1.22762
1901.375	1901.70137	0.326266	0.326266
1907.751	1908.84383	1.093132	1.093132
1915.343	1915.9863	0.643798	0.643798
	1923.12876		
1929.827	1930.27123	0.44443	0.44443
1937.5	1937.4137	-0.0863	0.086304
	1944.55616		
	1951.69863		
	1958.84109		
	1965.98356		
1973	1973.12603	0.126026	0.126026
1980.211	1980.26849	0.057532	0.057532
1987.8	1987.41096	-0.38904	0.389042
1994.917	1994.55342	-0.36376	0.363756
2001.696	2001.69589	0	0
2008.712	2008.83836	0.126056	0.126056
	2015.98082	avg dev	0.875354
		days	319.5041

Our next step (5) is to see how close our model predicts the actual data by subtracting the actual from the predicted to get a measure of the deviation from a perfect prediction. For instance if we subtract 1637.088 from 1637.43012 we have a positive 0.342524. We carry out this type of calculation for each of our actual panics or data points. As we see, sometimes the deviation is negative and sometimes positive. If we add up these deviations, a lot of them would cancel each other out and we would not have a clear picture of how well the model predicted the actual data. Therefore, we take the "absolute value" of each of our calculated deviations so that we can find out our average deviation. The average deviation tells us how much we must hedge our bets on accepting the results of our model as a true forecast of the future.

The average deviation for our 7.142 years interval model is 0.875354 years or 319.5 days. This means that if we add 7.142 to our last predicted value of 2008.98082 we have predicted the next panic to be 2015.98082, plus or minus 0.875354 years. So the panic could occur anywhere between 2015.105 and 2016.856 which is a 1.75 year period. Good but not good enough. There are a couple of things wrong with our 7.142 interval model based on my assumption that the rabbis would always want to keep the "Sabbath Day" holy. That is, the calculations must be multiples of 7 days. In this case 7.142 years represents 2608.78571 days or 372.683672 weeks, not whole numbers.

So to get an interval based on whole weeks, we picked intervals around 372.683672 weeks. We chose 373 weeks, 374 weeks, 375 weeks and 376 weeks. Then we went through the same process as we did in Table 4. The results for 375 weeks are presented in Table 5, 374 weeks in Table 6, 376 weeks in Table 7 and 373 weeks presented in Table 8. We calculated the average deviation for each model and placed them side by side in Table 10. A quick glance at the average deviation or days reveals that the 375 week model of 2625 days (avg. dev. 256.7529) is a better predictor than any of the other four. It is 85.5 days better than 373 week model, 62.7 days better than the 372.683672 week model, 10.2 days better than the 374 week model and 27 days better than the 376 week model.

Table 5

Step 6	Prediction	Dev.	Abs Dev.
Weeks	375		
Days	2625		
Panics	7.186858316		
1621	1620.792399	-0.2076	0.207601
	1627.979258		
1637.0876	1635.166116	-1.92148	1.921484
	1642.352974		
	1649.539833		
	1656.726691		
	1663.913549		
	1671.100407		
	1678.287266		
	1685.474124		
	1692.660982		
	1699.847841		
	1707.034699		
	1714.221557		
1720.6708	1721.408416	0.737616	0.737616
	1728.595274		
	1735.782132		
	1742.968991		
	1750.155849		
	1757.342707		
1763.668	1764.529566	0.861566	0.861566
1772.41889	1771.716424	-0.70247	0.702466
	1778.903282		
	1786.090141		
1792.167	1793.276999	1.109999	1.109999
1799.83504	1800.463857	0.628817	0.628817
	1807.650715		
1815.4627	1814.837574	-0.62513	0.625126

Panics	Prediction	Dev.	Abs Dev.
1819.41615	1822.024432	2.608282	2.608282
	1829.211290		
1836.91992	1836.398149	-0.52177	0.521771
	1843.585007		
	1850.771865		
1857.7502	1857.958724	0.208524	0.208524
1866.33128	1865.145582	-1.1857	1.185698
1873.668	1872.332440	-1.33556	1.33556
1882	1879.519299	-2.4807	2.480701
	1886.706157		
1893.33128	1893.893015	0.561735	0.561735
1901.3751	1901.079874	-0.29523	0.295226
1907.7507	1908.266732	0.516032	0.516032
1915.3425	1915.453590	0.11109	0.11109
	1922.640449		
1929.8268	1929.827307	0.000507	0.000507
1937.5	1937.014165	-0.48583	0.485835
	1944.201023		
	1951.387882		
	1958.574740		
	1965.761598		
1973	1972.948457	-0.05154	0.051543
1980.21096	1980.135315	-0.07564	0.075645
1987.8	1987.322173	-0.47783	0.477827
1994.91718	1994.509032	-0.40815	0.408148
2001.69589	2001.695890	0	0
2008.7123	2008.882748	0.170448	0.170448
	2016.069607	avg dev	0.703433
		days	256.7529

Table 6

Step 7	Prediction	Dev.	Abs Dev.
Weeks	374		
Days	2618		
Panics	7.167693361		
1621	1621.808320	0.80832	0.80832
	1628.976010		
1637.088	1636.143700	-0.9439	0.9439
	1643.311390		
	1650.479080		
	1657.646770		
	1664.814460		
	1671.982150		
	1679.149840		
	1686.317530		
	1693.485220		
	1700.652910		
	1707.820600		
	1714.988290		
1720.671	1722.155980	1.48518	1.48518
	1729.323670		
	1736.491360		
	1743.659050		
	1750.826740		
	1757.994430		
1763.668	1765.162120	1.49412	1.49412
1772.419	1772.329810	-0.08908	0.08908
	1779.497500		
	1786.665190		
1792.167	1793.832880	1.66588	1.66588
1799.835	1801.000570	1.16553	1.16553
	1808.168260		
1815.463	1815.335950	-0.126750	0.12675

Panics	Prediction	Dev.	Abs Dev.
1819.416	1822.503640	3.087490	3.08749
	1829.671330		
1836.92	1836.839020	-0.0809	0.0809
	1844.006710		
	1851.174400		
1857.75	1858.342090	0.59189	0.59189
1866.331	1865.509780	-0.8215	0.8215
1873.668	1872.677470	-0.99053	0.99053
1882	1879.845160	-2.15484	2.15484
	1887.012850		
1893.331	1894.180540	0.84926	0.84926
1901.375	1901.348230	-0.02687	0.02687
1907.751	1908.515920	0.76522	0.76522
1915.343	1915.683610	0.34111	0.34111
	1922.851300		
1929.827	1930.018990	0.19219	0.19219
1937.5	1937.186680	-0.31332	0.31332
	1944.354370		
	1951.522060		
	1958.689750		
	1965.857440		
1973	1973.025130	0.02513	0.02513
1980.211	1980.192820	-0.01814	0.01814
1987.8	1987.360510	-0.43949	0.43949
1994.917	1994.528200	-0.38898	0.38898
2001.696	2001.695890	0	0
2008.712	2008.863580	0.15128	0.15128
	2016.031270	avg dev	0.731419
		days	266.968

Table 7

Step 8	Prediction	Dev.	Abs Dev.
Weeks	376		
Days	2632		
Panics	7.206023272		
1621	1619.777890	-1.22211	1.22211
	1626.983890		
1637.088	1634.189890	-2.89771	2.89771
	1641.395890		
	1648.601890		
	1655.807890		
	1663.013890		
	1670.219890		
	1677.425890		
	1684.631890		
	1691.837890		
	1699.043890		
	1706.249890		
	1713.455890		
1720.671	1720.661890	-0.00891	0.00891
	1727.867890		
	1735.073890		
	1742.279890		
	1749.485890		
	1756.691890		
1763.668	1763.897890	0.22989	0.22989
1772.419	1771.103890	-1.315	1.315
	1778.309890		
	1785.515890		
1792.167	1792.721890	0.55489	0.55489
1799.835	1799.927890	0.09285	0.09285
	1807.133890		
1815.463	1814.339890	-1.12281	1.12281

Panics	Prediction	Dev.	Abs Dev.
1819.416	1821.545890	2.12974	2.12974
	1828.751890		
1836.92	1835.957890	-0.96203	0.96203
	1843.163890		
	1850.369890		
1857.75	1857.575890	-0.17431	0.17431
1866.331	1864.781890	-1.54939	1.54939
1873.668	1871.987890	-1.68011	1.68011
1882	1879.193890	-2.80611	2.80611
	1886.399890		
1893.331	1893.605890	0.27461	0.27461
1901.375	1900.811890	-0.56321	0.56321
1907.751	1908.017890	0.26719	0.26719
1915.343	1915.223890	-0.11861	0.11861
	1922.429890		
1929.827	1929.635890	-0.19091	0.19091
1937.5	1936.841890	-0.65811	0.65811
	1944.047890		
	1951.253890		
	1958.459890		
	1965.665890		
1973	1972.871890	-0.12811	0.12811
1980.211	1980.077890	-0.13307	0.13307
1987.8	1987.283890	-0.51611	0.51611
1994.917	1994.489890	-0.42729	0.42729
2001.696	2001.695890	0	0
2008.712	2008.901890	0.18959	0.18959
	2016.107890	avg dev	**0.77741**
		days	**283.7548**

Table 8

Step 9	Prediction	Dev.	Abs Dev.
Weeks	373		
Days	2611		
Panics	7.148528405		
1621	1622.966900	1.9669	1.9669
	1630.112730		
1637.088	1637.258560	0.17096	0.17096
	1644.404390		
	1651.550220		
	1658.696050		
	1665.841880		
	1672.987710		
	1680.133540		
	1687.279370		
	1694.425200		
	1701.571030		
	1708.716860		
	1715.862690		
1720.671	1723.008520	2.33772	2.33772
	1730.154350		
	1737.300180		
	1744.446010		
	1751.591840		
	1758.737670		
1763.668	1765.883500	2.2155	2.2155
1772.419	1773.029330	0.61044	0.61044
	1780.175160		
	1787.320990		
1792.167	1794.466820	2.29982	2.29982
1799.835	1801.612650	1.77761	1.77761
	1808.758480		
1815.463	1815.904310	0.44161	0.44161

Panics	Prediction	Dev.	Abs Dev.
1819.416	1823.050140	3.63399	3.63399
	1830.195970		
1836.92	1837.341800	0.42188	0.42188
	1844.487630		
	1851.633460		
1857.75	1858.779290	1.02909	1.02909
1866.331	1865.925120	-0.40616	0.40616
1873.668	1873.070950	-0.59705	0.59705
1882	1880.216780	-1.78322	1.78322
	1887.362610		
1893.331	1894.508440	1.17716	1.17716
1901.375	1901.654270	0.27917	0.27917
1907.751	1908.800100	1.0494	1.0494
1915.343	1915.945930	0.60343	0.60343
	1923.091760		
1929.827	1930.237590	0.41079	0.41079
1937.5	1937.383420	-0.11658	0.11658
	1944.529250		
	1951.675080		
	1958.820910		
	1965.966740		
1973	1973.112570	0.11257	0.11257
1980.211	1980.258400	0.04744	0.04744
1987.8	1987.404230	-0.39577	0.39577
1994.917	1994.550060	-0.36712	0.36712
2001.696	2001.695890	0	0
2008.712	2008.844418	0.132118	0.132118
	2015.992947	avg dev	**0.937827**
		days	**342.3068**

Table 9

Step 10	Prediction		
Weeks	365.25		
Days	2556.75	Dev.	Abs Dev.
Panics	7		
1621	1623.695890	2.69589	2.69589
	1630.695890		
1637.088	1637.695890	0.60829	0.60829
	1644.695890		
	1651.695890		
	1658.695890		
	1665.695890		
	1672.695890		
	1679.695890		
	1686.695890		
	1693.695890		
	1700.695890		
	1707.695890		
	1714.695890		
1720.671	1721.695890	1.02509	1.02509
	1728.695890		
	1735.695890		
	1742.695890		
	1749.695890		
	1756.695890		
1763.668	1763.695890	0.02789	0.02789
1772.419	1770.695890	-1.723	1.723
	1777.695890		
	1784.695890		
1792.167	1791.695890	-0.47111	0.47111
1799.835	1798.695890	-1.13915	1.13915
	1805.695890		
1815.463	1812.695890	-2.76681	2.76681

Panics	Prediction	Dev.	Abs Dev.
1819.416	1819.695890	0.27974	0.27974
	1826.695890		
1836.92	1833.695890	-3.22403	3.22403
	1840.695890		
	1847.695890		
1857.75	1854.695890	-3.05431	3.05431
	1861.695890		
1866.331	1868.695890	2.36461	2.36461
1873.668	1875.695890	2.02789	2.02789
1882	1882.695890	0.69589	0.69589
	1889.695890		
1893.331	1896.695890	3.36461	3.36461
1901.375	1903.695890	2.32079	2.32079
1907.751	1910.695890	2.94519	2.94519
1915.343	1917.695890	2.35339	2.35339
	1924.695890		
1929.827	1931.695890	1.86909	1.86909
1937.5	1938.695890	1.19589	1.19589
	1945.695890		
	1952.695890		
	1959.695890		
	1966.695890		
1973	1973.695890	0.69589	0.69589
1980.211	1980.695890	0.48493	0.48493
1987.8	1987.695890	-0.10411	0.10411
1994.917	1994.695890	-0.22129	0.22129
2001.696	2001.695890	0	0
2008.696	2008.695890	-0.00011	0.00011
	2015.695890	avg dev	1.448423
		days	528.6743

Lastly we thought that we should check one more possible interval of exactly 7.00 years, since Jonathan Cahn uses it in his book to predict the next great crash. Since he uses "9/11" as his starting point for his predictions, we produced a grid moving back in time from 2001.69589 using 7.00 year intervals back to 1623.69589. The results of using the 7 years or Shemittah cycle is presented in Table 9. When we do the calculations on the deviations between the actual panics and the predicted dates we produce an average deviation of 528.6743 days. This average deviation is a little over twice as large as the deviation for our 2625 day (7.18686) model, therefore we stand by our model as being the best predictor for the next big crash. Cahn's prediction of the crash hitting on September 17, 2015 is close but not close enough.

Table 10

Deviation Comparisons

Step 3	Prediction		Step 4	Prediction		Step 5	Prediction
Weeks	372.683672		Weeks	375		Weeks	374
Days	2608.78571		Days	2625		Days	2618
Years	7.142466		Years	7.186858		Years	7.167693361
avg dev	0.87535368		avg dev	0.703433		avg dev	0.731419231
days	319.504093		days	256.7529 ***		days	266.9680192
Step 6	Prediction		Step 7	Prediction		Step 8	Prediction
Weeks	376		Weeks	373		Weeks	365.25
Days	2632		Days	2611		Days	2556.75
Years	7.20602327		Years	7.148528		Years	7
avg dev	0.77741038		avg dev	0.937827		avg dev	1.448422692
days	283.75479		days	342.3068		days	528.6742827

So the mathematics has brought us right back to where we started from, the book of Daniel 12:11 and 12, which gave us our hypothetical interval of 2625 days. This being the case we can expect the big crash to occur around January 26, 2016 plus or minus 256.7529 days. So we can expect the big economic calamity to fall within May 12, 2015 and October 10, 2016 with the most likely date of January 26, 2016.

In Chapter 7 Donald Trump forecasted that the collapse of the

U.S. dollar would come when the National Debt hit the $21 or $22 trillion mark. Data provided on http://www.usgovernmentdebt.us shows that the U.S. should reach that mark somewhere between 2015 ($21.897 trillion) and 2016 ($22.805 trillion). In fact in 2008 the National Debt was less than the Gross Domestic Product (GDP) when the debt was $12.550 trillion and the GDP was $14.418 trillion. But that all changed after 2008 financial collapse. Now each year the debt is larger than the product. In business one would call this "**bankruptcy**."

Now that we have confirmed that the Jewish "insider" investors use 2625 days as the key to when they collectively act to crash the financial markets and rip off the unsuspecting "outsiders" who dare to venture into their corral called the "stock market", we want to take a closer look at the implications of the mathematics of our predictive model. When we made our calculations on the deviations of our predicted dates and the actual dates of recorded panics, we took the absolute values of these deviations and took their average so that we could compare one model to the next. However, if we take a look at the actual deviations, some positive and some negative, then add them all up, the negative values will cancel out some of the positive values. The sum of these values was -3.26 years and when we divide this number by the number of observations (26), we have an average directed deviation of -0.12539 years, which is about -45.77 days. This means that on average each of our predicted dates is about 46 days ahead of the actual dates. It is quite interesting that the difference between the two numbers taken from the book of Daniel to form the number 2625 is 45; 1335 minus 1290 is 45.

We know that the recorded panics except for September 11, 2001 were probably the result of some activities that transpired in the days preceding these panics. In other words when we are looking at the panics or crashes, we are looking at the results and not the cause. "9/11" was so dramatic and so powerful that it immediately caused the financial markets to crash. However, we don't know

343

exactly when they pulled the lever in the other cases, but 46 days is a good estimate of how long it may take a sudden move by the insiders to have enough effect in the financial markets to cause a panic. For instance, the tightening of credit by the Fed would cause a series of adjustments by the players in the economy which eventually would result in the strangling of a bull market, resulting in a crash and financial panic.

Even though the ultimate insiders know what time it is in the cycle and the signals to look for, there is still competition within the pack of thieves (raiders) as to how much of the booty they will ultimately run off with. So the big players still play games with each other. This reminds me of a book by one of the investment bankers William D. Cohan called **House of Cards** (2009) which gives a blow by blow account of the takeover of Bear Sterns by JPMorgan Chase in 2008. The men at the top of these firms, while they are ripping off the world, are still trying to become the "king of the hill" by taking over the companies of the other players. The author goes into details about how the head of Bear Sterns, Ace Greenberg picked his heir to the throne Jimmy Cayne, because he was a "world-champion-level bridge" (Cohan 2009) player, a skill that was admired by the corporate elite because it represented the type of skills needed to play the real game on Wall Street. In other words at the very top, the evil financial shepherds play a game with each other like playing cards where they try to bluff each other into making a mistake. Alan Greenspan even made a statement after the big crash of the stock market in 2008 to the effect that he did not feel sorry for the big players in Wall Street, who were taken down in the crisis, because they should have known when to get out.

The Federal Reserve has already told the market that it intends to hold their interest rate at zero "at least through 2015." The financial raiders will be watching to see how much the Fed increases interest rates to determine when they will make their exit and dump their stock on the market. So January 26, 2016, twenty-six days after the end of 2015, is a good predictor of when all hell will break loose. Minster Farrakhan warned us that the Most Honorable Elijah Muhammad said to us, "One day, you will see the rich lighting their cigars with $1,000 bills because the currency will have no more value." When the currency goes down, the government goes down behind the currency. Where will you be?

Chapter 10

Muhammad's Economic Blueprint: Elimination of Usury and Speculation

The Jews' Civilization

We hope that we have given you, the reader, insight as to how the so-called Jews, the "evil shepherds", control the world through their control of the people's minds with the Bible and manipulating financial markets using their secret codes. The Jews are not persecuted because of "who they are", but "what they do." They have fooled the world into thinking that they are "God's Chosen" people as they have stolen the identity, history and wisdom of the Black man. Now they have the financial world in their grips and intend to sink the masses into chaos.

They killed Jesus who was "their messiah" who was trying to help them stop doing the wicked things that they were doing at that time, which included turning the Jewish Temple into a den of moneychangers. They now want to kill The Messenger of Allah and his helper the Honorable Minister Louis Farrakhan because they are exposing these evil shepherds and are leading the "sheep", the original people, out of the shadow of death and into a world of freedom, justice and equality.

We have to thank the Jews for participating in Allah's plans, for He is the Best of Planners. The Jews were not enslaved in Egypt for 400 years, yet it was they who infiltrated Africa to start the trans-Atlantic slave trade which brought God's chosen people, the seed of Abraham, to a land that was not theirs to be afflicted for 400 years as the scriptures foretold. Allah came to America in the Person of Master Fard Muhammad and rose up the Most Honorable Elijah Muhammad to be our redeemer, Messiah and now Christ. It is time for our exodus.

The wise of these so-called Jews knew who Jesus was and they know about their 6,000 year limit to their civilization as evidenced by what their Rabbis wrote in the Babylonian Talmud:

I.89 A. *A Tannaite authority of the house of Elijah [said]*, "For six thousand years the world will exist.
B. "For two thousand it will be desolate, two thousand years [will be the time of]
Torah, and two thousand years will be the days of the Messiah.
C. **[97B]** but on account of our numerous sins what has been lost [of those years, in which the Messiah **should have come but has not come**] has been lost.

They admit that for their first 2,000 years they were "desolate" or locked up in the caves of Europe as taught to us by The Messenger. For 2,000 years they were under the teachings of Moses and the Torah. For 2,000 years they would be in the time of the "Messiah," which they claim was not Jesus, but yet calculate their time as though he was. How wicked can you be as to deny something happened, but use it to calculate what time it is? We are at the end of their 6,000 years.

The Jews used their knowledge of money and banking which they learned in Babylon along with their development of the "stock market" to corral and periodically fleece the non-Jews. They learned about the Sabbatical practice of allowing the land to rest every seven years and to relieve the debt of the people every seven years. They learned the secrets of mathematical cycles and how to read the "writings on the walls" of Ancient Egypt, yet they give credit for their education to Daniel from Jerusalem instead of from captured Egyptian priests who they forced to teach them while in bondage in Babylon. They use the knowledge of these cycles to take from the people instead of letting the people go free. They increase the money

348

supply to trick greedy people into speculation instead of legitimate commerce, then every 2625 days they contract the money supply, destroying the value of the stock or commodity that was the object of speculation. Without manipulative interest rates and the trading of stocks, their schemes would fail.

Let me give a little background understanding of what the "stock market" is and what it is not. When a corporation "goes public" or issues common stock to the public, it makes that initial offering based on a set price, let's say $25 per share. So if it issues 1,000 shares, it receives $25,000 for those shares. The holder of those shares can sell those shares to someone else and get his money back. However, this transaction has no effect on the company that offered those shares. Ownership of the stock certificate has changed, but that has no financial bearing on the company. If the original stock could not go up above $25 in a "stock market", then the only way to make money off of this company is to hold that stock and wait on a dividend payment from that company. If they wanted to receive more profits, they would have to buy more shares at $25 per share. These new shares would increase the investment money going to the company instead of feeding the speculators who have no ties to the company. There is a business model called the "cooperative corporation" which issues ownership stock but does not allow for speculation on the price of the stock. We will talk a little about it in this book, but more about it can be read in our previous book *Commonomics: The Development of a Post Yakub Economy*.

But now if we look at what happens with stocks in the corporations that we are all familiar with, the stage for the opportunity to speculate on stock prices is set. With stocks being traded on a stock market, investors become speculators where they are less interested in the dividend returns based on the profitability of the company than they are on what others may believe is the future possibilities of that company. As the price of the stock rises, speculators jump in with hope that it will continue to rise. They gamble whether to hold the stock for a long time or sell it short to make a profit before its value goes down. Insider traders (raiders) have information on when such stocks are going down before the general public. So the late-comers to the game invariably get taken. Of course the late-comers don't know what time it is, so they do not know that they are late. Without greedy suckers the stock market scams and swindles will not work.

We argue that the mechanisms that allows the Jewish international bankers to rule the world can be eliminated through following the five principles presented by The Most Honorable Elijah Muhammad in his Economic Blueprint, setting up an Islamic banking system to eliminate usury and removing the possibility of speculating on "stock prices" by setting up "Cooperative Corporations" instead of publically traded stock of modern corporations.

Muhammad's Economic Blueprint:

1. Recognize the necessity for **unity and group operation** (activities).
2. **Pool your resources**, physically as well as financially.
3. **Stop wanton criticisms** of everything that is black-owned and black-operated.
4. Keep in mind -- **jealousy destroys** from within.
5. Observe the operations of the white man. He is successful. He makes no excuses for his failures. He works hard in a **collective manner**. You do the same. (Elijah Muhammad)

The Most Honorable Elijah Muhammad gave us these 5 principles for establishing a sound economic base. Each one of these points is asking Black people to do what has historically been what was natural for the indigenous people of our planet until they have been tampered with by the white man. In particular the Jews practice these principles "religiously" among themselves but deceitfully with non-Jews, whether they are Black or White. We can practice all of these 5 principles without discriminating against or taking from others unlike what the Jews have done historically.

The Jews were taught civilization from one from among us and they have come back among us to learn more about civilization and science. However, Minister Farrakhan has admonished the Nation of Islam to not be like the Jews who were supposed to share their wisdom with their Gentile brothers, but instead used that wisdom to enslave them through their own ignorance. The question is whether we can practice economic development without exploiting other people or our planet?

The imbalance in economic development between the very rich and the poor peoples and nations has been due to the practice of war, usury and the luring of the unsuspecting wage earners, retirees, small business owners, pension funds and mutual savings into the crooked gambling casino called the "Stock Market." Muhammad's Economic Blueprint encourages us to pool our resources so that we can work collectively to improve our lives. We should invest in productive assets and ventures that over time will turn a profit. However, we are not to buy and sell stock just to gamble on the price of that stock going up. The profit to the society is through the jobs and income generated from those companies. The profits to the investors are the normal business profits that the firm generates by being productive, frugal and fair.

Islamic Banking

There is a good reason for the international bankers to hate Islam. Islam does not allow for the loaning out of money at interest. Usury is not allowed in Islam.

Islam is a way of life and not just a religion. One of the main differences between the Islamic world and the West is that Islam does not permit usury or loaning money at interest. Islamic Law is known as Shari'a. Shari'a is found in the Holy Qur'an, the Sunna of the Prophet and Hadith.

Islamic banking does not permit, interest *(riba)*, uncertainty *(gharrar)*, speculation *(maisir)*, unjust enrichment/unfair exploitation and unethical investments. However, all other business

351

activity is permissible and making a profit on investments is encouraged. The key here is that in Islam the person who puts up the capital must take the same risks as the person who receives the capital. You cannot loan out money, then if the business fails, go after the person's house or other possessions. This requires that the lender must be diligent in investigating the repaying ability of the person or business venture and not just checking out how much collateral the person has.

If a person has borrowed money to buy a house, but falls short on the payments because of a loss of income, it is incumbent on the lender to work with the borrower to get them on their feet without premature foreclosure proceedings. The lender should help that person get a job or develop some means of income generation.

If the bank wants to loan money to a business, it must get the individual deposit holders to agree to make the investment and be involved with the progress of the investment. The bank cannot invest the depositors' money without consulting them.

Our history of banking and Jews has shown us that the Jews like to use the power of the state to insure that their debtors pay them back their money. The Jews sullied up to kings and potentates in the past, but got real slick when they came to America. They got control of the banks through the Federal Reserve System (The Fed). They loaned money at interest to the government, then had the government set up the Internal Revenue Service (IRS) to service that debt. They set up the Federal Bureau of Investigation (FBI) to look out for anyone that understood their schemes. They set up the Anti-Defamation League (ADL) to brand whoever understood their schemes, but could not be convicted of some nonrelated crime, as an Anti-Semite and thereby "stink up" his reputation with the people who believed them to be God's chosen people.

The elimination of greed

Greed is the vice that feeds speculation. Islam teaches us to

352

want for our brother what we want for ourselves. The Muhammad Economic Blueprint says that we should "work hard in a collective manner." The operative words here are "work" and "collective." Remember that it was this desire for others to do our work instead of each putting in his share which led to the production of a "race of devils" by Yakub. We should produce and then trade with others to get the benefits of our work, but we should not desire to receive compensation from doing nothing. Then we should work "collectively" which is a form of socialism or really more exactly, "communalism" which was the natural way people lived before the capitalist mind of the white man led by the Jews forced their ways on the indigenous peoples.

Capitalism

According to www.Wikipedia.com:

> **"Capitalism** is an economic system in which trade, industry, and the means of production are largely or entirely privately owned and operated for profit. Central characteristics of capitalism include capital accumulation, competitive markets and wage labor. In a capitalist economy, the parties to a transaction typically determine the prices at which assets, goods, and services are exchanged."

This definition leaves out the real exploitative power behind "capital" in terms of banks and financing. The accumulation of wealth, competitive markets and wage labor have existed within many civilizations, but what makes this modern form of "capitalism" so viral is **usury and speculation** on corporate stocks.

Black people see doing business, i.e., buying and selling

353

goods and services as "capitalism" and anyone doing such is branded a "capitalist." However, the real civilization of the Jews is a world where "money" grows "money" without the production of a tangible product or service. Then the law or government is used to protect these ill-gotten gains. Stock ownership is not a problem, but speculation on the price of the stock allows for the type of market manipulation and thievery exemplified in the use of the Jews' secret code to make the markets rise and fall. They then use this "money" or capital to buy industries that are actually producing a tangible good or service. "Money" instead of being just a means of exchange has become the means of domination of a small elite minority who steal the people's labor by the manipulation of "money."

The word "capital" comes from a word meaning "heads of cattle." Wealth moved from land ownership to the ownership of a movable commodity, cattle. Now the idea of wealth has moved to even more movable and subtle instruments such as derivatives and other Jewish schemes. The Egyptians dominated their world with knowledge and food. The Greeks and Romans dominated their world with superior weaponry and military strategy. The Jews have dominated the modern world with their "Poison Book", money and tricknology which is their "civilization."

Look for the "Game" not the "Name"

We have asked and I think we have answered the question, "Are the Jews persecuted because of who they are or what they do?" The answer is of course "what they do." There is a corollary to this question which is, "Do all Jews practice financial raiding and moneylending?" and "Are all financial raiders and moneylenders, Jews?" The answer to both of these questions is "no", however not to recognize the dominance of the Jews in these professions, in light of what they have written with their own hands, would be ignorant.

Plus, the object of this book is not to go after the "Jews", but to change Black people's behavior so as not to be victimized by these

354

people and the civilization that they have set up. This means we must separate from them, not participate in their schemes and not perpetrate such schemes on each other or others. The issue is the "game" and not the "name." The "game" is "usury and speculation." The Jews' civilization of moneylending and gambling has spread throughout the world, so there are many non-Jews who practice these schemes now. To practice such exploitative schemes takes a certain mind-set that did not dominate our planet 6,000 years ago, but has now become standard behavior for most. In other words, everybody seems to be looking for a "sucker" or some way to make money without doing anything for it. This goes back to what The Most Honorable Elijah Muhammad taught about those who followed Mr. Yakub: "*Naturally, there are **always some people** around who would like to have others do their work. Those are the ones who fell for Mr. Yakub's teaching, 100 per cent.*" *(Muhammad 1965: 108)*

The Messenger was referring to Black people as well, because before Yakub there was no "race" of White people and certainly no Jews. So, any people who want others to do the work while they do nothing but yet benefit, must think that they are somehow "better" or more deserving than other people. The Holy Qur'an exposes this type of mindset in Surah 38: 75-78 (Muhammad Ali translation)

38:75 He said: O Iblis, what prevented thee from submitting to him whom I created with both My hands? Art thou proud or art thou of the exalted Ones?

38:76 He said: I am better than he; Thou hast created me of fire, and him Thou didst create of dust.

38:77 He said: Go forth from hence surely thou art driven away:

38:78. And surely My curse is on thee to the day of Judgment.

So how does one find this "Iblis"? Just watch his or her behavior. If he acts as though he thinks that "I am better", then he is a devil or satanic. The Honorable Minister Louis Farrakhan has warned us not to be like the Jews who were given divine wisdom, but did not share that wisdom with their other white brethren and used such wisdom to exploit their ignorance. He warned us as members of the Nation of Islam who have received divine wisdom from The Most Honorable Elijah Muhammad, not to fall into that same selfish behavior stemming from that feeling of "I am better."

In Chapter 3 of this book we discovered that anthropologist had identified the white invaders, "Kurgan culture", who came into Europe about 6,000 years ago by their practices: After Kurgan had conquered an area, the primary changes are said to have been "…the emergence of **ranked**, highly **competitive** societies **dominated** by localized **elites** who controlled local production and enriched themselves through **trade and war**." In other words they set up a caste or class system where the lighter-skinned ones felt "better" than the darker ones. Kurgan culture was a "devil" culture not because of its racial identity but because of its behavioral identity.

Also in Chapter 4 we discovered that the Babylonians raped Black women to produce half-breeds, mulattos, who were trained to feel that they were better than their former people and in fact when sent to Jerusalem, called themselves, "Pharisees", which means "set apart." We also discovered the Portuguese Jews who practiced this same type of race mixing to achieve their goals of infiltrating Africa and starting the trans-Atlantic slave trade. So mixing of genes and the changing of identities has been going on for some time now. We Blacks in America are all mixed up, genetically, therefore behavior and not race must be used to identify "devils."

And lastly, in Chapter 5, Money and Banking, we found that Jews were forced to convert to Christianity starting in 1391 in Spain and 1492 in Portugal. These "converts" were called "conversos" or "maranos" in Europe, but called "Donmehs" in Turkey. Many of these converted Jews were suspected of being "crypto-Jews" who secretly still held on to Judaism while outwardly practicing Christianity or Islam. Chapter 5 describes many cases where these converts continued to practice usury, set up banks and became very rich in many Christian cities, especially Amsterdam. They changed their ethnic names to "Christian names" and intermarried with other conversos, carrying on the family line and business under the guise of Christianity. There is much research going on to trace down the identity of some of the "non-Jewish" movers and shakers of today back to these families of Jews that converted to other religions, **only** to deceive.

This is why we say look for the "game" not the "name". And if you take larceny and laziness out of your heart, then you will not be suckered by players of the different "games." Islam forbids both usury and gambling (speculation).

To reestablish our civilization we need the correcting of our morals, like the elimination of greed; and we must have unity. However, one of the obstacles to our unity is the lack of community. We are a scattered people. Whenever the enemy saw us making progress towards self-determination and economic development, he would set up some scheme to break us up. After slavery when we tried to build our own communities, he lynched us and even used planes to bomb us out of "Black Wall Street" in Tulsa, Oklahoma and other methods to destroy viable communities across the country.

He forced us to live in segregated communities. Under segregation we developed our own churches, grocery stores, restaurants, clothing stores, shoe repair shops, bus companies, insurance companies, banks, cab companies, schools, hospitals, professional athletic teams, auto repair shops, janitorial services, home repair companies, construction companies, plumbing repair, farms, upholstery shops, tailor and seamstress shops, movie houses, night clubs, beauty supply manufacturers, newspapers, magazines, bakeries, music companies, record companies, hotels, lawn maintenance companies, barber shops, hair salons and catering services.

Then our "friends" the Jews came along and convinced us that we needed to integrate with Whites. We followed their advice and accepted their financial support to give up everything we had developed on our own for the opportunity of being accepted into the world of lower class white folk. The Jews never invited us into their banking and financial world, but left us with our churches. The white folk did not come to our Black businesses with their dollars, but came with their bulldozers. With the promise of "Urban Renewal" they practiced "Urban Removal" and mowed our businesses down, split our communities apart with four lane limited access freeways right through the heart of our neighborhoods and black business districts.

They were not yet finished. They capped off their slash and burn operations with their dispersal and skills removal plan. In the 1960s they began to remove life-skills training, such as home economics, shop and vocational agriculture classes from the high schools. In home economics we learned meal planning, food preparation, canning, sewing and taking care of the home. In shop we learned wood working, auto repair, electrical repair and plumbing. In vocational agriculture we learned how to grow a garden, care for animals and keep records for the farm. With these skills coming out of high school we were prepared to set up a home and make a living for ourselves, even if we did not go on to college.

Then they changed the mission of the Black Land Grant colleges from teaching to research, from practical to theoretical, from community development to the "global community." They took us out of our "blue collars" and gave us "white collars" and a briefcase. Soon we were running all over America, and later the world, after that same pot of gold that the "slave trader" promised us when they tricked us on to the slave ships. "Greed" allowed us to be tricked then and "greed" is the door that the enemy uses to keep us divided now.

The section in this book called "Deportation and Return???" is so significant for us to understand the "time and what must be done." In that section we pointed out that it was state policy in the ancient world for the White and Semite conquerors of the indigenous peoples to take the upper echelon of the conquered people away and place them on another side of the empire, never to return again. We think that we proved that this was their practice in both Jerusalem

358

and Egypt. And they have carried this same practice into effect in the Black communities of America.

They lured our finest and our best away from our communities and placed them behind "gated" mixed communities of "middle class" Whites, leaving the Black communities with the "losers" who could not get out. The Blacks that could not get out were not "losers", but were treated as such. Then the enemy brought into the community the destructive bombs of crack cocaine and heroin to further demoralize our communities and capture young Black men for the prison industrial complex.

Under segregation the poor, blue collar workers and even professional Blacks lived in the same community. But now all the professional and high income Blacks live over the fence with white people. Then for those professional white collar Blacks to move up in corporate America, they had to relocate about every five years to move up in the organization. When they retired or were simply let go, they found themselves in areas far away from their childhood communities and neighborhoods. They were far away from family and friends, just like the exiles from Jerusalem and Egypt.

The Most Honorable Elijah Muhammad said that we should "…work together in a collective manner." However, if we do not live together, how can we work together? This is what our enemy understood when he set up this plan of dispersal and exile. Now we must plan to move back home or make a new home, close to one another in communities of likeminded and industrious people. We must find a reason to be in common. Anything that we can use to find commonality between us, we should do so as an excuse to live together. Retirees should seek out areas to retire where their skills and remaining energy can be put to work to build businesses and train the next set of business owners, farmers and industrialists. The old need to put the young beneath their wings and guide them. When we "make it", we need to "make it" together and not apart. We do not need to live among our historical enemies, who are like vultures waiting to pick the meat off of our bones, when nobody is paying attention.

Our enemies have proven themselves to be skillful at conquering and using tricknology to raid the people's wealth. We must become skillful at healing and teaching the people. The enemy will not change his ways because those ways have been successful for his purposes. He will always cheat in any economic or business endeavor that he is allowed to control. And if he cannot cheat, he will attempt to take the people's wealth with his weapons. If he cannot do either, then he will just self-destruct.

Conclusions

In our "Western History" classes they give credit for the development of civilization to the Greeks. However, George G.M. James dispelled that lie in his monumental book, **Stolen Legacy,** where he shows that the "great thinkers" of Greece went to school in Ancient Egypt to learn science and mathematics. The West likes to talk about the progress of civilization from the Greeks to the Romans through the Dark Ages to reappear in the Renaissance, then the British Empire, but they fail to mention the Jews' Civilization. The Jews like it that way so that their control of the western world's leadership can stay hidden, like "Mystery Babylon." They manipulate the minds and purse strings of the super powers as they wield the ultimate power of money, Mammon, the "god" of this world.

The international bankers, acting as financial raiders, have the people of the world trapped in their corral of debt and speculation. These white people who call themselves Jews are the *mind* behind the *body* of white folk who were made and taught by Yakub to make the original people, dark people, of our planet their slaves. They first started out 6,000 years ago when they came back into the Holy Land of our people and began to cause mischief. When they were found out, the original people, Egyptians, ran them out from among us and bottled them up behind the Caucasus Mountains. Moses (Musa), a half-original, came 2,000 years later and civilized them. He left them a book of law which allowed them to organize themselves and swoop down on the indigenous people in Mesopotamia and Egypt.

They took women from among the dark peoples and made a mixed race or race of half-breeds, mulattos. In Babylon they taught this new race a new religion which had been made from what Moses had taught them, but mixed with Mesopotamian and Egyptian wisdom. They went into Egypt and wrote down all they could find, then destroyed all they could find and had Ezra and other scribes in Babylon produce what was called the Hebrew Bible. Half-breeds were trained to be spies and allies for Babylon/Persia, then sent to posts in Jerusalem and Elephantine with this new book and religion and called themselves "Jews."

While in Babylon they had picked up the science of money, banking and usury. They used their knowledge of money and became the moneylenders to the kings and aristocracy of the Gentiles. Over time the Jews amassed great wealth. However, some of the strict adherents to the law of Shemittah (Sabbatical Year) would relinquish the debts of their fellow Jews every seven years. Every time the Gentiles found out about this **practice**, they killed or ran the Jews from among them. The Jews were hated in Europe not because of "who they are", but "what they do", **practicing** usury and tricknology.

When the Jews arrived in America, they thought up a new strategy to rob the Gentiles, but get away. They kept the heat off of themselves by using Blacks as "scapegoats" for all the ills of the American society, so that the Gentiles/Goyim/sheepdogs, would busy themselves beating up and oppressing the black people, sheep, while they took control of America's money supply by setting up the privately owned Federal Reserve System in 1913. As they set up the Fed they also set up the FBI, IRS and ADL to protect their interests and to make sure that they got their money.

In the early 1600s the Jews set up the publically traded corporation and stock markets to trade stock, which are nothing but gambling houses. They would play the outsiders for fools by first producing a bubble then pulling the strings behind the scenes to take the suckers' money every 2625 days. Their greatest "magic" was "9/11", scapegoating Muslims. They sunk America's economy in 2008/2009, scapegoating Blacks. Their next big financial raid, is predicted to be in January of 2016. They have already begun the process of allowing the sheepdog to attack the sheep with the intention of starting a race/civil war in America as they walk off with the loot one more time. This time America may be in for a 25 year depression after the "Great Snake" strikes in 2016.

The Honorable Minister Louis Farrakhan has been attacked by the so-called Jews because he represents the Messiah, Christ, The Most Honorable Elijah Muhammad. The Messiah is here to put the Black man and woman back on top of civilization, replacing the imposter who called themselves Jews. This is why these Jews hate Farrakhan and the Nation of Islam. They would love to kill him but are afraid of "the people" and the Mother Plane which protects The Minister.

Black people know that Minister Farrakhan is teaching and is offering to our people the right solution for their problems. However, they are afraid to work with him for two reasons: fear of their open enemy and dependence on that same enemy for sustenance. Like the "sheep" who fear the wrath of their shepherd, but love him because they believe that he leads them to "green pastures and still waters," they accept this life of bondage. The sheep could stop listening to their bell-wether castrated Negro leaders and follow a "ram with testicles."

Minister Farrakhan has instituted Muhammad Economic Blueprint to eliminate poverty and want. We hope that this book encourages you to support him and help yourself. The Jews are not the only ones who know economics and money. They are not all wise, because they got caught "crawling across the road" on 9/11. They had a good thing going until they attacked Minister Farrakhan and brought out his researchers who have tracked this "snake" down. We don't need to kill the "snake", evil shepherd, just separate from him and his wicked world. He needs us more than we need him. Trust me.

When the Jews come among Black people they claim to empathize with us, because they say they were once enslaved in Egypt for 400 years. Now we know that they lied. Then they encouraged us to push for social integration with Whites while the Jews knew well that whites would retaliate against us. Recessive white cannot mix with dominant black and stay "white." So they lynched, burnt, shot and sent their dogs against us.

When the Jews go among non-Jewish Whites, they claim their "whiteness" and even change their names to "good Christian" names to mix in among them, until it is time to strike. And they have struck repeatedly over the last 400 years using a secret Biblical code of 2625 days or 7.1869 years. The white folk (sheepdog) just use force to enslave and steal from black folk (sheep). The Jews wait until the white folk have stolen and accumulated substantial wealth (the Golden Fleece), then they lure them into their world of financial speculation and fleece them stealthily as a shepherd would shear the wool off of sheep.

Stolen Identity, Usury and Financial Raiding

Now that we have caught these liars and raiders, what is the remedy or penalty? Let's point out their three major crimes: 1. Stolen Identity, 2. Usury and 3. Financial Raiding.

This "Stolen Identity" is the identity of the legitimate heirs to God's kingdom. To steal the birthright of the Black man, the Jews lied on God Himself by tampering with His words. Of course we have a problem right from the start. Anyone that would lie on God, either does not believe in God or has accepted an adversarial relationship to God, i.e. accepts being Satan. Satan does not repent

363

or pay reparations. As Muslims say in our daily prayers, Satan or Iblis would come in God's (Allah's) straight path, the **"aṣ-Ṣirāṭ al-mustaqīm."** So he in the person of wicked scribes has slid right up into the Word of God and corrupted it in order to lead His children astray.

How does one measure the value of millions, nay billions, of lives lost (black, white, red, brown, yellow) due to wars and starvation caused by misrepresentation of God's word since the production of the Poison Book, 2500 years ago? How does one measure the loss of human identity due to a misrepresentation of the Creator and thereby the reason for existence of his creation and creatures? How does one measure the difference between being blind, deaf and dumb to the knowledge of God and self to being enlightened?

How does one measure the value of labor stolen from God's legitimate children, Black people, for the last 400+ years? How does one value the mineral resources stolen from Africa? How does one measure the value of our suffering at the hands of Nebuchadnezzar, King of the Magi, being stolen and used by the Jews to gain world sympathy and political and economic favors? How does one measure the leverage gained by Jews using their Biblical claim on the "Promised Land" to force the American government to fund and militarily back Israel's conquest of the Palestinians' lands? How does one measure the value of the protection of America for Jews all over the world, as they stole mineral resources from less developed countries?

These are very difficult questions, so let's ask some easier ones. In terms of "usury", how much is the "bite" of that snake? We highlighted an article in Chapter 5 by Ellen Brown entitled "It's the Interest, Stupid! Why Bankers Rule the World." In it she quotes an estimate that from 35 to 40% of the cost of the goods we buy goes to those who loan the money to the modern system of production and distribution. In other words for every dollar that Americans spend about $0.40 goes to the moneylenders. So if the GDP is $16.8 trillion, then the moneylenders get $6.72 trillion EACH YEAR.

If we look at the National debt, an extra $400+ billion of interest is paid each year to those who own the debt including the privately owned Federal Reserve System. According to http://www.truedemocracy.net/hj34/18.html in the fall of 2010 **"The total interest paid to the Federal Reserve since 1913 is over TWENTY SEVEN TRILLION DOLLARS (that's a "27" with twelve zeroes!). And as of this writing, we still owe 8.875 TRILLION dollars more!"** I would say that everybody in America is a slave working for the financial raiders.

Now we have discovered that the financial raiders use the stock and commodity markets to fleece their sheep and sheepdogs about every 2625 days (7.1869 years). We know that the bankers walked off with at least $4.7 trillion just from the Federal Reserve and the Treasury in the last big raid in 2008/2009. This does not include the money they stole from the suckers who lost their retirement in the stock market where the DJIA fell from 13,058 in May of 2008 to 6,547 in April of 2009. The estimated loss of the total market value of publically traded corporations worldwide dropped by $34.4 trillion, which is more than the 2008 annual gross domestic product (GDP) of the US, the European Union and Japan combined (http://www.rooseveltinstitute.org/new-roosevelt/crisis-wealth-destruction).

Let's just deal with the $4.7 trillion raided from the Federal Reserve and Treasury first. It would take 200 million people working 40 hours per week, 58.75 weeks or a little over a year to make that much money. In other words, the financial raiders stole a year's worth of labor from each American worker in one year, and they repeat this cycle every 7.1869 years.

Now to replace the loss of wealth due to the reduction in the value of stocks, $34.4 trillion, would take these same 200 million workers 430 weeks or 8.27 years. However, before we reach 8.27 years from 2008/2009 the world will be hit with another raid, crash and panic. Guess what white folk? "We are all niggas to these raiders."

Of course you will get no reparations from these financial raiders and identity thieves because they do not feel that they have done anything wrong. They do not see us as even being human and they see themselves as "I am better." And what court would we carry them to anyway? Therefore, Black people must depend on God (Allah) and repair ourselves.

And how the evil shepherd and their sheepdogs will get along with each other at the brink of the "lake of fire," after their true relationship has been exposed to the world, is anybody's guess? However, we would be wise to separate and be far away from both of them, when they go after each other. The Holy Qur'an states in Surah 41:29:

"And those who disbelieve will say: Our Lord, show us those who led us astray from among the jinn and the men that we may trample them under our feet, so that they may be the lowest."

Peace, Doc

Appendix to Chapter 10

A. Taking land with debt
Colonization by Bankruptcy: The High-stakes Chess Match for Argentina

Ellen Brown
August 25, 2014

(www.webofdebt.com)

If Argentina were in a high-stakes chess match, the country's

366

actions this week would be the equivalent of flipping over all
the pieces on the board.

– David Dayen, Fiscal Times, August 22, 2014

Argentina is playing hardball with the vulture funds, which
have been trying to force it into an involuntary bankruptcy.
The vultures are demanding what amounts to a 600% return
on bonds bought for pennies on the dollar, defeating a 2005
settlement in which 92% of creditors agreed to accept a 70%
haircut on their bonds. A US court has backed the vulture
funds; but last week, Argentina sidestepped its jurisdiction by
transferring the trustee for payment from Bank of New York
Mellon to its own central bank. That play, if approved by the
Argentine Congress, will allow the country to continue making
payments under its 2005 settlement, avoiding default on the
majority of its bonds.

Argentina is already foreclosed from international capital
markets, so it doesn't have much to lose by thwarting the US
court system. Similar bold moves by Ecuador and Iceland
have left those countries in substantially better shape than
Greece, which went along with the agendas of the
international financiers.

The upside for Argentina was captured by President
Fernandez in a nationwide speech on August 19th. Struggling
to hold back tears, according to Bloomberg, she said:

When it comes to the sovereignty of our country and the
conviction that we can no longer be extorted and that we can't
become burdened with debt again, we are emerging as
Argentines.

. . . If I signed what they're trying to make me sign, the bomb
wouldn't explode now but rather there would surely be
applause, marvelous headlines in the papers. But we would

enter into the infernal cycle of debt which we've been subject to for so long.

The Endgame: Patagonia in the Crosshairs

The deeper implications of that infernal debt cycle were explored by Argentine political analyst Adrian Salbuchi in an August 12th article titled "Sovereign Debt for Territory: A New Global Elite Swap Strategy." Where territories were once captured by military might, he maintains that today they are being annexed by debt. The still-evolving plan is to drive destitute nations into an international bankruptcy court whose decisions would have the force of law throughout the world. The court could then do with whole countries what US bankruptcy courts do with businesses: sell off their assets, including their real estate. Sovereign territories could be acquired as the spoils of bankruptcy without a shot being fired.

Global financiers and interlocking megacorporations are increasingly supplanting governments on the international stage. An international bankruptcy court would be one more institution making that takeover legally binding and enforceable. Governments can say no to the strong-arm tactics of the global bankers' collection agency, the IMF. An international bankruptcy court would allow creditors to force a nation into bankruptcy, where territories could be involuntarily sold off in the same way that assets of bankrupt corporations are.

For Argentina, says Salbuchi, the likely prize is its very rich Patagonia region, long a favorite settlement target for ex-pats. When Argentina suffered a massive default in 2001, the global press, including *Time* and *The New York Times*, went so far as to propose that Patagonia be ceded from the country as a defaulted debt payment mechanism.

The *New York Times* article followed one published in the Buenos Aires financial newspaper *El Cronista Comercial* called *"Debt for Territory,"* which described a proposal by a US consultant to then-president Eduardo Duhalde for swapping public debt for government land. **It said:**

[T]he idea would be to transform our public debt default into direct equity investment in which creditors can become land owners where they can develop industrial, agricultural and real estate projects. . . . There could be surprising candidates for this idea: during the Alfonsin Administration, the Japanese studied an investment master plan in Argentine land in order to promote emigration. The proposal was also considered in **Israel.**

Salbuchi notes that **ceding Patagonia from Argentina was first suggested in 1896** by Theodor Herzl, founder of **the Zionist movement**, as a second settlement for that movement.

Another article published in 2002 was one by IMF deputy manager Anne Krueger titled "Should Countries Like Argentina Be Able to Declare Themselves Bankrupt?" It was posted on the IMF website and proposed some "new and creative ideas" on what to do about Argentina. Krueger said, "the lesson is clear: we need better incentives to bring debtors and creditors together before manageable problems turn into full-blown crises," adding that the IMF believes "this could be done by learning from corporate bankruptcy regimes like Chapter 11 in the US".

These ideas were developed in greater detail by Ms. Krueger in an IMF essay titled "A New Approach to Debt Restructuring," and by Harvard professor Richard N. Cooper in a 2002 article titled "Chapter 11 for Countries" published in *Foreign Affairs* ("mouthpiece of the powerful New York-Based Elite think-tank, **Council on Foreign Relations**"). Salbuchi writes:

Here, Cooper very matter-of-factly recommends that *"only if the debtor nation cannot restore its financial health are its assets liquidated and the proceeds distributed to its creditors – again under the guidance of a (global) court"* (!).

In Argentina's recent tangle with the vulture funds, Ms. Krueger and the mainstream media have come out in apparent defense of Argentina, recommending restraint by the US court. But according to Salbuchi, this does not represent a change in policy. Rather, the concern is that overly heavy-handed treatment may kill the golden goose:

. . . [I] n today's delicate post-2008 banking system, a new and less controllable sovereign debt crisis could thwart the global elite's plans for an *"orderly transition towards a new global legal architecture"* that will allow orderly liquidation of financially-failed states like Argentina. Especially if such debt were to be collateralized by its national territory (what else is left!?)

Breaking Free from the Sovereign Debt Trap

Salbuchi traces Argentina's debt crisis back to 1955, when President Juan Domingo Perón was ousted in a very bloody US/UK/mega-bank-sponsored military coup:

Perón was hated for his insistence on not indebting Argentina with the mega-bankers: in 1946 he rejected joining the International Monetary Fund (IMF); in 1953 he fully paid off all of Argentina's sovereign debt. So, once the mega-bankers got rid of him in 1956, they shoved Argentina into the IMF and created the "Paris Club" to engineer decades-worth of sovereign debt for vanquished Argentina, something they've been doing until today.

Many countries have been subjected to similar treatment, as John Perkins documents in his blockbuster exposé *Confessions of an Economic Hit Man.* When the country cannot pay, the IMF sweeps in with refinancing agreements with strings attached, including selling off public assets and slashing public services in order to divert government revenues into foreign debt service.

Even without pressure from economic hit men, however, governments routinely indebt themselves for much more than they can ever hope to repay. Why do they do it? Salbuchi writes:

Here, Western economists, bankers, traders, Ivy League academics and professors, Nobel laureates and the mainstream media have a quick and monolithic reply: because all nations need "investment and investors" if they wish to build highways, power plants, schools, airports, hospitals, raise armies, service infrastructures and a long list of et ceteras . . . .

But more and more people are starting to ask a fundamental common-sense question: why should governments indebt themselves in hard currencies, decades into the future with global mega-bankers, when they could just as well finance these projects and needs far more safely by issuing the proper amounts of their own local sovereign currency instead?

Neoliberal experts shout back that government-created money devalues the currency, inflates the money supply, and destroys economies. But does it? Or is it the debt service on money created privately by banks, along with other forms of "rent" on capital, that create inflation and destroy economies? As Prof. Michael Hudson points out:

371

These financial claims on wealth – bonds, mortgages and bank loans – are lent out to become somebody else's debts in an exponentially expanding process. . . . [E]conomies have been obliged to pay their debts by cutting back new research, development and new physical reinvestment. This is the essence of IMF austerity plans, in which the currency is "stabilized" by further international borrowing on terms that destabilize the economy at large. Such cutbacks in long-term investment also are the product of corporate raids financed by high-interest junk bonds. The debts created by businesses, consumers and national economies cutting back their long-term direct investment leaves these entities even less able to carry their mounting debt burden.

Spiraling debt also results in price inflation, since businesses have to raise their prices to cover the interest and fees on the debt.

From Sovereign Debt to Monetary Sovereignty

For governments to escape this austerity trap, they need to spend not less but more money on the tangible capital formation that increases physical productivity. But where to get the investment money without getting sucked into the debt vortex? Where can Argentina get funding if the country is shut out of international capital markets?

The common-sense response, as Salbuchi observes, is for governments to issue the money they need directly. But "printing money" raises outcries that can be difficult to overcome politically. An alternative that can have virtually the same effect is for nations to borrow money issued by their own publicly-owned banks. Public banks generate credit just as private banks do; but unlike private lenders, they return interest and profits to the economy. Their mandate is to serve the public, and that is where their profits go. Funding through their own government-issued currencies and publicly-owned banks has been successfully pursued by many countries historically, including Australia, New Zealand, Canada, Germany, China, Russia, Korea and Japan.

Countries do need to be able to buy foreign products that they cannot acquire or produce domestically, and for that they need a form of currency or an international credit line that other nations will accept. But countries are increasingly breaking away from the oil- and weapons-backed US dollar as global reserve currency. To resolve the mutually-destructive currency wars will probably take a new Bretton Woods Accord. But that is another subject for a later article.

(Ellen Brown is an attorney, founder of the Public Banking Institute, and author of twelve books, including the best-selling Web of Debt. In The Public Bank Solution, her latest book, she explores successful public banking models historically and globally. Her 200+ blog articles are at EllenBrown.com.)

B. The Cooperative Corporation as a Business Model

Cooperative Success Confounds Liberals, Analysts Alike

By Matthew Martin Staff Reporter

The Exponent (Purdue - West Lafayette,Ind)

February 17, 2012

(http://www.purdueexponent.org/campus/article_cea97626-7952-521c-a743-6d798191d245.html)

Analysts said it couldn't happen and liberals said it was too early to come, but the Spanish cooperative of Mondragon has grown into a global powerhouse.

The Mondragon cooperative of 120 different companies was the focus of Carl Davidson, a writer and the national co-chair of the Committees of Correspondence for Democracy and Socialism, who talked on Thursday to a sparse audience in Lawson Hall. The speech was sponsored by the Committee on Peace Studies and the Latin American and Latino Studies Program.

Mondragon is the largest cooperative in the world. The cooperative has been successful in a wide array of businesses including industry, research, and education.

"Think about a platypus. When they discovered them (Mondragon), it wasn't supposed to exist," Davidson said.

An unusual aspect of the cooperative is all the workers are owners of the company. Every worker gets one vote and a paycheck based on the company's profits rather than a wage.

"The workers in Mondragon are not normal workers. They are not wage laborers," Davidson said.

Davidson spoke of how the cooperative has become the seventh-largest business group in Spain because of the core principles made by the founder, José María Arizmendiarrieta Madariaga. Arizmendiarrierta was a priest who first founded a small credit union that grew into Mondragon.

Davidson said Mondragon operates on several principles including application, pay solidarity, and the soverignty of labor. Davidson said Mondragon has its own bank to keep money within the cooperative.

"Capital is subservient to labor. That's why the bank is owned by the cooperative," Davidson said.

Davidson said the workers of Mondragon are paid well and the differences in pay between an executive and a janitor are not very broad.

"In Mondragon the average spread is one to nine from the guy who sweeps the floor to the head honcho. In the U.S. it would be one to 9,000," Davidson said.

One of the main principles of the cooperative is to take a three-in-one approach to business said Davidson. Davidson said the cooperative prides itself on its factory, school and credit unit aspects. He said it's possible for companies to become a cooperative but that they need to accomplish a few goals.

"First, the workers have to want to do it. Second, the workers have to trust each other. Third, you need a decent business plan," Davidson said.

Mondragon is working in other countries than Spain. Mondragon recently made an agreement to work with the United Steel Workers of the United States but things are moving slowly. Davidson said several other cooperatives, such as the Cleveland Evergreen Cooperatives, were influenced by Mondragon.

"The U.S. is a very easy place to start a co-op and a

very easy place to fail," Davidson said.

Audience members seemed very interested in the idea of a cooperative. Elena Benedicto, an associate professor in the College of Liberal Arts, said she thought it was an interesting idea for workers to own their positions and jobs.

"Those companies are household names and you would never expect that they are cooperatives," Benedicto said.

Bibliography

Adkins, Leslie and Roy. <u>The Keys to Egypt</u>. HarperCollins Publishers, Inc.: N.N., NY. 2000.

Ali, Abdullah Yusuf. <u>The Holy Qur'an.</u> Sh. Muhammad Ashraf: Lahore Pakistan, 1969.

Ali, Maulana Muhammad. <u>The Holy Qur'an</u>. Ahmadiyyah Anjuman Isha'at Islam: Lahore, Inc.: Columbus, Oh. 1991.

Allan X.<u>Mathematical Theology and the Physics of God.</u> Dog Ear Publishing: Indianapolis, IN. 2012.

Bernays, Edward. <u>Propaganda.</u> Ig Publishing: Brooklyn, NY. 2004.

Brown, Ellen Hodgson. <u>Web of Debt.</u> Third Millennium Press: Baton Rouge, La. 2007.

Budge, E.A. Wallis. <u>The Egyptian Book of the Dead.</u> Dover Publications, Inc.: N.Y., NY. 1967.

_____. <u>The Gods of the Egyptians.</u> Dover Publications, Inc.: N.Y., NY 1969.

_____. <u>An Egyptian Hieroglyphic Dictionary.</u> Dover Publications, Inc.: N.Y., NY. 1978.

Butler, Alfred J. <u>The Arab Conquest of Egypt.</u> A&B Books Publishers: Brooklyn, NY. 1992.

Cahn, Jonathan. <u>The Harbinger.</u> Frontline Charisma Media: Lake Mary, FL 2010.

Cohan, William D. <u>House of Cards.</u> Doubleday Publishing Group: New York, NY 2009

De Selincourt. <u>Herodotus: The Histories.</u> Penguin Books: London, England 1954.

Denver, William G. <u>Who were the Early Israelites and Where did they come from?</u> Wm B. Eerdmans Publishing Co.: Grand Rapids, Mi. 2003

Dover, K.J. <u>Greek Homosexuality</u>. Harvard University Press: Cambridge, Mass, 1978.

El-Daly, Okasha. <u>Egyptology: The Missing Milennium.</u> UCL Press: London, England, 2005.

Farrakhan, Min. Louis. <u>A Torchlight for America</u>. FCN Publishing Co: Chicago, 1993.

_____. <u>Self-Improvement: The Basis for Community Development</u>. Final Call: Chicago, Study Guides beginning 1986.

_____. <u>Closing the Gap.</u> FCN Publishing, Co.: Chicago, 2006.

Farrell, Joseph P. <u>Financial Vipers of Venice.</u> Feral House Books: Port Townsend, WA, 2010.

_____. <u>Babylon's Banksters.</u> Feral House Books: Port Townsend, WA

2010.

Finklestein, Israel and Neil Asher Silberman. <u>The Bible Unearthed.</u> Touchstone Books: N.Y., NY. 2002.

Fleckenstein, Willam A. <u>Greenspan's Bubbles.</u> McGraw Hill, New York, NY 2008.

Freud, Sigmund. <u>Moses and Monotheism</u>. Alfred a. Knopf: N.Y. 1947.

Gadalla, Moustafa. <u>Exiled Egyptians.</u> Tehuti Research Fondation: Greensboro, NC, 1999.

Greider, William. Secrets of the Temple. Simon & Schuster Paperbacks: New York, NY 1987.

Griffin, G. Edward. The Creature from Jekyll Island. American Media: Westlake Village, CA. 2010.

Guthrie, Paul Lawrence. Making of the Whiteman. Beacon Communications: San Diego, 1992.

Hancock, Graham. The Sign and the Seal. Crown Publishers, Inc.: New York, NY 1992.

Hoffman, Michael. Usury in Christendom. Independent History and Research: Coeure d'Alene, Idaho. 2013.

_____.Judaism Discovered. . Independent History and Research: Coeure d'Alene, Idaho. 2008.

Holy Bible: King James Version. Oral Roberts Evangelistic Assoc.: Tulsa, Okla. 1970

Hull, Richard. Jews and Judaism in African History. Marcus Wiener Publishers: Princeton, NJ 2009.

James, George G. M., Stolen Legacy. Julian Richardson Associates: San Francisco. 1954, 1985.

Knight, Christopher and Robert Lomas. The Hiram Key. Fair Winds Press: Gloucester, Ma. 1996.

Kindleberger, Charles P. Manias, Panics, and Crashes. John Willey & Sons, New York, NY. 2000.

Krugman, Paul. The Return of Depression Economics and the Crisis of 2008. W. W. Norton & Co, Inc. 2009

Koestler, Arthur. The Thirteenth Tribe. Random House Inc.: New York, NY 1976.

Licht, Hans. Sexual Life in Ancient Greece. Barnes & Noble, Inc.: N.Y. 1952.

Marable, Manning. Black Routes to Islam . Palgrave McMillan 2009.

Marsden, Victor E. Protocols of the Learned Elders of Zion. 1934

Massey, Gerald. Book of the Beginnings. Health Research: Mokelumme Hill, CA. 1987.

Mayani, Zacharie. Les Hyksos et Le Monde De La Bible. Payot: Paris. 1956.

Mu'min, Ridgely A. Amen: The Secret Waters of the Great Pyramid. A. M. Distributors: Greensboro, NC & Bronwood, Ga. 1988.

_____. Image of the Beast. K.R.I.S.T.: Bronwood, Ga 1999.

_____. No Farms, No Food. Muhammad Farms. Bronwood, Ga. 2001.

_____. America's Secret War Against Blacks. Muhammad Farms: Bronwood, Ga 2002.

_____. I will not apologize: Resurrection of the Master Architect.
        K.R.S.T.: Bronwood, GA 2003.

_____. Commonomics: Developing a Post Yakub Economy. K.R.S.T.:
        Bronwood, GA 2009.

Muhammad, Cedric. The Entrepreneurial Secret to Starting a Business,
        vol,1&2. CM Cap Publishing: Washington, DC. 2009.

Muhammad, Elijah. Message to The Black Man. Muhammad Mosque No. 2: Chicago, 1965.

_____. The Fall of America. Muhammad Temple of Islam No. 2: Chicago,1973

_____. Our Saviour has Arrived. United Brothers Communication Systems: Newport News, VA. 1992.

_____. The Theology of Time. Abass Rassoull, UB&USCS: Hampton, Va. 1992.

Muhammad, Master Fard. The Supreme Wisdom. Final Call Publishing: Chicago, 1992.

Muhammad, Wesley. Black Arabia & The African Origin of Islam. A-Team Publishing: Atlanta, GA 2009.

Mysliwiec, Karol. The Twilight of Ancient Egypt. Cornell University Press: Ithaca, NY. 2000.

Neusner, Jacob. The Babylonian Talmud. Hendrickson Marketing LLC.: USA 2009.

NOI Historical Research Department. The Secret Relationship between Blacks and Jews, V2. Latimer Associates: USA. 2010.

NOI Research Group. Defending Farrakhan Book 2. Historical Research Department: USA. 2013.

O'Reilly, Kenneth. "Racial Matters". Free Press: N.Y. 1989.

Peled, Miko. The General's Son. Just World Books: Charlottesville, Va. 2012.

Perkins, John. Confessions of an Economic Hit Man. Penguin Group: NY, NY 2004.

Polakow-Suransky. The Unspoken Alliance. Pantheon Books: New York, NY. 2010.

Prins, Nomi. All The Presidents' Bankers. Nations Books: N.Y., NY 2014.

Redford, D. B. Egypt, Canaan, and Israel in Acient Times. Princeton University Press: Princeton 1992.

Samuelson, Paul A. Economics: An Introductory Analysis. McGraw-Hill Book Company: New York, N.Y., 1967.

Sand, Shlomo. The Invention of the Land of Israel. Verso Books: Brooklyn, NY 2012.

_____. The Invention of the Jewish People. Verso Books: Brooklyn, NY 2009.

Schama, Simon. The Story of the Jews. Bodley Head: London, England 2013.

Shaw, Ian. The Oxford History of Ancient Egypt. Oxford University Press: Oxford 2000.

Sheeham, Peter. Babylon of Egypt. The American University in Cairo Press: New York, NY 2010.

Siddiqui, Dr. Nejatullah. Banking without Interest. Markazi Maktaba Islami: Delhi, 1994.

Sitton, Thad and James H. Conrad. Freedom Colonies. University of Texas Press: Austin, Tx. 2005.

Stiglitz, Joseph E. Freefall. W. W. Norton & Co. New York, NY 2010.

Sorek, Susan. The Emperor's Needles: Egyptian Obelisks and Rome. Britol Phoenix Press: Exeter, UK 2010.

Tenney, Merril C. Editor. Pictorial Bible Dictionary. The Southwestern Co.: Nashville, Tenn. 1976.

Thompson, Thomas L. The Bible in History. Pimlico: London, UK 2000

Thorn, Victor. <u>9-11 Brand Terorism</u>. Sisyphus Press: State College, Pa. 2011.

Velde, H. Te. <u>Seth, God of Confusion</u>. 1977.

Vennard, Wickliffe B. <u>The Federal Reserve Hoax.</u> Omni Publications: Palmdale, CA, 1963.

Williams, Chancellor. <u>The Destruction of Black Civilization</u>. Third World Press: Chicago, 1976.

_____. <u>The Re-Birth of African Civilization</u>. U.B. & U.S. Communication Systems: Hampton, VA 1993.

Index

385

312, 313, 322, 331, 332, 336, 362

Business: 7, 8, 14, 112, 144-148, 152
  164, 175, 181, 182, 188, 190
  198, 200, 203, 208, 218, 243, 246
  247-251, 264, 271, 285, 287, 288
  290, 291, 298, 301, 308, 310, 311
  313, 319, 321, 324, 332, 333, 343
  349, 351, 352, 354, 357, 358, 360
  368, 372, 374-376

C

Cambyses: 97, 118-120, 127-129, 132
  133, 135, 136
Capital: 7, 18, 69, 79, 96, 118, 120
  145, 157, 169, 170, 173, 178, 179
  182, 187, 188, 190, 197-202, 244
  245, 250, 259, 283, 298, 301-303
  312, 352- 354, 367, 372, 373, 375
Captivity: 4, 45, 46, 75, 78, 98, 107
  109-111, 113-115, 122, 126, 212
Cattle: 2, 8, 14, 18, 19, 57, 86, 106,
  112, 270, 273, 274, 354,
Caucasus: 17, 18, 44, 54-56, 59, 60, 76
  82, 85, 88, 111, 123, 124, 138,
  139-141, 271, 361
Chosen People: 1, 5, 17, 46, 95, 105, 125
  147, 347, 353

Cipher: 8

Civilization: 1, 6, 17, 35, 40, 43, 44, 46
  60, 76, 77, 78, 82, 88, 90, 91, 99
  110, 124, 127, 143, 240, 250, 347
  348, 351, 354, 355, 357, 360, 362

Code(s): 1, 21, 136, 137, 145, 241, 243
  247, 250, 251, 253, 267, 294, 347
  354, 363

Colchians: 82, 84, 88, 123

Commonomics: 1, 8-10, 156, 349

Cooperative Corporation: 349, 350, 374

Corral: 8, 25, 273, 343, 348, 361

Crashes: 274-276, 298, 333, 344

Credit: 60, 108, 121, 137, 149, 158, 160
  164-168, 170, 173-175, 182, 184

185, 186, 201, 202, 216, 217, 219
  220, 247, 283-286, 290, 294, 298
  303, 304, 306, 314, 315, 317, 320
  321, 323, 335, 346, 350, 362, 369
  371, 372, 375, 377
Crisis: 64, 149, 150,167, 178, 202, 243,
  246, 248, 252, 268, 269, 270, 271,
  276, 277, 280-282, 285, 286-288,
  291, 292, 298, 299, 303, 305,
  309-315, 321, 324, 325, 326, 344,
  366, 370, 371
Cycles: 215, 217, 248-251, 259, 261, 262
  329, 334, 335, 350, 351

D

Daniel: 113, 118, 132, 137, 173, 255, 257
  258, 323, 327, 334, 342, 343, 348
Darius: 59, 113, 119, 120-122, 124, 127
  133-137
Dark energy: 46-48
Dark matter: 46-48
Debt: 8, 17, 150, 155, 159, 160, 164, 166
  167, 171-174, 181, 194, 207, 213,
  214, 215, 218, 219, 229, 230, 239,
  244, 245, 247, 262, 271, 275,
  279-282, 296, 301, 305, 311, 343,
  348, 352, 361, 365, 367-373
Depression: 194, 243, 244, 269, 284.
  286, 287, 288, 297, 311, 362
Devil: 3, 7, 17, 39, 42, 43, 50, 99
  112, 121, 122, 156, 157, 159
  242, 334, 353, 356
DNA: 16, 51, 122, 266
DuBois, W.E.B.: 148-151

Duhl-Karnan (Zul-Quarnain): 57
  58-60, 104

E

Economic Blueprint: 7, 9, 156, 211
  347, 350, 351, 353, 363
Economics: 7, 9, 143, 144, 156, 157
  158, 243, 247, 249-252, 303
  321, 359, 363

390

About the Author

Dr. Ridgely Abdul Mu'min (Muhammad) was born in Winston-Salem, N.C. in 1951. He received his bachelors and masters degrees in Agricultural Economics from N.C. A&T State University. He received his Ph. D. in Agricultural Economics from Michigan State University. He has a minor in Finance with a specialty in Systems Science. He was an Assistant Professor of Agricultural Economics and Principle Investigator on small farm research projects at North Carolina A&T. Along with numerous papers and publications he has written six books. He writes feature articles in the Final Call Newspaper and other Black newspapers related to food security and the survival of the Black farmer. He lectures at colleges and universities on the African origins of agriculture and the agricultural functions of the pyramids of Ancient Egypt along with giving food security and survival seminars to churches and community organizations.

Dr. Ridgely is presently the Minister of Agriculture and farm manager of a 1600 acre farm is southwest Georgia owned by the Nation of Islam. He is also the Agricultural Economist and Vice-President of the National Black Farmers and Agriculturists Association. He is the founder of the Kemetic Research Institute of Science and Technology located in Bronwood, Ga.

Books published include: "Amen: The Secret Waters of the Great Pyramid", "Image of the Beast", "I Will Not Apologize: Resurrection of the Master Architect", "Commonomics: Developing a Post-Yakub Economy", "The Science and Business of Farming vs the Art and Hobby of Gardening" and "Recipes For/From Life".

Email him at: drridge@noimoa.com